The Italian Factor

THE
ITALIAN
FACTOR

The Italian Community in Great Britain

TERRI COLPI

MAINSTREAM
PUBLISHING

EDINBURGH AND LONDON

Front Cover   Left to right:
1. Angela Corsini, Aliens Book, London, 1940. Credit: A. Corsini.
2. Ice-Cream Cart in a London Park, *c*1910. Credit: *La Voce*.
3. Italy wins the World Cup, Bedford, 1982. Credit: *Bedfordshire Times*.
4. The Brig Restaurant, Alyth, Perthshire, 1930s. Credit: M. Dorà.

Back Cover
The *Madonna del Rosario*, Manchester Whit Walk, 1984. Credit: A. Rea.

The Moral Right of the Author has been asserted
First published in Great Britain 1991 by
MAINSTREAM PUBLISHING COMPANY (EDINBURGH) LTD
7 Albany Street
Edinburgh EH1 3UG

ISBN 1 85158 334 0 (cloth)

A catalogue record for this book is available from the British Library

Typeset in 10/12pt Times by Blackpool Typesetting Services Ltd., Blackpool
Printed and bound in Great Britain by
Butler & Tanner Ltd, Frome and London

In memory of my grandfather

Dolfè di Stagnedo

Acknowledgments

The Italian Factor represents the culmination of research into, and work within, the Italian Community in Great Britain. As a third-generation Italian Scot, I am myself a proud member of the Community and my interest in its history and development is therefore 'life-long'. From my early experiences and research within the Scottish Italian Community to my doctoral research at Oxford University on the southern Italian Community in Bedford, during my professional involvement with the Italian consular authority in London and, in 1990–91, there have been many individuals who have helped me. People have given generously of their time, have answered my probing questions, have told me their personal and family histories, have opened their family archives, have divulged details on the internal workings of businesses, have invited me into their homes to carry out 'interviews', both in this country and in Italy, have shown me their back shops and restaurant kitchens, have participated in the ghastly rigours of the 'questionnaire survey' and finally have allowed me access to official files and documentation. I am grateful to them all because, without the breadth of vision that such wide-ranging insight has allowed me, I could never have written this book.

Unfortunately, I cannot list everyone; such a list would in itself fill the pages of a book. Below, I acknowledge many who, in the last year or so when I have been specifically engaged in drawing together many threads in order to write *The Italian Factor*, have given me generous and constructive assistance. I apologise for any omissions.

The Aceto family, Bedford; Giuseppe Alcorano, Watford; Anna Alonzi, Edinburgh; Lucio Alzetta, London; Roland Antonelli, Manchester; Michele Arpaia, Bedford; Aldo Bacchetta, Porth; *Dott.essa* Tosca Baldini, Milano; Bruno Bartolomei, Barga; the Bavaro family, Bedford; Rodolfo Benacci, Greenock; *Rev. Padre* Silvano Bertapelle, Woking; *Cav.* Rando Bertoia, Glasgow; *Cav.* Bruno and Olive Besagni, London; *Cav.* Luigi Beschizza, London; *Cav.* Pietro Beschizza,

5

Middlesex; Edwin Bicocchi, Aberdeen; Joseph Boni, Edinburgh; *Dott.*
Luigi Bottaro, Edinburgh; Elida Morelli Brooks, Aberdeenshire;
Tommaso Bruccoleri, London; Wolfango Bucci, London; Pino Buglione,
Derby; *Console Generale* Rodolfo Buonavita, Edinburgh; Vincent
Capaldi, Bearsden; Rosario Capozza, London; Luciano Caprio, Cheadle;
Cav. Enrico Casci, Falkirk; Sofia Casci, Barga; *Dott.* Lorenzo Castello,
London; Monty Cattini, London; Alberto Cavalli, London; *Dott.* Luigi
Cavandoli, Manchester; *Dott.* Bruno Cervi, London; Dr David Cesarani,
London; *Dott.essa* Marta Cherchi, London; *Cav.* Romolo Chioconni,
Glasgow; Amilcare Cima, Padivarma; Emelda Cima, Drymen; Paul
Coia, Glasgow; Armo Collini, London; Martin Colpi, Milngavie;
Rodolfo Colpi, Milngavie; Bishop Mario Conti, Aberdeen; *Dott.essa*
Verina Conti, Bedford; *Cav.* Philip Contini, Edinburgh; Silvio
Corciolani, Glasgow; Peter Corvi, Glasgow; Angela Corsini, London;
Carlo Cosentino, Stockport; Victor Crolla, Edinburgh; Guido Cruci,
Barking; *Cav.* Nicola Cua, Wallington; Domenica De Marco Cullen,
Edinburgh; *Console Generale* Gabriele De Ceglie, London; *Avv.* Pietro
Del Giudice, London; *Rev. Padre* Mario Della Costa, Bedford; *Cav.*
Richard De Marco, Edinburgh; *Rev. Padre* Carmelo Di Giovanni,
London; Ann Marie Di Mambro, Hamilton; *Cav.* Teodoro Di Nardo,
London; the late *Cav.* Giuseppe Dorà, Beith; the Dorà family, Beith;
Maria Grazia Dorian, Glasgow; Dr Mario Dutto, Roma; Carlo Edoni,
Glasgow; Ronald Farrants, London; Antonio Fatica, Bedford; Teresa
Fazio, Reading; Sandro Fazzi, Glasgow; Lillie Ferrari, London; *Prof.*
Remo Finaldi, London; Silvana Fishlock, Glasgow; the Honourable
Rocco Forte, London; the late *Avv.* Osvaldo Franchi, Glasgow; *Dott.*
Giuseppe Franco, London; Kathleen Fusco, Portobello; Michela Galelli,
London; Patrizia Galleotti, Barga; Giorgio Garofalo, Bedford; *Avv.*
Francesco Giacon, London; *Comm.* Giuseppe Giacon, London; *Dott.*
Carlo Giglio, Edinburgh; Mario Giovanacci, Greenock; Angelo
Giovanazzi, Glasgow; *Cav.* Fulvio Giretti, Nottingham; Luigi and Rosa
Giso, Bedford; Gabriele Grandi, London; *Cav.* Gino Guarnieri, London;
Colin Hughes, Gerrards Cross; Nadia Iacovazzi Dalziel, Peeblesshire;
Cav. Fortunato Iannetta, St Andrews; Raffaele Iannucci, London; C.T.
Isolani, London; Teresa Jocklick, London; Nunzio La Fratta, Oxford;
Cav. Riccardo Lombardelli, Leicester; *Comm.* Benedetto Longinotti,
London; *Comm.* Lorenzo Losi, London; Battista Lussana, Newport;
Damiana Maestri, Manchester; Pino Maestri, London; the Mancini
family, Ayr; Peter and Olga Marchetti, Glasgow; Flavio Mazzi, London;
Console Sergio Mercuri, Manchester; Dr Eileen Ann Millar, Glasgow;

ACKNOWLEDGMENTS

Michael Minchella, South Shields; Gina Mortellaro, Chertsey; *Comm. Avv.* Tino Moscardini, Glasgow; *Cav.* Roberta Mutti, London; Jean MacDonald, Inverness; Prof. J.S. MacDonald, London; Dr Remo Nannetti, Glasgow; *Vice Console* Fabrizio Necchi, Aberdeen; Gianfranco Nobis, Poole; *Prof.essa* Laura Oliveti, London; Joan Ottolini, Glasgow; the late *Cav.* Alessandro and the late Charles Pacitti, Glasgow; Gina Pacitti, Glasgow; Nello Paoletti, Dumfries; *Rev. Padre* Gaetano Parolin, London; Domenico Pascale, Enfield; Giorgio Pettinelli, Bedford; Frank Pignatelli, Glasgow; *Cav.* Elio Poli, Tarbolton; *Comm.* Lino Quaradeghini, London; Silvia Quarantelli, Aberdeen; Olga Raffaeta, Pietrasanta; Amerigo Razo, Glasgow; Antony Rea, Manchester; Maria Renucci, Glasgow; Elpidio Rossi, Chiavari; *Mons.* Gaetano Rossi, Glasgow; Gina Rossi, Padivarma; Dr Gino Rossi, La Spezia; Sir Hugh Rossi, London; *Prof.* Vincenzo Rossi, London; Archie Salvini, Edinburgh; Elena Salvoni, London; Giuseppe Sammarco, London; *Avv.* Salvatore Sammarco, London; Amadeo Sarti, Glasgow; Gaetano Scappaticci, Manchester; *Cav.* Maria Schiavo, Cardiff; *Cav.* Giorgio Scola, Reading; *Comm.* Renzo Serafini, Inverness; the late Bruno Sereni, Barga; *Dott.essa* Rita Sidoli, Swansea; *Prof.* Antonio Spallone, London; Dr Lucio Sponza, London; Franca Torrano, Bradford; Walter Toscano, London; Dr Arturo Tosi, London; Alan Toti, Glasgow; Paolo Trainotti, London; Dr John Vergano, London; Daniela Versace, Reggio Calabria; Lidia Vignapiano, Edinburgh; Dr Andrew Wilkin, Glasgow; Adolfo Zaccardelli, Edinburgh; Antony and Norina Zanrè, Aberdeen; Ronaldo Zanrè, London; Anna Zanusso, Bedford; *Rev. Padre* Pietro Zorza, Glasgow.

I am grateful also to Martin Lubowski for his diligent research help throughout the project.

In addition to these people my greatest single debt is to my husband, Michael, for his never failing support and assistance. His help on the detail of the book was invaluable, particularly in the statistical sections. I am also eternally grateful to my brother, Martin, who read every chapter in draft form and gave superb overall advice on the content and the historical 'sweep' of the book.

Contents

CONTENTS

List of Tables

Table of Maps

List of Figures

13

Introduction

The Italian presence in Great Britain today, a population of approximately 250,000 people, represents one of the country's longest established immigrant groups, with a rich and varied history over the last 150 years.

The current situation of total integration into British life, with varying degrees of assimilation based on individual choice rather than on any societal constraint, puts the Italian Community in a unique and favoured position compared with other immigrant groups. In the early days of their settlement, however, the ordinary Italian immigrants experienced many hardships in both social and economic terms; the struggle to the current level of prosperity and social integration has not been problem free, and in fact has taken more than a century to achieve.

The history of the Italian connection with Britain is not only long and fascinating; most importantly it is ever evolving. Each new era has brought a new wave of immigrants and a new development. *The Italian Factor* covers all of the main phases of immigration, describes the different waves of immigrants and offers an overall history of the Italians in Britain.

Today, Italians are spread geographically across the entire country, from the Cillo family at St Just near Land's End to the Cabrelli family of Stornoway in the Outer Hebrides. Most towns have at least one Italian family and many towns and cities have a sizeable Italian presence. The greatest concentration of Italians is, however, in the south east where over 60 per cent of the Community are resident. London has always hosted the largest Italian concentration and indeed throughout the nineteenth and first half of the twentieth centuries the Clerkenwell Italian Colony formed an Italian *ghetto* or 'Little Italy' of considerable size. Traditional Italian Communities are also still visible in Glasgow, Edinburgh, Manchester and in many smaller towns.

These 'old' Communities all date to the nineteenth century and can be contrasted with the 'new' Italian Communities of the post Second World

War era, such as those in Bedford, Peterborough, Nottingham and Loughborough. It was the 'old' Communities which developed the catering industry, and which are now in the third, fourth and even fifth generation of Italians. Amongst these 'old' Italian settlers and their descendants, assimilation is often advanced and economic prosperity is normally marked. The more recent immigrants are rather less prosperous and less integrated. They are also without the same catering connection since their immigration was in response to demand for labour in the restructuring of British industry after the war. These new arrivals of the 1950s established entirely 'new' Communities and now form over two-thirds of the total British Italian Community.

The 1970s and 1980s introduced another two waves of migrants. Firstly, in the 1970s there was a small influx of young, student-age, people who arrived after British accession to the European Community. Then, in the 1980s, a wave of high-status professionals arrived, particularly in London, changing the fabric of the Italian Community, giving it an 'upper crust'.

At the national level it is interesting to consider to what extent such an entity as the British Italian 'Community' exists. With so many disparate groups making up the whole, how much cohesion and co-operation between the different geographical, temporal, occupational and social groups is there? In this context, the word 'Community' is used loosely to cover all these groups. Perhaps the Italian word, *collettività* – collectivity – is more apt since it contains the idea of many distinct groups less cohesively comprising a whole – like the European Community.

There are in fact at both local and national levels a number of forces or structures which bind together the various sub-groups into a 'Community'. One of the main developments of recent years has been the upsurge of Italian associations, circles and societies within the Community. The associations, together with a wealth of Italian institutions, both privately and government funded, or based around the ethnic churches, have all had a great influence on preserving the stability and distinctiveness of the British Italian Community. The notion of the ethnic 'Community' implies a certain harmony or sense of self-definition and of belonging. In the 'old' Communities, because of the passage of time, and assimilation, many people have been lost to the Italian fold and no longer feel themselves to be Italian. This book is not directly concerned with those who have opted or drifted out of the Community; it is concerned with those who have an Italian way of life, are linked with Italy and who feel at least partly Italian. *The Italian Factor* takes, therefore, an insider's view and describes this interesting facet of British society.

The main aim of *The Italian Factor* is to provide, for the first time, a book which traces the history of the Italians in Britain from their humble origins in the 1830s to the prosperous present in the last decade of the twentieth century. It is concerned with offering the reader, especially the British Italian reader, a total picture of the Community, past and present. The heritage and evolution of the Italian Community in this country over the last 150 years has an important bearing on the current structure. By working systematically and chronologically through the various phases of the immigration and describing the different types of immigrants, the occupations they followed and how they lived their lives, *The Italian Factor* charts the evolution of one of Britain's oldest and most interesting ethnic communities.

Three initial questions

Before beginning this exposition, let us deal with three questions which tend to be asked by everyone beginning to focus on the Italian presence in Britain for the first time.

(1) How many Italians are there in Britain?
(2) Why did they come to Britain?
(3) Why and how did they develop such strong links with the catering industry?

Often to the surprise of the questioner, none of these questions permits a simple definitive answer.

How many Italians are there?

An indication of the overall size of the Community has already been given at roughly a quarter of a million people. In other words, approximately one in every 200 people in Britain today is Italian. We must be aware, however, that the main problem with trying to estimate the number of Italians surrounds the definition of who is Italian. How does one define Italian? From 1861 onwards, the British census has enumerated only foreign-born people as foreign – that is to say Italian-born as Italian. Individuals born in this country of Italian parentage are counted as British. In a Community such as the Italian one, which has well over a century's history, second, third, fourth and even fifth-generation Italians are thus not accounted for in the British census Italian figures, although family ties and connections with Italy are still strong. There are fifth-generation Italians living in London and Manchester today whose blood is 100 per cent Italian, who are economically and socially very attached to Italy, but neither they nor their forefathers figure in the British statistics.

This generational problem can be alleviated somewhat by referring to Italian statistical sources. Both the Italian census and the figures compiled by the Italian Ministry of Foreign Affairs on the world-wide expatriate communities of Italians include those Italians born abroad, i.e. second and subsequent generations of Italians.

Although it is not a straightforward task to estimate the size of the British Italian Community, available census figures, estimates and guides will be utilised throughout the book to give an indication of numbers and geographical distribution.

Why did the Italians come to Britain?

Many people ask this, in itself perfectly reasonable, question. The answer needs, however, to be set within a much wider context. It must be remembered that few nations in the course of recent international migration history sent so many emigrants to all corners of the earth with such sustained consistency as Italy. Few countries that have received immigrants since the beginning of the mass global migrations of the late eighteenth and early nineteenth centuries did not admit Italians, so strong were the 'push' factors which forced people to leave Italy in this period. A description of Italian migration, by the historian Foerster in 1919, still provides an eloquent starting point for a study of contemporary Italian migration:

> *Emigration from Italy belongs among the extraordinary movements of mankind. In its chief lineaments it has no like. Through the number of men it has involved and the courses it has pursued, through its long continuance on a great scale and its role in other lands, it stands alone. (Foerster 1919, p.3)*

With the current population of Italy standing at around 57 million, it has been estimated that there are some 40 million Italians and people of Italian descent living outside Italy. Thus, the answer to the initial question posed above is simply that the Italians who came to Britain were part of a larger exodus from Italy, the vast mass of whose emigrants were destined for the Americas, Australia and elsewhere in Europe.

This answer does not necessarily satisfy the more persistent questioner who will insist that the Italians' arrival in Britain cannot have been by chance. It is true that some of the 'pioneer' migrants of the early nineteenth century may have 'chosen' Britain, being specifically 'pulled' by the opportunities of this land rather than others and, in those cases, London, at that time the largest city in the world, was the usual destination. But most Italians who came to Britain did not actually make a positive choice to do so. There were a number of reasons for this, most of which are related to the mechanisms of migration, the methods of transfer which actually brought people out of Italy. By focusing on the mechanism rather than the rationale, 'how?', not 'why?', we gain a far better overall understanding of the Italian Community resident in Britain.

These so-called 'mechanisms' of migration are the crucial devices which have enabled the transference of large numbers of people from Italy to Britain in the last 150 years. There have been two main mechanisms – **chain migration** and **impersonal recruitment migration** – both very easy to understand.

The concept of chain migration was defined by Australian geographers John and Leatrice MacDonald in 1964 as a process whereby families from particular villages or regions move to a new country or to a city, from which they instigate a 'chain of migration' by assisting their relatives to join them. We can describe chain migration as the process by which prospective migrants learn of opportunities, are provided with transportation, and have initial accommodation and employment arranged for them by contacts already established abroad.

Impersonal recruitment on the other hand, as the name suggests, is an impersonal form of migration where migrants have no personal contacts at their destinations. They are recruited by agencies who work on behalf of various sponsors and industries, and sometimes in very large batches or groups.

Both chain and impersonal recruitment migration have brought Italians to Britain. Both have been responsible, however, for producing very different types of Italian Communities – different in terms of their geographical and social origins in Italy, their period of arrival, destination in Britain and their occupational groups. This simple distinction between these two mechanisms and the different Communities they spawned is important in helping us to understand the Italians in Britain, past and present.

One of the main results of chain migration from Italy has been the establishment, not only in Britain but all over the world, of particular Italian Communities which have links with specific source areas, and even villages, in Italy. Within Britain, because of chain migration, the Italian Community is not a cross section of Italians mixed up in a random way but is composed of distinct subcommunities and subgroupings.

On the other hand, because impersonal recruitment casts its net wider and recruits people through bureaucratic rather than personal means, it results in a greater variety of people from a far greater variety of source areas. There are many Italian Communities in Britain which owe their origin to this form of recruitment and which are therefore not characterised by distinct origin groups. These Communities tend instead to consist of people from a vast range of villages throughout Italy, although, as will be seen as our tale unfolds, in later phases of development in these Communities, chain migration often also came into play leading to a predominance of certain groups of people over others.

The distinction between the two migratory mechanisms is crucial, not only in understanding how different groups of Italians came to Britain at different points in the history of Italian migration, but also in understanding the different Italian Communities which are present today. Anyone who thinks all Italian Communities are the same, or even similar, should read on to discover just how far from the truth that view is.

Why the catering connection?

This final general question again has no straightforward answer. Chapters 1 and 2 which chart the arrival of the early immigrants, who were mainly street entertainers, and describe their gradual move into street vending of food, do, however, hold some answers. These and Chapter 3 set the backdrop for the subsequent development of this particular occupational niche, which is again monitored in Chapter 5. Apart from the London Community, and in the 'old' Italian Communities of Scotland, however, the catering connection is not the dominant one.

The 'mass' Italian migration to Britain in the post-Second World War period had nothing to do with catering and was almost exclusively to do with industry. These migrants and their descendants, although now mainly skilled workers, still have little connection with catering. In general terms, therefore, the catering link is perhaps an exaggerated stereotype which, although it cannot be overstated for London, should not be overemphasised in the rest of the country.

Organisation of the book

Although *The Italian Factor* looks across an expanse of history, in fact from 1800 to 1992 and beyond, there are a number of themes which run through the book and which are relevant regardless of time. Of greatest interest are the occupations of the migrants, where they came from in Italy and their areas of settlement and way of life in this country. These are the factors which have been influential in the founding, merging and molding of the different Italian Communities through history.

The book divides into two parts, with four chapters in each: the ending of the Second World War in 1945 forms the dividing date. Part One covers the historical period from 1800 and Part Two brings the story up to the early 1990s. Part One takes a strictly chronological approach, each chapter looking at a different period and dealing with the factors relevant to that particular period of time. Part Two of the book, while again moving through time from 1945 to the present, adopts a more thematic approach. Each of the four chapters discusses a major aspect of the Community during this period.

Chapter 1 begins with a brief review of the long historical period from 1000 until the point where our main story begins – at the turn of the nineteenth century. The chapter discusses the various types of immigrants of the nineteenth century, introducing the foundations of the present-day Italian Community. Chapter 2, building on the framework set out in the opening chapter, moves forward to the First World War and in the process of covering the period from 1880 to 1918 sets out the manner in which the catering industry evolved. The type and number of Italians who settled in Britain in this period are also reviewed. In Chapter 3 the two decades of the 1920s and 1930s are described as a golden era, since it was in this period that the Italians consolidated their Community and, most importantly, business structures. The rise of fascism and the build-up to the Second World War are also discussed in this chapter.

Chapter 4 forms the heart of the book, covering the previously uncharted topic of the Italian experience during the Second World War. The material is presented from the Italian point of view and part of the aim of this chapter is to document a previously unwritten episode of Second World War history. As we will learn, the war had a profound effect on the 'old' Italian Communities.

Part Two of the book, Chapters 5 to 8, is concerned with the growth and development of the Community in the post-war era. Chapter 5 opens by reviewing, in the same way as Chapter 1, the main new flows of immigrants to arrive, in this case in the 1940s and 1950s. It was in this decade that Britain experienced its first true 'mass' influx of Italians, the result being the foundation of entirely new Italian Communities. The second theme of the chapter is occupations. The catering connection is brought up to date and the new industrial connections of the migrants from southern Italy are explored.

Chapter 6 takes a global view of the Community offering an analysis of its size, its distribution in this country and its origins in Italy. The structure and composition of each of the main Communities are then examined. Chapter 7 concentrates on the individual and the family, explaining how people lead their lives, particularly in the 'new' Communities, and discussing the question of assimilation in the 'old' Communities. The final chapter, Chapter 8, builds up to the Community level and looks at the all-important institutions which bind the Italians into an organised structure and provide a framework for life.

Although only around a quarter of a million people resident in Britain today are either Italian-born or of Italian origin, they are a distinct presence within British society. Their long history in this country, their specialist development of the catering industry, their continued contact with Italy, their ever evolving migration picture and finally their strong Italian 'ethnic memory', which makes them cling even after generations to aspects of their Italianness, all contribute to Community tradition. In this era of closer European integration the Italians in Britain are probably the most European section of British society – a position which is giving them increasing prominence. *The Italian Factor* in British life has truly come of age. Let us see how all this has come about.

PART ONE:

UNTIL 1945

Chapter One

Historical heritage

Introduction

This chapter is primarily devoted to the key elements of the foundation of the present-day Italian Community in Britain which occurred from 1800 onwards. However, it seems of interest in a work such as this to mention something of the Italian contribution to British life in the preceding 800 years. The Roman invasion, which in any case generally involved colonists from parts of the Roman Empire outside the Italian peninsula, is, however, outside our scope!

The distant past: 1000 until 1800

The Italian immigrations to Britain of the medieval (1000–1500), the early modern (1500–1750) and the modern period from around 1760, and in this case until 1800, comprised élite and high-status men who came from all over Italy, but mainly the north. These men settled mostly, but not exclusively, in London and during such a long period there were a number of distinct phases and types of migrants.

The first of these groups began to appear from the late 1200s and early 1300s. A commercial colony of Italians grew up in London, on the left bank of the River Thames, near the Tower of London, based on the *Veneziano* and *Genovese* mercantile trading connection. From this commercial centre, set up by these seafaring traders, links were also established with the rest of the country. There was also a similar colony in the port of Southampton in this very early period of settlement.

In addition to the trading colony, by the early second half of the fourteenth century, Italians had become responsible for introducing banking and an understanding of financial matters – known as *il commercio del denaro*, the commerce of money – to London. When

25

Edward I expelled the Jews in 1290, the Italians were able to enter this sector and develop a considerable niche. Some Italian banking firms of the era were Bardi & Peruzzi, Medici, Pallavicini, Cavalcanti. The most famous bankers of all were the *Lombardi*, from whose working area Lombard Street in the City derives its name. The terms 'bankrupt' (from the Italian *banca rotta*) and the old £.s.d. (from *lire, soldi e denari*) also came to us from this period of Italian commercial colonisation. Later, after this initial commercial phase, the type of Italian who entered Britain was connected more with the arts, culture and learning.

During these early periods the numbers of people present in Britain from the Italian peninsula were very small and transitory in nature. They were independent individuals – artists, writers, musicians, scholars and churchmen – who migrated from one part of Christendom to another to take up an appointment or commission at the court, the abbey, the great church or university.

Before the industrial revolution (1760) it was the abbeys, located across the country, which formed centres of population. As great centres of learning they formed focal points for scholars and men of letters. Many Italians came to live in and work at the abbeys. One such example was the *Piemontese* scholar Giovanni Ferreri who had two periods as a teacher at the remote Kinloss Abbey in Morayshire in the 1530s and 1540s. The courts of the kings of Scotland and England also attracted many Italians of ability and talent. One of the most illustrious of these was Pietro Torrigiani (1472–1528) the Florentine artist who sculpted the tomb of Henry VII in Westminster Abbey.

Perhaps the best known of these was Davide Riccio (Rizzio). The Queen of Scotland, Mary, 'Queen of Scots', as she later became known, had a charming voice and enjoyed singing. Her general interest in music and her own musical talent influenced her choice of valets and secretaries. In 1561 she had five *viola* and three flute players attached to her court. Rizzio, her French secretary, also, as the son of a musician, possessed considerable musical abilities and skills. He was murdered by those jealous of his influence over the queen.

Attached to the court of Queen Elizabeth I of England was Petruccio Ubaldini the scholar and illuminator from *Toscana*. Apart from his skill in calligraphy, he was a great writer of treaties and indeed has the distinction of writing the first Italian book to be printed in England (*Vita di Carlo Magno Imperadore*) in 1581. Also worthy of mention is the family Ferrabosco, three generations of whom – all named Alfonso – were attached to the Royal court. All three (the son and grandson of the original

Alfonso Ferrabosco were born at Greenwich) were noted musicians and composers and had a considerable influence on the development of music, particularly composition, between 1625 and 1660.

In addition, many artists and scholars arrived at the great houses and their works often took many years to complete. As exponents of the Italian *renaissance* all of these individuals at the courts, abbeys and houses did not in any sense form a community, but rather moved freely and frequently throughout Europe at the highest level of society.

By the end of the seventeenth century the first Italian craftsmen and artisans began to arrive in London. For example, a group of glass blowers were summoned by Edward VI. Clock-makers too had reached London. It was these migrants who formed the basis for the Italian Colony of Clerkenwell, and, in the nineteenth century, as we shall see below, initiated the development of barometer and scientific instrument-making.

During the eighteenth century it was again predominantly the cultural influence of Italy which prevailed in the type of migrants who arrived in England. Antonio Canaletto (1697–1768) and many others visited and painted here. Cipriani, who came to London in 1756, together with Capezzuolo, built the Gold State Coach for coronations. Cipriani was a founding member of the Royal Academy in 1768. In addition to art, the influence of Italian architecture was considerable with a return to the style of Palladio. Giacomo Leoni and Leon Battista Alberti were responsible for the translation of Palladio's works into English, and, under the general patronage of Lord Burlington, Italian architecture became very prominent. Also, during the eighteenth century, over 100 composers and performers of music came to Britain. Bononcini and Ariosti with Handel were founding directors of the Royal Academy of Music.

By around the turn of the nineteenth century, however, this long period of élitist Italian immigration was drawing to a close and by 1800 a new era, the main historical period of interest to our story, was about to begin. From small artisan-based Colonies of Italians in London and Manchester from 1800, these cities would soon witness the arrival of masses of poor Italian immigrants, and by 1880 the foundation of the Italian Community as we know it today had been laid.

The recent past: 1800–1880

During this second and main historical phase of Italian immigration to Britain, there were four different types and waves of migrants who reached the British Isles. In Italian immigration to this country, there is normally a relationship between the time of arrival, the occupation and the area of origin of each group of migrants. If these three points are borne in mind, it becomes relatively straightforward to distinguish one group from another. On this basis the four groups to arrive in Britain during the nineteenth century in chronological order of initial arrival were as follows:

(1) highly skilled craftsmen and artisans;
(2) political refugees;
(3) poor unskilled immigrants;
(4) skilled and semi-skilled itinerant craftsmen.

The highly skilled craftsmen from northern Italy arrived first. They were present in some locations from 1790 but their numbers increased and they had settled across the country by the 1820s. They were followed by the political refugees, who fled from all over Italy and had a short but important presence mainly between 1820 and 1848.

The third group, the most important for our study, were the poor unskilled immigrants who first appeared in London in the 1830s. Their numbers built up in the middle decades of the nineteenth century, but it was not until the 1880s and towards the turn of the twentieth century that this influx of poor Italian immigrants reached significant levels and laid down the foundations across the country for the British Italian Community as we know it today. (This second post 1880 phase is discussed in Chapter 2.) The final group, the travelling semi-skilled craftsmen, arrived from 1850 or 1860 and, although their numbers were never great, they too formed an important factor in the overall heritage.

The highly skilled craftsmen and artisans

Skilled Italian craftsmen had been present in Britain from around 1790. The numbers of these artisans, who collectively possessed a vast range of skills, built up in the 1820s and, by the 1830s, they were to be found in all major urban centres including Liverpool, Glasgow and Edinburgh, and also in smaller cities such as Hull. These artisans were moving to all countries of Europe at the time in search of markets and were essentially economic migrants. Their geographical origins in Italy were almost exclusively in the north – mostly in *Lombardia* and *Liguria*. The clock-makers from *Como* became particularly well known.

The kinds of skills were two-fold. On the one hand were the scientific, mathematical and 'philosophical' instrument makers and on the other were the specialists in fields such as decoration, design, illustration, engraving, mirror-making, carving, gilding and framing. Some sold prints in combination with framing. These were all specialist crafts which did not interfere with any of the local craft unions and societies. Although not directly connected with the arts as such, many of these activities perpetuated the tradition of Italian art, promulgated in one form or another by the immigrants of the previous centuries.

The scientific instrument makers were more specialist than their compatriots, since more precise and complicated skills were required in their work. The instruments included barometers, thermometers and hydrometers; surgical and optical equipment, such as eyeglasses, microscopes; surveying instruments, such as theodolites and telescopes (see Plate 1); mathematical instruments for accurate drawing; experimental or philosophical instruments; and a range of gauges and devices for measuring temperature and pressure of machines, of importance to the ever developing industrial revolution.

One of the very earliest craftsmen was Molinari from *Como* who arrived in Edinburgh in 1752 as a glass-blower. Glass-blowing was an essential requirement for the making of the early instruments. Thermometers and stick barometers, for example, included glass tubes. Other firms in Edinburgh in this period were Zenone & Butti who in 1823 were listed in the Post Office Directory as a looking-glass manufacturer in Cowgate. Butti later set up as a carver and gilder in Leith.

In Glasgow one of the earliest firms to be established in 1805 was Antoni & Galletti who were carvers and gilders. In 1828 they moved to the newly built Argyll Arcade, and by this time were also producing mathematical instruments. Also in Glasgow, in 1828 at the Saltmarket, was Gerletti, a looking-glass manufacturer and maker of barometers and thermometers. Riva in Glasgow was another carver and gilder established in 1823. Not all of the gilders made instruments; many bought them from the increasingly more specialist makers.

Some of the instruments intended for domestic use included a number of features. A piece, now owned by a prominent member of the Manchester Italian Community, and made by Augustine Maspoli of Hull between 1825 and 1846, includes a barometer at the top above a round and gilded mirror, and a thermometer, a humidity gauge and a spirit-level at the bottom. The multi-functional instrument is shapely, cased in mahogany and designed as a wall-piece. The masters of the craft could combine the individual skills in a quite remarkable fashion.

29

Manchester was a main centre for instrument makers from around 1800. There were three main family firms, two from *Tavernerio, Como*, and the other from near *Lago di Garda*. The first to arrive was Giovanni Battista Ronchetti from *Tavernerio* (Co) in 1790 who set up as a weather-glass (barometer) manufacturer at High Street. In 1805 he was joined by his son Charles Joshua and relative Luigi Antonio Casartelli, who worked both in Manchester and Liverpool. The main branch of the Casartelli family emigrated to Liverpool in 1834 and the firm founded there was in business until the 1980s. Although ownership passed out of family hands in 1933, the Casartelli name remained in use. The Casartelli and Ronchetti families in Manchester became heavily interrelated; in 1851 Casartelli took over the Ronchetti firm, and this firm traded until the 1960s. One branch of the family in Manchester, under John Casartelli Limited, set up in 1939, still trades today.

The third Manchester family was Zanetti. Vittorio Zanetti had arrived in Manchester from Lake *Garda* in 1803. He was a glass blower who made weather-glasses. Zanetti gave a partnership to Thomas Agnew (much to the disappointment of a certain Domenico Bolongaro and one of the Ronchetti family) and the business moved more towards carving, gilding and eventually fine arts by the middle of the nineteenth century. This firm is still enormously successful and prominent, now based in London. One of the main partnerships founded in London was Negretti & Zambra, barometer makers of Cornhill in the City, Holborn Viaduct and latterly of Regent Street, which traded until the late 1970s.

In London these artisans were concentrated occupationally and residentially in the Clerkenwell district of the city and they laid the foundations for the Italian Colony which developed and flourished in the next two decades. Most of these craftsmen tended to die out with their skill and their descendants either merged into the local population or into the rest of the Italian Community. Many married English women. As well as these craftsmen there were also a number of specialist traders by the 1840s in London, some supplying the royal household. The 1838 Post Office Directory lists 60 Italian firms of a general commercial nature.

The political refugees

It is worth reminding ourselves for a moment of the broader sweep of historical developments in Europe at this time. After almost 25 years of the French Revolutionary and Napoleonic Wars, Napoleon was finally defeated in 1815 at the battle of Waterloo. The treaty of Vienna in 1815 led to further upheaval with increased imperialism by the Austro-Hungarian Empire in northern Italy. Italians opposed to the designs of Austria on their territory wished to see the unification of Italy under the Kingdom of *Piemonte*. Thus began the Italian 'nationalist' movement whose struggles produced a new type of migrant who was obliged to flee. Many of these political refugees and *émigrés* left Italy for London. It was not until 1861 that the nationalists succeeded in their cause and the unification of Italy occurred.

With a common reason for emigrating, unlike the craftsmen who came individually and were economically motivated, and most of whom settled on a permanent basis, the political refugees were mostly temporary migrants.

The first of these Italian patriots to arrive, in 1818, was Ugo Foscolo, writer and poet. However, following the strife of 1820-1, hundreds of Italian political *émigrés* sought sanctuary and assistance for their cause in London. The most famous of these exiles was Giuseppe Mazzini, nationalist *par excellence*, who also made the greatest contribution to the organisation and welfare of the mass of poor Italian immigrants who began to flood into London in the 1830s. Antonio Panizzi, who became the Director of the British Museum and designed the famous reading-room, was the first Italian to be knighted in this country. Both he and Gabriele Rossetti, the poet and painter, settled permanently. In total between 1820 and 1860 there were almost a thousand of these exiles living in London.

The political migrants of this period, like their élitist predecessors of earlier centuries, were well received by British society, particularly within liberal circles. They sought entry into the cultural and political world in order to mobilise public opinion in favour of their cause as well as to find means of supporting themselves. Many were in desperate economic circumstances and were dependent on British sympathy. Somehow they had to keep themselves alive and promote their cause. For occupations, reliance was placed on their background, and incomes were earned by giving singing, music, painting and Italian language lessons. The arrival of these men in England coincided with a growing love and 'need' of the arts by the upper classes of society – a movement which manifested itself in the 'grand tour' of Europe. To learn about and appreciate music and art, an understanding of Italian language was, and indeed is, extremely useful.

For the first time, in London where the patriots congregated, there was a sense of 'Community' or at least common purpose amongst this group of Italian immigrants. If they stayed there for any length of time they usually became very well integrated into English life, often marrying English women. However, this group was estranged from both the craftsmen and the poor and uneducated Italian immigrants, although their presence did give a certain leadership to the embryonic Italian Community. It was the most famous of these immigrants, Giuseppe Mazzini, who set up the first Italian club in 1840 and, in 1841, a school for the poor Italian immigrants in Hatton Garden, London.

The numbers involved in this *émigré* migration were not great and it was a transitory phenomenon. However, the significance of this early 'pioneer' movement was not its size, but the example it set. It was the immigration of the political *émigrés*, taken together with the contemporary presence of highly skilled Italian craftsmen, which helped to break the ice and clear the way for the later immigration which included quite different classes. By the 1830s the first real 'wave' of Italian immigrants was beginning to reach London: the poor and the unskilled.

The poor and unskilled immigrants

The origins of the British Italian Community as it is today can be traced to the influx into London from 1830 of impoverished and completely unskilled land peasants and small-holder farmers from the Emilian and Tuscan Appenine mountain regions. This was the most numerous and most important of the nineteenth-century Italian immigrations to Britain.

The major source of these migrants was the *Tosco–Emiliano* mountain area of northern Italy. They first began to arrive in London in the late 1820s and the early 1830s but only from the 1840s and 1850s did their numbers begin to build up significantly. Almost all of them walked to England following a route north up through Italy to the Alps, crossing at Chambéry into France and then on to Paris before crossing the Channel. From rural origins, these migrants became street entertainers and later street vendors and hawkers in the growing urban centres of Britain. They also took up a number of other unskilled occupations wherever they could find work.

Forced to leave their mountain hamlet and village communities because of poverty resulting from an increasing population living within an archaic agricultural system, they formed part of the beginnings of large-scale emigration from Italy at this time. At first the migrants, who were mostly men, had travelled within Italy wherever work could be found. Of course, initially, they sought agricultural or general labouring work, but developed an increasing resourcefulness as circumstances demanded. Generally they migrated in the late spring in the hope of finding work for the summer so they could earn enough money to see themselves and their families through the winter at home. Gradually, pioneers began to move further and further afield, until the season was spent abroad in many different locations. Migrants thus began to spread out across Europe and indeed the world. Owing to the increasing distances involved in these migrations, it became inevitable that the communities these migrants established became more permanent and less seasonal or temporary. This became true for London as much as it did for Moscow and San Francisco in the middle of the nineteenth century.

It is from this era that the notion of the chain of migration first springs. A pioneer or group of men from a particular source village in Italy would find and establish a connection with a particular destination. In this context, we can begin now to discover how and by what means the mass of migrants were able to transfer themselves or, as was more often the case, were transferred by others from remote mountain communities of Italy to this country.

Chain migration

The notion of chain migration was explained in the Introduction. Now, we can expand this idea and apply it to the migrants of the nineteenth century.

The development of the first British 'Little Italy', in London, was due entirely to the phenomenon of chain migration in its various forms. Almost every migratory flow begins with the adventuring pioneers or groups of individuals who set off from their place of origin to a particular destination. The most significant attribute of pioneers, as in other areas of life, is that they blaze trails that others follow, and sometimes the number who do so grows into a broad stream. The idea is that after a pioneer has established himself at a given location, he then sends for his family, his relatives, and even his fellow villagers or *paesani*. In the case of *paesani* their actual recruitment can take various forms from the personal to the impersonal. These people follow and, in this way, particular destinations develop links with particular sources. From this period of Italian emigration, particular villages have links, through expatriates, all over the world. Thus, for example, migrants and their descendants from *Barga* (Lu) are found in Glasgow, Boston, Chicago and Caracas. Migrants from the Upper *Val Taro* (Pr), most notably from the *comuni* of *Borgo Val di Taro* and *Bardi* are found in London, Wales, the north-east of Scotland and New York.

One of the most notable types of pioneer in Italian migration was the *padrone*. These men had an enormous influence over the subsequent migratory flows from their villages and, throughout the nineteenth-century Italian immigration to Britain, they were among the most influential figures in the process of chain migration. The type of *padrone* and his role in the immigration took several forms over the period 1830–1939.

The early *padrone* and street musicians

The early *padrone* was often a pioneer who had been successful in establishing himself at a destination. To develop his activities further, the next step was often to bring over people from Italy to help him expand the enterprise. Those pioneers who took this step thus became *padroni*. Other migrants also, followers rather than pioneers, saw the potential in becoming *padroni*.

The *padrone* transformed the process of emigration into a business; he offered work contracts to people in Italy, sought volunteers to fulfil them, organised transport and employed people himself once at the destination. Unlike his counterpart in America – the 'labour boss' who hired and controlled the newly arrived Italian immigrants on behalf of an indigenous employer and who therefore acted as a sort of broker – the British Italian *padrone* was normally himself the employer of recruits that he had been responsible for bringing over from Italy. In these early days, and this is rightly quite contrary to present-day moral standards, often the workers were not adult volunteers exercising a judgment to come; they were children, children parted from poor parents with false promises, treated badly, and prevented from leaving. At its worst, this process could become virtual slavery. During the mid-nineteenth century when most Italian immigrants were dependent for a living on street music in urban locations, the *padrone* was not only the importer of labour, but at the same time the man who controlled and exploited that labour.

The procurement of these young workers took several forms. Often the *padrone* himself would return to Italy for recruitment purposes. This most often meant to his own village or at least area of Italy, where he and his connections were known. Parents agreed to 'contracts' for their offspring which promised them work, food and lodgings and normally a lump sum payment at the end of the agreed period, usually two or three years. After this time the boys would be free to take up work elsewhere, return to Italy, or perhaps set up in a business of their own. This process is described by the *Graphic* newspaper of 1875 in an article on boy organ-grinders in London:

> *As a rule, they live in parties of from forty to fifty in one house under the fatherly care of a* padrone, *who has imported them from Italy (chiefly from* Parma*). They are bound to him for a term of two to three years, the conditions being that he shall take all their earnings, and in return provide them with food and lodging, and at the end of the term send them home with a large fortune of eight or ten pounds.*

In a court case entitled 'Cruel Treatment of Italian Boys' reported in the *Morning Chronicle* newspaper of 1840, the solicitor who attended for the complainant, a boy called Antonio Petinatti, explained to the courtroom how the system of the *padrone* operated:

> *The masters entered into an agreement with these boys, and brought them to this country to go about with pianos and organs, but paid them no money until the expiration of their term of service.*

In this case the complainant came from *Parma* and the defendant, a certain Stefano Conte, had agreed to pay him nine francs per month, and to provide him with board and lodging. Apparently 'before he crossed the Alps he was well treated, and the agreement was fulfilled in every respect, but afterwards the conduct of the master was entirely changed, and he then only received a piece of dry bread in the morning, and at night a small quantity of rice boiled up with a little bacon'.

With regard to living conditions in Little Italy and in the organ-grinders' quarters in particular, it is worth conjuring up in the mind's eye the character of Fagin from Charles Dickens's novel *Oliver Twist*. Written in 1838, *Oliver Twist* is set in precisely the same area of London as the Italian Colony and, although Fagin is engaged in training boys to be thieves and this was not the case with the *padroni*, the setting, notion and organisation of a large group of boys is very similar. Saffron Hill, the heart of the Italian Colony, had been a place of notoriety during the early nineteenth century and was where the fictitious 'Fagin's Den' was situated. The Artful Dodger led Oliver Twist into the den of thieves by the following route:

*They crossed from the Angel into St John's Road; struck down
the small street which terminates at Sadler's Wells Theatre;
through Exmouth Street and Coppice Row; down the little court
by the side of the workhouse; across the classic ground which
once bore the name of Hockley-in-the-Hole; thence into Little
Saffron Hill; and so into Saffron Hill the Great. . . . A dirtier
or more wretched place he [Oliver] never had seen. (Dickens
1838, p.68).*

The journey thus traced followed a route through the Parish of
Clerkenwell into the heart of Little Italy; the focal point of the Italian
quarter was centred on Saffron Hill, Hatton Garden, and Leather Lane.
This was an area of densely packed housing with a myriad of little alleys
and back courts. Dickens goes on to say:

*The street (Saffron Hill the Great) was very narrow and muddy,
and the air was impregnated with filthy odours. There were a
good many small shops; but the only stock in trade appeared to
be heaps of children, who even late at night were crawling in and
out of doors, or screaming from the inside.*

Often a *padrone* would have a large number of boys, kept in poor
conditions, the youngest of whom were really little more than beggar boys.
The Graphic of 1875 said that:

*The accommodation is wretched in the extreme, all sanitary laws
being set at defiance. Some of the sleeping rooms contain as
many as sixteen beds, upon each of which three or four boys lie
huddled together, dreaming of the sunny skies of their native
country.*

In general, the scandal of organ-grinders was one which occupied
much debate and discussion throughout the Victorian era. The *Morning
Chronicle* newspaper of 1840, under the court case about the treatment
of Italian boys, reported that: 'A few days ago an Italian named Luciano,
who for several years endeavoured to protect Italian boys from the
ill-treatment of their masters, applied to Mr Hall (the judge) on behalf
of a boy of the name of Antonio Petinatti, whose master had, without
provocation, knocked him down and kicked him'. The worst part of it was
that the master always took the boys' passports and kept them until the

agreement expired, so that they could not return to their country without the *padrone*'s permission. If a boy left the service of his master because of ill treatment, he had little chance of obtaining employment from any other person, for the masters were 'combined amongst themselves to prevent the boys leaving, and they were severely punished if they quitted their employer's service'. Boys could, and did, however, run away to other parts of the country either to seek their fortunes alone or to join other *padroni*. There was concern too at the other end of the migratory chain about the number of children being sucked into the emigratory process, and in 1873 legislation concerning the exportation of child labour was passed in Italy. In Britain, not just in connection with Italian boys and girls (remember this is the era of human chimney brushes and child factory workers), legislation was passed in 1889 limiting the exploitation of child labour.

The control of the *padroni* over the Colony in terms of immigration and occupation was thus very powerful in these early days. This was especially true with regard to the organ-grinders, where the *padrone* controlled large numbers of boys who wandered the streets on his behalf. Grinding organs required no skill other than simply turning a crank handle to activate the hammer which struck the cords for the tune. Playing the *zampogne*, an Italian bagpipe instrument, required more musical skill and training, and fewer boys were involved. This was a tradition among the migrants of the *Ciociaria*. Organs, especially the upright piano variety, were an expensive item. Many adults who were no longer under the direct control of the *padrone*, having completed their contracts, or migrated independently, were nevertheless unable to buy an organ and hired one out on a daily basis from a *padrone*.

Mostly the type of *padrone* described above and the organ-grinders were associated with London, although a similar smaller Colony developed in Manchester's Ancoats. Most of these migrants had started out in, or at least passed through, London and all headed for urban centres. The barrel organs, on wheels, were pushed and pulled around the country. Plate 2 was taken in Bradford around 1890 and shows also the popular combination of performing animals and street music. Virtually all the barrel organs were made by Chiappa, Spinelli & Rossi and Gaviolli of London from 1860 and either Rubino or Antonelli of Manchester from 1894.

Other unskilled groups

Although organ-grinding and other forms of street entertainment were predominant in the middle of the nineteenth century, there were also other

37

occupations, again with specific origins in, and working from, the Colony. One early occupation was that of artist's model. It was generally believed that these people were mainly 'Neapolitans'. Actually, they came from the *Ciociaria* area – people from the village of *Picinisco* (Fr) were particularly famous in this field. In an amusing article on the Italian Colony in London, the *Graphic* newspaper of 1875 described how one of their reporter-sketchers entered a house occupied by Neapolitans and, when he produced his sketchbook, all the occupants suddenly became as motionless as statues, and so remained until he had finished sketching. Many of these immigrants had been in Paris, involved in a similar occupation, before they came to London. Here, they were employed by the various art schools such as the Royal Academy, the Royal College, the Slade School and Westminster School as well as the art schools in other cities such as Edinburgh, Manchester and Liverpool. By the turn of the century there were around 200 Italian artists' models in Britain.

Domenico Mancini, born in *Picinisco* in 1889, became the most famous of all the artist's models. He posed for many well-known paintings and sculptures including the 'Light of the World' by Holman Hunt, now in the chapel at Keble College, Oxford, and the bronze artillery at Hyde Park Corner in London. While he worked in London he supplemented his modelling income by running an ice-cream stall in Hammersmith, outside the Lyric Theatre, in the summer. In 1930 he moved to Edinburgh and worked for many years at the College of Art. In 1964, he was still working and at 75 was the oldest artist's model in the country.

In London, unskilled members of the Italian Colony also took up labouring jobs for which there were increasingly few local volunteers. Two of the most common were paviours, paving the roads; and asphalters, covering roads and roofs. Ghirardani became the largest Italian asphalt contractor based at Goswell Road in the Clerkenwell Colony. The development into the itinerant street selling of crudely prepared food was, however, the major development of the Colony into which the organ grinders naturally evolved.

Skilled and semi-skilled travelling craftsmen

The last group of arrivals, completing the pre-1880 Italian Community, were several types of itinerant semi-skilled craftsmen, specifically the *figurinai* and *arrotini* from the 1860s and mosaic and *terrazzo* workers from slightly later.

Figurinai

The *figurinai* were makers and sellers of small statuettes and figurines. They were itinerant, manufacturing and selling their wares as they travelled from place to place. These migrants formed an interesting group who originated almost exclusively in the province of *Lucca*, *Toscana*. They came mostly from the two *comuni* of *Barga* and *Coreglia Antelminelli*. (Plate 3 illustrates the monument to the *figurinai* in *Coreglia*, erected in 1990.) During the mid- to late-nineteenth century these *figurinai* travelled and settled throughout the world – most notably in Chicago. A large number reached Britain.

These men travelled and worked in groups of between five and seven, responsible to their own *padrone*. This was a very different type of *padrone* from the one controlling large numbers of boys in a much more impersonal and exploitative context as described in the previous section. This *padrone* would select a group of men from his village, allocate each a specific task, and they would set out together, again by foot, on a two- to five-year journey from their village of origin. The troupe was thus occupationally entirely self-sufficient. Travelling around, on a planned route, the *figurinai* had all the equipment, tools, moulds and paints they needed to produce their chalk statuettes to sell as they travelled. Several basic models could be painted and named to fit with local traditions and popular figures of the day. Garibaldi could become St Patrick, Abraham Lincoln, Tsar Nicholas of Russia or Prime Minister Gladstone of Britain depending on the routes taken by the troupe of *figurinai*.

This itinerant manufacture and selling did lead, however, to permanent settlement in certain locations, usually at the end points of journeys. This partly explains the relatively large presence of the *Barghigiani* in Paisley and Glasgow and the almost non-existence of such a Community in London today. Many of the *Barghigiani* present today in Scotland are the descendants of *figurinai* who arrived in Britain in the 1850s, initially in London, and who worked their way northward. Having walked the length of the country making and selling their wares as they went, it is logical that they would have stopped at the last main centre of population on this northward journey. Perhaps after an initial intention to stop only for a while, perhaps to work another season, eventually inertia on the one hand and the availability of other types of opportunity on the other led to the development of a permanent Community.

Arrotini

The *arrotini* were the knife-grinders from the *Val Rendena*, now in the *Trentino*. Like the *figurinai* they came mostly from two specific source villages: *Pinzolo* and *Carisolo*. (Plate 4 illustrates the monument to the *arrotini* in *Pinzolo*, erected in 1969.) The *arrotini* spread out across Europe, having a particular connection with Eastern Europe and the Austro-Hungarian Empire, to which the *Val Rendena* belonged at this time. They emigrated on a seasonal basis: in winter when agriculture in their Alpine valley was impossible. Each knife-grinder pushed his *moleta*, a sort of wheelbarrow fitted with grindstone and sharpening equipment, to towns and cities with large households, hotels and restaurants.

By 1850 the first *arrotini* had arrived in London. In what used to be the largest city in the world, with the fastest-growing tertiary sector, there was more business than the grinders could cope with in a season. Almost from the outset they established a presence in London all year round. They would park their barrows outside the rear entrances of hotels and shops and offer to grind all the cutlery then and there. London became an increasingly popular destination with the growth of the Italian Colony and, from the 1880s onwards, the growth of the catering trade.

The *arrotini* still exist in London today and have a monopoly on knife sharpening in the capital, supplying a much needed service to the entire catering industry. Anyone who has ever seen the speed, skill and precision with which the Italians of the London sandwich bars cut and make up various sandwiches will fully realise the importance of perfectly maintained knives.

Mosaic and *terrazzo* workers

From around 1870 another specialist but more skilled sort of Italian craftsman began to arrive in Britain. These were the mosaic and *terrazzo* workers. Their origins were almost exclusively in the *Friuli* region of northern Italy. Unlike the earlier groups of skilled artisans and craftsmen who had tended to congregate in London and Manchester, these men quickly dispersed throughout the country, being called for important works both in private and public buildings – churches, theatres, museums, town halls, hospitals, banks and hotels. Some of their works included St Paul's Cathedral, Brompton Oratory, Westminster Cathedral, the National Gallery, the Tate, the Bank of England and Fife Castle.

Noteworthy amongst the firms founded in this era were the Art

Pavement Co Ltd which employed 250 Italians with Federico D'Angnolo in charge. The firm Diespeker, which was founded in 1881 in Hamburg by Luigi Oderico, soon set up a branch in London under Carlo Oderico and Domenico Bertin, also employing 250 Italians. Art Pavement undertook much Roman mosaic restoration work in Chichester, Colchester, Bigmore and for the Bank of England. Nearly all of the workers of these firms were from the villages of *Sequals, Fanna, Spilimbergo, Solombero* and *Cavasso Nuovo* in *Pordenone, Friuli*. Other important firms sprang up in Birmingham, Bristol, Newport, Glasgow, Belfast, Dublin, Liverpool, Manchester, Bournemouth, Hull, Leeds and Brighton.

The *Friulani*, later to arrive, continued to be in demand right up until the Second World War, by which time there were around 700 of them in Britain. This particular tradition survives today in the form of *terrazzo* and tiling, with many of the old firms still in business such as Grossi of Lewisham in London, Toffolo (Jackson) of Glasgow and Quiligotti of Manchester. Other firms which spring from this era also still operate today in the adapted business of ceramic tiles, for example Minoli of Oxford.

The early Community and its institutions

In the 1830s and 1840s the male–female ratio of the Italian presence in this country was very imbalanced and it was not until the middle of the second half of the century, the 1860s and 1870s, that women began to arrive in sufficient numbers to balance the sex-structure of the Colony in London. By this time the role of the *padrone* as described on pages 34–7 was declining but a new type of *padrone* began to emerge. Apart from the three groups of semi-skilled craftsmen described in the previous section, the general immigration of the poor Italians with no trades, training or skills continued to be the largest portion of the flow and in the late 1870s this began to follow a more classical pattern of chain migration where the *padrone* and others began to bring over female members of the family. The Community thus became more sedentary and stable and it is interesting to look at some other aspects of Community life at this time.

The Italian schools

The institution of an Italian school in London is perhaps the oldest of the Colony. In fact, from 1817 under the Catholic church of Sardinia Street, Lincoln's Inn, known as *La Cappella Sarda*, subsidised by the government of the *Regno di Piemonte*, there was *una scuola popolare* – a popular

41

school. Not much is known about this school in its early days, however, and it is not until 1841 when Giuseppe Mazzini founded a school for the poor Italians that the Colony had its first proper school. This was at 5 Greville Street, Hatton Garden, and was free to Italians in the area. Mazzini and his compatriots, mostly political exiles, conducted the lessons every evening and in the afternoons of holidays. As well as Mazzini himself, one of the well-known teachers was Filippo Pistrucci, the engraver. Antonio Gallenga and Gabriele Rossetti were also involved with the school. A few months after its foundation, the school had 160 pupils – a sign of its success. Not only children but also illiterate adults attended.

During the 1840s, the school of Sardinia Street was still in operation and from 1837 was under the direction of a priest called *Padre* Angelo Baldacconi of *Siena*. There was a degree of hostility between the two schools with Sardinia Street being extremely suspicious of the 'liberal' and anti-religious views being imparted at the Mazzini school. There was much friction and a particular incident involving a mob from Sardinia Street, which set out with apparent intent to do damage to the Mazzini school, gained considerable coverage in the British press. The *padroni* objected to both schools since they feared that some of their boys were being lured away from their street occupations, and they were also aware that Mazzini and the Italian patriots did not approve of their activities. It was the Mazzini school which made the first request in 1846 for a law protecting children from exploitation.

When Mazzini returned to Italy in 1848, his school inevitably declined and was finally forced to close. This left the school at Sardinia Street as the only school within the Community for most of the second half of the nineteenth century. It was taken over by the Pallottini Fathers, Raffaele Melia and Giuseppe Faà, who arrived in London in 1844 and later founded the Italian Church. Later this school transferred across the street to 14 Greville Street, Hatton Garden, and then to George Yard where a house was purchased for its occupation. Finally, with the demolition of George Yard in 1878 and with the opening of Clerkenwell Road, it moved to Little Saffron Hill and was still there as a day school, but with Italian language evening classes, up until the Second World War. Today the premises are still standing and used as a ballet and dance school.

The Italian Benevolent Society

The Italian Benevolent Society is the oldest association of the Italian Community in London. It was founded in the same year as the unification of Italy, 1861, by the first Italian ambassador to the Court of St James, *Marchese* d'Azeglio, and was under the patronage of the first king of Italy, Vittorio Emanuele II. It was established to help the poor and needy Italians in general – in finding jobs, helping people return to Italy, offering help in cases of sickness and most of all working against the exploitation of Italian children in this country. In this last capacity one of the main reasons for the foundation of the society was to try to check the flow of boys, *garzoni*, into London and, most of all, to help alleviate the often miserable conditions under which they were housed.

Indeed, significantly, as a result of much of the work of the Society in collaborating with the government commission of inquiry, the Children's Protection Act was passed in 1889. This Act prohibited boys under 14 and girls under 16 years from professional begging. In addition, the society petitioned the London Schools Board to extend the obligation of schooling to foreign children.

The Italian Benevolent Society is still in existence today and has naturally undergone changes in more than a century of life. Its stated aims, however, remain the provision of help to needy Italians. These are harder to identify now and the Society has an enormous surplus of funds in its bank account.

La Società per il Progresso degli Operai Italiani

Founded in 1864 and still in existence today, known as the *Mazzini Garibaldi Club*, this is one of the oldest and noblest institutions of the British Italian Community. Although officially inaugurated, named and given a constitution at the time of the triumphal visit of Giuseppe Garibaldi to London in 1864, a looser society or association of Italian workers had been in existence from about 1840 onwards under the auspices of Mazzini: the *Unione degli Operai Italiani*. The overall concern of the society at this time was in giving assistance to the poor, and organising the Italian immigrants.

The first club house was at 106 Farringdon Road and the first committee consisted of Leopoldo Cristiani, Giacomo Geminazzi, Andrea Vaccani, Giacomo Crista, Battista Arrigoni and Pietro Nelli under the presidency of Domenico Lama. One of the early initiatives taken by the society was to have a plaque mounted on the outside wall at 5 Hatton Garden, the house where Mazzini had lived during his stay in London. This stone carving can still be seen today.

St Peter's Italian Church, Clerkenwell

In 1844 when San Vincenzo Pallotti sent two of his missionary priests, Fathers Raffaele Melia and Giuseppe Faà, to help the Italian Colony in London, his hope was to establish a church for them in the British capital. This dream took 20 years to realise and, in 1864, the now famous Italian Church of St Peter's was founded in Clerkenwell, providing a physical and spiritual heart for the London Italian Community from then until today.

The original plan for the church showed five entrances: two on either side of the altar (which are still visible today) and three at the rear of the church with a huge façade and stairway leading onto Herbal Hill (then Little Saffron Hill). There were still five houses awaiting demolition on Herbal Hill and this main entrance was rarely used, so the two smaller side entrances were used, one leading onto George Yard (running into Hatton Wall which in turn ran into the famous Hatton Garden) and the other on to Back Hill. In 1878 the construction of Clerkenwell Road was passed and its opening, forged through the middle of the Colony, was to be a great advantage to the church as George Yard was subsequently demolished, and consequently the entrance of the church opened on to the new road. It was on this entrance, still the main entrance today, that the grand *portico* and *loggia* were later constructed.

The splendid interior, which represents the architectural lines of the *Basilica* San Crisogono in *Roma*, is rich in mosaics and side chapels and has a wonderful concert organ which was bought in 1887. The marble for the building of the altar, tabernacles and inside steps was imported from Italy. Although originally conceived to hold 3,400 people, the design was scaled down to a capacity of 1,500. The Bell Tower is 100 feet high and the bell, which weighs 4 tons, was exhibited at the International Exhibition in 1862.

Apart from the role St Peter's assumed in the Italian Colony, one of the most interesting aspects of its presence as an Italian, as opposed to Irish or indigenous Catholic, church was the part that it helped play in the reintegration of the Catholic religion into mainstream society in Britain. This Italian church, obviously more festive and colourful in its tradition, helped to dismantle the persecution and guilt complex of the local Catholics which had resulted from the Reformation. In fact, according to Marin (1975) it was only from such a church that it was conceivable for a procession of a *Madonna* or saint to have been born. When the *Madonna del Carmine* left St Peter's in a glorious procession in 1883, it was in fact the first procession of its kind in Britain since the Reformation.

44

In addition to the spiritual role of the church in the midst of the Italian Colony, it also acted as a social core to the Community, giving it a sense of identity. The important life-cycle rituals of birth, death and marriage were centred upon the church and this more than any other institution gave the Colony a means to enact its social cohesiveness. The priests acted as social workers and helped new migrants in their adaptation to the urban environment. Elsewhere in the country, no Italian churches were founded at this time, mainly because of the smaller numbers of immigrants and the smaller scale of residential concentration. It would be over 100 years before the next Italian church was established in Britain.

Having completed our review of the development of, and institutions of, the early Community, it is time to move on. The Community was in fact poised for large-scale expansion, not just in London, but across the country, due to the development of an entirely new field of occupation – one which would employ the large majority of members of the Colony and be responsible for much new migration – the catering connection. The 1880s formed something of a watershed in terms of both the type of immigrants who were arriving and more importantly the sorts of occupations followed by the Italians who were by this time becoming an increasingly permanent aspect and factor in the make-up of British society.

Chapter Two

Firm foundations 1880–1918

Introduction

The original building blocks of the Community were described in Chapter 1. The reasons for, and the mechanisms of, migration were explained and the occupational activities and some of the early Community institutions were highlighted.

This chapter moves the story forward and introduces the numerical development of the Community, summarises the Italian geographical origins of the migrants in terms of the key areas and villages and then traces both these factors through into the build-up of the individual Italian settlements in Britain. This leads naturally into a review of the main occupational developments during 1880–1918, the move from itinerant and informal street entertainment and hawking to permanent settlement and sedentary catering ventures. Indeed, it was not until this second stage of development that the Community was assured of a future: an Italian factor would become an enduring facet of British life.

Growth of the Italian presence

Before 1851, no statistics on the size of Italian presence are available; nor, frankly, given the transitory nature of the Community, is it easy to see what means of counting the immigrants there might have been. The British census only began its enumeration of foreign-born residents in 1851, and in fact figures were only collected for London. A total of 1,604 Italian-born were found to be present in the capital. From 1861, figures were compiled for the whole country. Unfortunately, however, as mentioned in the Introduction to the book, the British census enumerates only people born in Italy and does not, therefore, take account of the descendants of the original immigrants – that is to say people born in this country of

Table One

Italian-born population in Britain, 1861–1911

Year	Great Britain	England & Wales	Scotland
1861	4,608	4,489	119
1871	5,331	5,063	268
1881	6,832	6,504	328
1891	10,934	9,909	1,025
1901	24,383	20,332	4,051
1911	25,365	20,771	4,594

Source: British census 1861–1911.

Italian parentage. The statistics for Italian-born people resident in Scotland, England and Wales, 1861–1911, are presented in Table 1. From the 1861 figure of 4,608 for the whole country we can assume that the Community had been steadily growing since the 1820s and 1830s; more than half of these people were, however, located in London. Between 1861 and 1871, the decennial increase was not enormous at around 700 people, but rose to an increase of 1,500 people between 1871 and 1881. By this decade the number of migrants flowing in from Italy was increasing rapidly and the Community was set for substantial growth between 1881 and the turn of the twentieth century. As can be seen from Table 1 there was an increase of over a third between 1881 and 1891, with the main growth decade for the British Italian Community in the nineteenth century clearly being between 1891 and 1901 when the numbers present more than doubled from 10,934 to 24,383.

Italian sources of statistics on the number of Italian citizens resident abroad became available in 1870. For the whole of the British Isles at this time the Italian Ministry of Foreign Affairs gave a total of 11,000 Italians – double the British census figure. This difference is due to the fact that the Italian figures, unlike the British census figures, include British-born Italians – that is, the second, third and subsequent generations of Italians.

This general pattern of growth was mirrored in Scotland where, although the numbers were much smaller, the rate of growth was more marked with a tripling in size of the Community between 1881 and 1891 and then a tripling again between 1891 and 1901. The largest absolute increase was again in the decade 1891–1901, with the significant increase of 3,026 people.

This substantial increase in the British Italian Community at the end of the nineteenth century and the beginning of the twentieth century was due primarily to the explosion of emigration from Italy in the 1880s and 1890s caused by the ever increasing demographic pressure on the archaic agrarian structure. The mass of emigrants at that time were destined for the Americas. The increasing flow into Britain was due also, however, to the changing nature of the Italian Community and the fact that new immigrants could be accommodated.

Strangely, between 1901 and 1911 the Community seemed to stagnate somewhat. This is difficult to explain since Italian immigration was little affected by the 1905 Aliens Act, which was mainly aimed at stemming the flow of Russian and Eastern European Jews into Britain and, as we shall see below, limiting itinerant commercial activity. The Italians were not affected by the Act since the vast majority who entered the country were sponsored either by *padroni* or extended family networks and could therefore prove means of support. Emigration from Italy in fact reached its peak in 1913. In concurrence with this trend, records held at the Italian Consulate General in Edinburgh show that 1913 was also the peak year of Italian immigration to Scotland.[1] Inexplicably then, the census figures show very little further growth in the Community between 1901 and 1911.

It is now interesting to look in some detail at the geographical origins in Italy of the early Community.

Origins of the migrants

As indicated in the Introduction to the book, the area, and often even the village, of origin in Italy have been important in the type of Italian Communities which have emerged in this country. Indeed, we have seen from our survey of pre-1880 migrants in Chapter 1, many of these groups came from specific locations and brought with them very specific and individualistic skills. As the century progressed, the migrants increasingly arrived as a result of chains established between their villages in Italy and particular places in Britain. Some of these chains continued to operate until the 1960s and 1970s, interrupted only by the Second World War.

In this first major phase of immigration the migrants came mostly from northern and central Italy. The 1861 British census and a study by Henry Mayhew, published in the same year, indicated that almost all of the Italians resident in Britain were from northern and central Italy, especially *Liguria, Lombardia*, and most significantly the *Tosco-Emiliano* Appenine mountain area. In an important book on the Italian presence in nineteenth-century Britain, the historian Lucio Sponza (1988) confirmed that the main movement of the poor immigrants was from mountainous communities in Italy and that the Upper *Valtaro* in *Parma* was the main area of emigration to Britain for the best part of the nineteenth century. The nearby *Val Ceno* of *Piacenza* as well as the *Lunigiana* and *Garfagnana* areas of the *Toscana* mountains were also major sources. (See Map One). Hamlets such as *Bratto, Braia* and *Grondola* in the *comune* of *Pontremoli*; *Grezzo* and *Casanova* in the *comune* of *Bardi*; *Val Dena* and *Rovignalia* in *Borgo Val di Taro*; *Sommacolonia* and *Tiglio* in *Barga* were just some of the most common mountain sources.

There were also, however, considerable contingents from further south in Italy, especially after the 1850s, *Val Liri*, the *Val Comino* and the isolated mountainous villages and hamlets of the *Abruzzi* mountains, an area of Italy known as the *Ciociaria* (see Map Two): places such as *Fontitune* and *Valle Porcina* in the *comune* of *Picinisco* and *Mortale* in *Casalattico*. According to the Italian census of 1871, southern Italians made up about 15 per cent of the overall total present in Britain. This proportion of the total was steadily maintained until 1915, and largely consisted of people from the *Ciociaria* which at that time came under the region of *Campania*. This area is now in the province of *Frosinone* in the region of *Lazio*. The *Toscana* and *Emilia* contributions were fairly similar and together these gave the Community its strong central-northern Italian character, accounting for between 35 per cent and 55 per cent of the total over the period 1877 until 1914.

Table Two

Main regions of origin of Italians in Great Britain, 1877–1914

Years	Total	Lombardia		Emilia		Toscana		Campania	
		Tot.	%	Tot.	%	Tot.	%	Tot.	%
1877–90	8,104	788	9.7	1,860	23.0	2,726	33.6	1,041	12.8
1891–1905	26,476	1,756	6.6	5,052	19.1	4,517	17.1	6,404	24.2
1906–14	32,308	2,140	6.6	8,070	25.0	4,847	15.0	5,822	18.0

Source: *Annuario Statistico della Emigrazione Italiana, Roma* 1926.

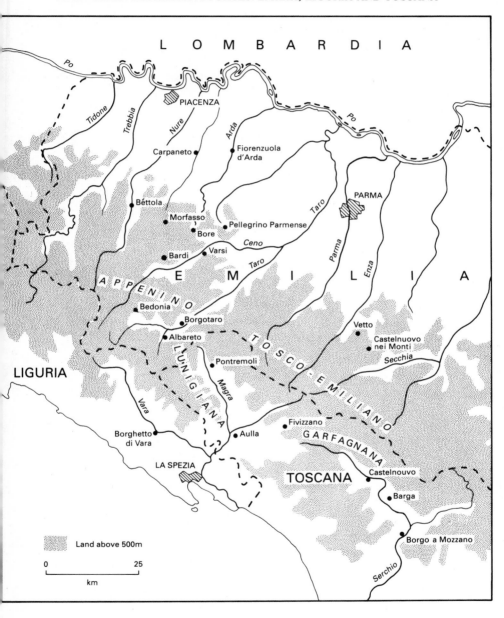

MAP ONE:
MAIN CHAIN MIGRATION SOURCES: *EMILIA, LIGURIA AND TOSCANA*

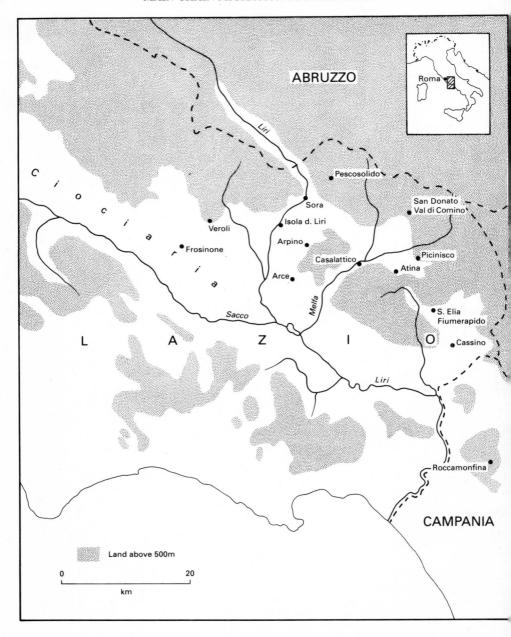

MAP TWO:
MAIN CHAIN MIGRATION SOURCES: *LAZIO*

ABRUZZO

Roma

Liri

C i o c i a r i a

Pescosolido

Sora

San Donato
Val di Comino

Veroli

Isola d. Liri

Arpino

Picinisco

Frosinone

Casalattico

Atina

Arce

S. Elia
Fiumerapido

Sacco

Melfa

L   A   Z   I   O

Cassino

Liri

Roccamonfina

CAMPANIA

Land above 500m

0   20

km

During the specific period of 1891 to 1905, however, as we can see from Table 2, the proportion of people from the south was the largest at 24 per cent of the total while both the *Emilia* and *Toscana* contributions declined. The *Lombardia* proportion remained more consistent over the whole period; many of these migrants came from the *Como* area.

The fact that most of the migrants came from mountainous communities is significant since this served to exaggerate their sense of local loyalties, or *campanilismo*. Meaning literally the spirit of the bell tower (*campanile*) of the church, *campanilismo*, or localism, resulted from the mountainous character of Italy, which isolated village communities to the extent that even adjacent areas developed their own characteristics, customs, speech patterns and loyalties. At the peak time of emigration, just after the turn of the twentieth century, local allegiance in Italy was still stronger than any feeling of national identity. National sentiment was artificial, or at least still novel, and second to local loyalty in a nation state as recently created as Italy (1861). Few migrants had experienced life beyond their villages and they were suspicious of outsiders, trusting only people they knew. When migrants moved abroad this sense of *campanilismo* was transported with them where, if anything, it became even stronger as a social force. The extent and retention of this local feeling abroad is summed up by the Italian American historian Lopreato (1970, p.104):

> *When the Italians came to the United States they imported a pitiful tendency to mistrust and avoid all those who did not share their particular dialect and customs*

in other words all those who did not come from their village or region of origin.

The notion and operation of *campanilismo* was particularly relevant in the early Italian Community of Britain. Also, as we have noted in Chapter 1, the different origin groups were often divided further by their different occupations. In London, within the Colony itself, little subgroups and separate social and economic entities and networks grew up based around these origins and skills. There was little or no opportunity, for example, for an Italian who came from outside the *Lucca* area to be apprenticed into the statuette trade by a *Lucchese padrone*.

The geographical origins in Italy of the various groups also influenced the paths they chose in their movement and settlement across Britain.

53

Growth of the Communities

Throughout the nineteenth century and until 1914, half of the Italian population was located in London. However, from the 1880s, with the build-up in numbers, dispersal from London began to gain momentum and the Italians began to settle permanently in urban locations. Because of the nature and range of occupations, initially organ-grinding and later street selling of food, it was necessary for the Italians to locate in towns and cities where they had a captive audience. The main centre for Italians in the north was Manchester which, by 1835, had formed its own 'Little Italy'. Manchester in fact was the only true Colony outside London before 1880. By 1891 there were around 600 Italians in Manchester and in addition to the organ-grinders there were *terrazzo* workers, plasterers and stone masons who had been called to help build the town hall in 1877. By the turn of the twentieth century the number of Italians in Manchester had doubled and Italian sources estimate a presence of 1,250 Italians in 1901.

By the end of the nineteenth century, Newcastle, Leeds, Bradford, Sheffield and the other northern cities also became significant destinations for Italians. In 1901, the Italian Consul General in Liverpool, responsible for the north of England, estimated that there were 300 Italians in Liverpool, 800 in Newcastle, 250 in Sheffield, 150 in Bradford, 140 in Leeds and 110 in Hull.

Few Italians had settled in Scotland by the middle of the nineteenth century but, as we have seen, their numbers increased rapidly in the 1880s and 1890s. Until 1881 there were roughly similar numbers of Italians in Glasgow and Edinburgh but by 1891 the Glasgow Community had grown to three times that in Edinburgh, a pattern maintained until 1911 and beyond. The Glasgow and Edinburgh totals taken together over this period accounted for around half of the Scottish Italian population. Similarly, the first Italians began to settle in Wales at this time, and by 1901 their numbers had reached around 400.

The oldest Italian families of the present-day Manchester, Glasgow and Edinburgh Communities trace their origins to the 1880s period. Identifying families which are able to trace their roots to the previous period, 1800s–1870s, is impossible, unless they are connected to the migration of the skilled craftsmen and artisans of the early 1800s. (Examples of the latter abound, especially in Manchester.) Strangely, even in the London Community, there seems to be a lack of continuity between the two periods 1800–1880 and 1880 onwards. Partly this bears out the fact that the early Community was very transitory, with few people settling on a permanent basis. On the other hand, it is puzzling that no well-known London Italian families can trace their roots to before 1870. Any information on this would be most interesting.

Thus the majority of Italians who reached the provinces in the 1880s and 1890s dispersed through the London Colony. Since most had in any case walked to Britain from Italy, they simply continued their northward journey in this fashion, although sometimes complete with an organ, hurdy-gurdy, or some other musical instrument in order to earn their passage. This was not always the way, however, with coastal locations. In Liverpool, for example, there was an Italian Colony during the nineteenth century composed mainly of *Liguri* (*Genova*) and *Campani* (*Napoli*) sailors who had arrived directly by sea.

During the early phase of settlement within each of the main cities, the Italians tended to congregate residentially and there were Colonies in several cities. In Manchester the Italians concentrated in the Ancoats area; in Edinburgh in the Grassmarket; in Glasgow in several small nuclei at the Cowcaddens and Garnethill area of the city, the Gallowgate and the Gorbals. The most noted Italian *ghetto* was still, undoubtedly, 'Little Italy' of Clerkenwell and Saffron Hill in London. By the 1880s, however, owing to demolition, slum clearance and the building of new roads, many Italians had already left the area and moved northwards to Finsbury, Kings Cross and Islington. The Colony was then centred inside a triangle formed by the new roads, Clerkenwell Road, Farringdon Road and Rosebery Avenue, which had cut through the original Colony.

By the 1890s a second London Italian Colony began to emerge in Soho, centred on Frith Street, Old Compton Street on one side of Shaftesbury Avenue and around Gerrard Street on the other. This was composed mainly of northern Italians – *Piemontesi* and *Lombardi*. The arrival of this new group was dependent, as we shall see below, on the rapid growth of the tertiary sector, especially from around the turn of the twentieth century onwards. In general, the new arrivals were rather more sophisticated and better off than the, often still street-roving, *Emiliani*, *Toscani* and *Campani* of Clerkenwell. The two London centres of Italian population were quite different and a good deal of jealousy and non-interaction developed between the two Communities. Many of the residentially displaced Italians from Clerkenwell did, however, seek new accommodation in Soho and the more upwardly mobile took advantage of the changing times and moved into the growing West End catering industry themselves. Generally though, the two Communities had their own sense of identity, their own networks, shops and support services.

It was due to the embryonic catering connection that the migrants were able, in the 1880s and 1890s, to spread out, forging much further afield than the organ-grinders had ever gone. Not only did the outlying Colonies of Glasgow, Edinburgh and Manchester significantly build up numbers in this period, but the migrants travelled further and the northern Communities of Aberdeen and Dundee were also established. The Aberdeen Colony, for example, was centred around Market Square and Justice Street. Firm source and destination links based on chain migration were established and the fabric of our 'old' Italian Communities put into place. Not all destinations received all groups of migrants.

As the migrants pushed north from London, in search of new pitches and markets, distinct routes were followed by the different groups. One of the strongest, and probably one of the pioneering flows out of London, was that of the *Ciociari* migrants. People from the *Val Comino* and *Val Liri*, from places like *Arpino*, *Arce*, *Isola Liri*, *Atina* and *Picinisco* (see Map Two), had been the founding fathers of the Manchester Colony. They were also the first to settle in Newcastle, Glasgow, Edinburgh, and in addition the first to cross the Irish sea to Dublin and Belfast. Their dispersal across the country was numerically the greatest and also the most multi-directional in its flow. Almost all, although there are exceptions as we shall note below, of the 'old' Italian Communities in Scotland and England outside of London were founded by this group of migrants in the 1880s era. Such was the extent of departure of the *Ciociari* from the capital that they left the Colony firmly dominated by the *Toscani* and *Emiliani*.

The second most important group to leave London were one of the *Emiliani* groups: the *Parmigiani*. They headed to the far north, and west to Wales. Their northerly journey was uninterrupted until they reached Perth, Dundee and more particularly Aberdeen, Stonehaven and Fraserburgh on the north-east coast of Scotland. They by-passed Manchester and, perhaps more notably, Glasgow and Edinburgh. No more than three or four *Parmigiani* families settled in Manchester – Manfredi, Federici and Molinari – and one or two in Glasgow, notably Giovanazzi. There are no families resident in Edinburgh from *Parma* who trace their origins to this period. As a result, in Aberdeen today links with the London Italian Community are stronger than with either the Glasgow or Edinburgh Italian Communities. In the westward movement from London, the Welsh Valley Italian Communities of Porth, Treorchy, Tonypandy and Merthyr Tydfil were established by migrants from *Borgo Val di Taro* but more especially *Bardi* (Pr).

Thus the Italian Communities of Wales and surprisingly the north-east of Scotland were direct off-shoots of the London Italian Community. On travelling up the country from London and on finding Italians – not from their source area – already established in Manchester, Edinburgh and Glasgow, it appears that the *Parmigiani* decided to leap-frog these Communities and continue northward until they found virgin territories. Aberdeen, the grey granite city of the north must, however, have seemed very different from the mountain hamlets of the Upper *Val Taro*.

Another group moving through London, but not settling there, were the *Lucchesi* statuette sellers. They reached Scotland by the 1880s and settled primarily in the west coast area. Paisley and Glasgow were the most prominent destinations, but a sprinkling of their descendants are to be found on west coast routes as far north as Inverness. They avoided the east coast routes almost totally and there are no families of *Lucchesi* descent in Edinburgh, Dundee or Aberdeen for example. On the road northward from London, not all of the *figurinai* reached Scotland and residual groups of *Barghigiani* are to be found in Leicester, Carlisle and Barrow-in-Furness. We know that very few of these *Lucchesi* statuette sellers settled in London because there are no more than a handful of families, descendants of the original migrants, living in the capital today.

Otherwise not many of the other *Toscani* and *Emiliani* groups left London. The vast majority of people from the *Lunigiana*, from *Piacenza*, remained in London. There are very few traces of descendants from these groups in the 'old' Communities of Glasgow, Edinburgh and Manchester. However, there are some outstanding exceptions; the most astonishing perhaps being the families from *Pontremoli* still resident in Elgin, Stornoway, Nairn and Banff in the extreme north of Scotland.

Let us now move on and see how the activity of the Italians changed and how they achieved this remarkable geographic dispersion.

The catering connection

It had always been necessary for the Italians as an alien immigrant group to identify their own occupational niches and adapt their unique skills to the local market. This they had successfully done in a range of skilled, innovative and even 'exotic' ways in the early phase of settlement from the early craftsmen in the first decades of the nineteenth century through to the organ-grinders of the middle of the nineteenth century. Owing to hostility and solidarity from the local trades unions and craft societies, the

Italians were only tolerated if they offered something distinctive and non-competitive. Even in the labouring sector, only asphalting, a particularly dirty and arduous job, was open to Italians, since opposition to immigrant labour was strong and, in any case, the Irish had a monopoly on most areas of heavy unskilled work.

The first development

The late 1870s and early 1880s saw the culmination of a fundamental change in the occupational structure of the Italian Community. There was a gradual decline in begging boys and then in street entertainers from the 1850s onwards. Indeed, according to the *Leisure Hour* news magazine of 1856, young Italian boys had virtually disappeared from the streets of the metropolis and the writer asked the questions: 'Where is the little pipe and taber doll dancer?', 'Where is the monkey bearer?', 'Where are the Italian white mice boys?' Apparently they were to be found only rarely in that year. Also, by the 1880s organ-grinding began to decline in popularity. The once popular informal entertainment increasingly became a nuisance as the numbers and varieties of grinders expanded. Public opinion turned against the grinders and discussion of how to effect their removal from the streets of London became a hotly debated topic. Both the itinerant street musicians and statuette sellers began to move towards a new trade, one which was to spawn an enormous and nationwide activity: catering.

It began this way. The *Garfagnana, Lunigiana, Val Taro*, and *Val Magra* were all great chestnut-growing areas. As the migrants left on their journey, they began to bring chestnuts from their villages when they came to London. In the autumn when the harvest was ready, *padroni* organised further consignments which duly arrived in the Colony. Throughout the winter, barrows were pushed around the streets in the same way as the organs. The barrows had braziers to roast the chestnuts, and many vendors were accompanied by some music, usually a small hand-organ, to announce their presence. This added a new and more lucrative dimension to the organ business. However, it was the innovation ingeniously conceived to improve the fortunes of the *padroni* in the summer which made the greatest impact on the Italians in general and on the Italian factor in British life; in the summer, they made and sold ice-cream.

According to Achille Pompa, the great guru of the ice-cream industry who safeguarded its development and organised the trades associations in the period just after the First World War, a certain Gatti, initially an importer of ice from Norway, was responsible for the introduction of ice-cream to the Colony in the 1850s. Domenico Santorelli from *Longarone* (B1), then brought with him from Italy in 1864 a beautiful painted hand-cart decorated with little mirrors and *stucco* which was shaped like a *gondola*. Thus began the idea of selling ice-cream around the streets.

At first the ice-cream was made in the domestic kitchen, the milk boiled and left to cool overnight and then frozen with ice and salt, bought from the 'ice men', in the back courtyards in the mornings, before being taken out in barrows and carts to be sold around the streets. The first vendors, like the chestnut sellers, were itinerant street hawkers and again this activity was carried out in conjunction with the organs. Gradually, however, as ice-cream became popular, especially with children, there was increasing controversy over its manufacture in the slum conditions of Clerkenwell. More than this, the vending of ice-cream in 'licking glasses' came under scrutiny from advocates of public hygiene. The little glasses from which the public 'licked' and 'sucked' the ice-cream could not be adequately washed out between customers and a lobby grew to ban its sale. Around 1905, the introduction of the 'ice biscuit', later known as the cone and wafer, saved the industry.

In London the barrows were pushed to the better residential and commercial areas of the city. Positions near or in the parks were good for trade. The *padroni*, of course, owned the fleets of barrows both for ice-cream and chestnuts, employed the staff and, as a syndicate, collectively organised and controlled the various territories. There were apparently over 900 ice-cream barrows in Clerkenwell at the turn of the twentieth century. As the industry grew and began to prosper, the barrows and hand-pushed carts became horse-drawn carts (and eventually of course the ice-cream van of today). In Scotland and northern England, this development was especially common since, with less dense centres of population, more ground had to be covered to attain the same level of sales (see Plate 5).

The embryonic food industry was further threatened by campaigns against itinerant street hawkers and pedlars, and foreigners generally, which began in the late 1880s. It was then inevitable that the Italians would begin to organise and rationalise their enterprises. The Aliens Act of 1905 effectively removed the possibility of itinerancy and after this date the Italians in London were forced to enter the formal economy. By this time the sex structure of the Community had become balanced and the organisation of 'business' changed. Independent family-based businesses became the norm and the old style of *padrone* controlling large numbers of people died out.

Setting up in business premises required a high degree of organisation and not a little capital. But for those who could make this transition from itinerancy there were high profits to be made. These small-scale family-based businesses were not beyond the resources, financial and psychological, of the ambitious ex-small-holding farmers who understood the notion of a family all pulling together in a common enterprise upon which their group survival depended.

The chestnut sellers had begun to sell hot potatoes and this combination with other foods, such as hot peas, provided the basis for the first café–restaurants. The ice-cream sellers and on a smaller scale, in London, the *arrotini* also began to establish business premises. The *arrotini* had operated from barrows and it was not long before they recognised the advantages of bringing cutlery to a workshop base rather than taking their *moleta* to the customer in all weathers. They also began to branch out into the wholesaling and retailing of cutlery. Ferrari of Soho was established by such a family in 1901 and still trades today as a specialist supplier of equipment to the catering industry.

For the London ice-cream trade, manufacturing moved to business premises although barrows at fixed points, for which licences now had to be obtained, remained the most common method of selling. Lodging-houses, barber shops, ladies' hairdressers, and provisions shops servicing the Italians, all became common in the 1890s. Indeed, Terroni of Clerkenwell and Gennari of Soho were both established in the late 1880s and early 1890s (see Plate 6).

In the Ancoats Italian Colony in Manchester, the pattern of the ice-cream trade tended to follow the one established in London: a manufacturing base with barrows for selling. Certain families gained control over certain territories and on this basis the ice-cream industry in the north evolved and remained unchanged until the 1960s. The little café or ice-cream shop, which became prevalent in Scotland and Wales, was not the main focus of development in either London or the north. The most prodigious development in ice-cream was on the coast. By the turn of the century there was a Colony of ice-cream men in Ramsgate and the industry, based on these growing seaside resorts, was poised for substantial growth.

In Scotland and the rest of the north of England too, the Italians became sedentary as the itinerant street sellers established themselves in permanent shops around the turn of the century. The period of transition from wandering musicianship and hawking to settled small business entrepreneurs took less than 20 years, the first permanent business being set up in the 1890s. In Scotland the transition to catering was more natural for the *Ciociari* who had already sold hot potatoes while playing the *zampogne* but the *Lucchesi* statuette sellers soon followed and by the 1880s and 1890s almost all of those who decided to remain in Britain had made this transition.

The new businesses led to the development of yet another type of *padrone*. The large increase in the Italian population in Scotland around the turn of the twentieth century was due to this move into the catering sector of the economy. A single shop established at this time would often employ up to ten boys. The owner of such a business, and often a small chain of similar outlets, became the prime mover in the migration process responsible for bringing over boys from Italy to work in his shops. One of the most famous of these *padrone* was Leopoldo Giuliani from *Barga*. He had been a member of a group of *figurinai* and had travelled as a boy to Chicago in the 1860s. By the 1880s he had organised his own troupe of *figurinai* and reached Glasgow where he decided to settle. By the turn of the century he had become the wealthiest Italian in Scotland with an empire based on sixty cafés and shops. A very large number of boys had to be transferred from *Barga* in order to keep the empire operational. The boys in turn grew and aspired to their own businesses. If successful, they too spawned considerable chains of migration.

In Wales, the best-known *padrone* was Giulio Bracchi who, although perhaps not the first Italian to arrive in Wales, was almost certainly the first to open a café. This he did in Tonypandy in 1890 and soon his little empire had grown to several shops dotted across the Rhondda Valleys. He was also responsible for large-scale transferral from his village, *Bardi* (Pr). Although not as outstanding an entrepreneur as Giuliani, his name has been immortalised. All Italian cafés and businesses in Wales became known as 'Bracchi's'. This term is still used there to refer to the local Italian shops regardless of the name of the owning family. In a family business such as the one owned by the Bacchetta family of Porth, which today consists of a café, a restaurant, a confectioner's and a gift shop, local people still say 'I'm going to Bracchi's'. The usage of the French term – café – and the adoption of 'Bracchi' illustrate how new words had to be invented and popularised to cover the new phenomenon.

This type of *padronismo*, which began around 1880 or 1890, continued until the late 1920s. The majority of *padroni* brought boys from their own villages in Italy and the arrangement was much more personal than it had been under the *padroni* of the previous era. Despite this, the living and working conditions of the boys were often little better than half a century before. Descriptions from men still alive today of their own and their parents' experiences in this period are readily available to justify the point. Although exploitation was common, with boys and girls as young as 10 and 11 years being brought over to work very long hours in the Italian family business environment, cruelty was rarely a feature. Members of the second generation from *la vecchia emigrazione*, people now in their 70s and 80s, tell stories of overcrowding into dormitory-style rooms or, worse still, sleeping under the counters, overwork and little, if any, schooling. Many children who were born in this country to Italian parents in the early 1900s and 1910s had nannies. In the same way that boys were brought from Italy to work in the shops, girls became domestic servants and nannies to children of the *padroni*. The compensatory side of all of this was that most people did eventually succeed, often with the help of their *padrone*, in opening their own shops.

The second development

There was a second and equally important strand of development occurring at this time which consolidated the Italian dominance of the catering industry. Unlike the small business development described above, which not only occupied Italians across the country but had in fact been responsible for that very dispersal, this second development was concentrated entirely in London.

Arriving later, the Italians of Soho rarely became organ-grinders and were not so much connected with the itinerant street selling of food. Almost all the Italians of the Soho Colony were drafted into the rapidly expanding hotel, restaurant and club (i.e. gentlemen's clubs) sector of London's West End. Initially at least, their employers were non-Italian. They became kitchen hands, porters, cooks and eventually waiters. The women of the Colony were employed to take care of the vast amounts of linen laundry. Many who started out in this sector soon moved, however, into ownership of the small café–restaurants as described in the previous section.

At this time hotels and restaurants were strictly for the upper echelons of society. It took a very long time for the boy of 12 or 13 arriving in the early 1900s to climb his way up the employment hierarchies from the back kitchens into the salons and dining-rooms. But it could be done, and not only did the majority achieve this, but to such an extent that soon the best hotels sought and would employ only Italians, thereby clinching the catering niche entirely for their compatriots. In addition, as we shall see in Chapter 3, by the 1920s Italians from the Soho Colony began to open high-class Italian restaurants in Soho and Mayfair. In order to found such a restaurant (catering to a mainly British upper-class clientele), or a hotel rather than a lodging- or boarding-house, the aspirant would have to undergo a long apprenticeship, often lasting decades, both to gain experience and to accumulate the necessary starting capital.

By the turn of the twentieth century the two London Italian Colonies were engaged in the catering industry in one form or another. Let us now confirm all of the above by making reference to some official sources.

The *Elenco Generale degli Italiani Residenti nel Regno Unito* published by the Italian Chamber of Commerce in London in 1895, and the British census for 1861–1911 allow us to gain some idea of the magnitude and changing nature of Italian occupational activity in the period before the First World War. By 1881 the main categories of occupation for the Italians in Britain were connected with catering. The number of people employed as cooks, waiters , in board and lodgings, as domestic servants, and as food dealers and confectioners, all rose dramatically between 1861 and 1911. The largest increases were, however, in 1881–91 and 1891–1901. Combining the catering categories, the numbers for England and Wales were 386 people for 1861; 583 for 1871; 1,333 for 1881; 2,930 for 1891; 8,244 for 1901 and 9,273 for 1911. Between 1881 and 1901 the number of ice-cream vendors tripled and then tripled again, slightly outstripping the general trend.

For Scotland, under the main catering category of 'food and lodgings', which was a general catch-all heading and included 'confectioners', most of whom made ice-cream, there were only 38 in 1881, 272 in 1891, 1,637 in 1901 and 2,344 in 1911. The largest increase anywhere in the country, by a factor of six between 1881 and 1901, was thus registered in the catering sector for Scotland.

In England and Wales, the number of street musicians, mainly organ-grinders, continued a gradual increase from 872 in 1861, to 852 in 1871, to 1,240 in 1881, to 1,441 in 1891 and 2,237 in 1901, before dropping dramatically to 464 in 1911. These figures show that the period of transition was over and the new era of catering established.

The *Elenco Generale* of 1895 also indicates, however, that in London there were still considerable numbers of people employed in the traditional specialised crafts of the early nineteenth-century immigration: instrument-making and carving and gilding. There were also people employed in the arts. But by far the largest number of businesses owned by Italians were clustered in retail and catering roles: there were 317 confectioners;

217 proprietors of 'dining and refreshment rooms'; 39 hoteliers; 55 proprietors of boarding-houses; 70 general merchants; 45 hairdressers; 19 beer retailers; 7 private clubs and several fish-and-chip shops. This particular Italian factor of the British economy was now irreversibly established and the Community, accordingly, part of society at large.

Institutions of the Community

By the end of the nineteenth century, the now well-established Italian Community in London had achieved a considerable level of internal organisation and had its own church, hospital and schools. In addition, several political, economic and social associations had been founded and a number of Italian language publications and community newspapers had been put into operation. Added to the growing economic prosperity, these new institutions helped give the Community a growing institutional completeness or self-sufficiency. The founding of associations and circles was very vigorous in the two London Italian Colonies at around the turn of the twentieth century, reflecting a desire from within the Community to organise and provide Italian institutions.

The Italian Hospital

The Italian Hospital in London was founded in 1884 in Queen's Square, Bloomsbury by *Comm.* Gianbattista Ortelli, a wealthy London Italian merchant originally from *Lecco* (Co), for the Italians of Great Britain, but also 'open to all nationalities' as proclaimed on the façade of the building. Instrumental in establishing this institution, which for over a century was one of the largest and most prestigious of the Italian Community, were Emilio and Lazarro Allatini, Giovanni and Giacomo Beghino, the Baring family, *Comm.* L. Bonacina, the Hambro family, the Heath family, *Avv.* Dalton, T. Miller, Leone and Arturo Serena, *Prof. Comm.* Melandri, *Cav.* L. Naintre and *Ambasciatore* Chiaramonte Bordenaro.

The original hospital was completely rebuilt on the same site and reopened in 1900 by Angiola Ortelli, the widow of Gianbattista. (The hospital remained in this distinctive building until its closure in 1989.) Soon after its establishment, the hospital attracted widespread support from within the Community – Italian authorities and immigrants alike – and its annual fund-raising ball soon became the most prestigious event of the Community's social season. After the Italian Church, the hospital formed a focal point for the Italians and its wide-ranging role within the Community assured its long future.

Camera di Commercio

The Italian Chamber of Commerce was founded in London in 1886, becoming affiliated to the London Chamber of Commerce in 1890. In its first decade of life it was extremely active, notably in 1888 with the organisation of the Italian Exhibition at Earl's Court, and in 1895 with the publication of its *Elenco Generale* of Italian commercial and professional entrepreneurs resident in Britain. Its presence provided a stimulus to assist the development of importers and the first commercial wholesalers from the ranks of the Italian Community.

Clubs and societies: London

The *Società Italiana di Mutuo Soccorso*, founded in 1886 in Soho by a woman, Lucia Jemini, was an association for restaurant and hotel employees. Within its initial premises at Soho Square it also housed the associate organisations of the *Circolo dei Mandolinisti* and the *Circolo dei Velocipedisti* both founded in 1891. By 1897 the hotel and restaurateurs association was extremely active and was organising a total of eight courses for its members.

In 1909, there was an internal split within the association because of a growing conflict of interests between the 'worker' members and the increasing number of members who were 'proprietors', as well as the desire by some members to develop activities into sectors other than catering. The breakaway group founded the *Club Cooperativo Italiano* which became one of the main centres for the London Italian Community. The success of the *Club Cooperativo* was due to the spaciousness and the amenities of its premises at 15 Greek Street, in the heart of the Soho Colony. Accordingly, many other circles and associations, including the original *Società di Mutuo Soccorso*, used these facilities and based their meetings and club administration here.

The *Mazzini Garibaldi Club (Società per il Progresso degli Operai Italiani)* was still very active in this era. It had moved from its original premises to 10 Laystall Street, just off Clerkenwell Road, and formed the heart of social activity for men of the Clerkenwell Community. These premises are still there today (in different usage) and the plaque mounted on the outside wall to Mazzini can still be seen. One or two small societies which had existed in the last decade of the nineteenth century, such as *Società Regina Margherita* and *Unione Sociale* founded in 1897, amalgamated into *Il Progresso degli Operai*. The *Mazzini Garibaldi Club* in Clerkenwell and the *Club Cooperativo* in Soho had become the two most active social and political centres of the Community.

Clubs and societies: Manchester and Glasgow

Two main initiatives were taken by the Italians in Manchester to organise their Community. In 1889 the Manchester Italian Catholic Society was founded, closely followed by the Manchester *Società di Mutuo Soccorso*, in 1900. Local Catholics in Manchester had organised an annual Whit Walk from 1834, five years after the Roman Catholic Emancipation Act had restored civil rights to Catholics for the first time after the Reformation. Founded by *Cav.* Domenico Antonelli from *Picinisco* (Fr) who had arrived in Manchester via London in 1894, the main activity of the Manchester Italian Catholic Society was to organise the Italians to join the Whit Walk. This he achieved by commissioning a statue, the *Madonna del Rosario*, behind which the Italians proudly gathered for the walk. The tradition of the Whit Walk has been popular with the Italians in Manchester ever since, passing its centenary in 1989. The Mutual Aid Society was non-religious in its remit and like the similar society in London (p. 42–3) was established to help the poorer Italians of the Ancoats Community. In 1986, its long life ended and the Society merged with the Manchester Italian Catholic Society.

The first collective activity of the Italians in Glasgow was the foundation of a *Società di Mutuo Soccorso* in 1891. As with the similar society in Manchester and the Italian Benevolent Society in London, its brief was welfare and assistance and it followed the constitution of the *Mazzini Garibaldi Club*. Until the establishment of the *Casa d'Italia* in Glasgow in 1935, this society was responsible for any organised social activity amongst the Glasgow Italians. Generally, however, there was little associative life. In Glasgow and the other cities the Italians had spread out because of the nature of their businesses. Because of this dispersal and the long hours worked there was little time for socialising. For a year, 1908 until 1909, a newspaper called *La Scozia* was published which helped keep the Italians in touch and aware of issues of mutual interest. The first visit of an Italian Ambassador to the Scottish Italian Community in 1908 was a major event and was extensively reported in *La Scozia*.

London was therefore not completely alone at this time in the establishment of Community institutions and activities. Just as the Italians were aspiring to new levels of respectability and organisation, there came the First World War.

The First World War 1915–18

The First World War caused a degree of upheaval within the Italian Community, as indeed it did to people all across Europe, but, as will be seen in Chapter 4, there was by no means the devastation which was wreaked by the Second World War. Italy and Britain were allies, not enemies, in the Great War.

When Italy joined the allies in 1915, the response of the Italians resident in this country was both patriotic and one which showed solidarity with the allies. There were massive demonstrations of support at London's Piccadilly Circus, at Great Ancoats Street in Manchester and in George Square, Glasgow. The demonstration and march of Italians in London was led by the two famous *ex Garibaldini*, Stinghi and Geloso, who had helped establish the nation state of 'Italy' in 1861. Such was the degree of patriotic fervour that no fewer than 8,500 men returned to Italy to take up arms and fight for their country between 1915 and 1918. Many of those who left from London were given a send-off from the *Mazzini Garibaldi Club*. The men were attached to the Italian regiments which fought on the Austrian front. A large number of *Croce di Guerra* were awarded to British Italian men for their bravery during these campaigns.

Generally these men who returned to fight were young and without family ties. Most of them had arrived in this country in the last decade of the nineteenth century or the early 1900s. One outcome of their temporary return to Italy was that, after the War, most took the opportunity of returning to their villages to visit relatives and friends. As a consequence, many men subsequently returned to Britain in the immediate post-war period with brides from their villages of origin, thus giving another new injection of migrants to the Italian Community in this country.

Not all, however, returned safely to Britain, and indeed the monument at the entrance of St Peter's Italian Church in London bears testimony to this fact, displaying the names of 175 London Italian men who lost their lives in the Great War. The Italian Hospital took in wounded men of all nationalities and the British government awarded a Diploma of Honour to the hospital for all the work done in this period.

A number of Italian men from Glasgow had also gone off to fight for Italy and ten men were lost. A monument to those men was later erected inside the *Casa d'Italia*. These ten names were as follows:

ALFIERI Angelo
CAMATTARI Francesco
GIANNOTTI Fausto
GIOVANNINI Angelo
JACONELLI Mario
LAVEZZARI Giulio
LAZZERINI Tosello
MAZZUCCHELLI Sante
RAVELLINI Luigi
TROGI Riccardo

An Italian Red Cross committee was formed during the war in Glasgow which collected money to send to Italy. In addition, a propaganda committee was set up which gathered and distributed information and material relating to Italy and the war. With the *Società di Mutuo Soccorso* these committees helped build the first feelings of 'Community' in Glasgow when the Italians were for the first time united in a common cause.

In London, the Italian Chamber of Commerce had to step up its activities to help Italian wholesalers identify new sources for their products since importation from Italy had been closed off because of the war. Businesses in the Community inevitably suffered a set-back, but the majority were able to continue trading. Only the ice-cream makers were affected and their product was almost banned in 1918 due to the shortage of sugar.

In Manchester, a stone which commemorated 'Our Italian Allies' was laid next to the British First World War Memorial in St Peter's Square. Sadly, this stone was removed during the Second World War and destroyed by the local authorities in Manchester. It was not until November 1990, on the fiftieth anniversary of Italy's entrance into the Second World War, that a new stone was commissioned and laid again beside the British First World War Memorial.

There is one further interesting aspect of the First World War and the British Italian Community. As we have seen in Chapter 1, the *arrotini* came to London from the *Val Rendena*. At this time the *Val Rendena* and other Alpine valleys in the *Trentino* area were part of the Austro-Hungarian

Empire, and the *arrotini* were thus classed as enemy aliens and hence interned with many other groups, mostly German and Austrian Jews, living in London. In order to combat internment in 1915, the *Unione Trentina* was founded in London to unite and assist the Italians of these provinces. Also formed, with support from the Italian authorities, was an Italian Information Committee to help disseminate information and assist families and relatives. Many were thus saved from internment, whilst those who were interned generally gained their liberty after a short time.

By 1920, life was returning to normal and the Community was poised for two decades of growing maturity and prosperity.

Chapter Three

The golden era 1920–39

Introduction

The 1920s and 1930s were partly a period of further growth but mostly a period of consolidation for the Italian Community in Britain. This was the time when the migrants from the 'old' emigration – *la vecchia emigrazione* – really settled in, progressed and became an integral part of the fabric of British society. The initial phase of establishment was over, the trauma of the First World War had been surmounted and the Community settled down to hard work, and growing prosperity.

There was a continuing trickle of immigrants but, as it became harder to leave Italy and also at the same time to enter Britain, the Community did not expand greatly. Those who had 'come over', been 'brought' or 'sent over', in the period before the First World War began to pioneer further afield, opening their family-based businesses. Every small town in even the more remote areas of Scotland, Wales and the north of England accepted as normal and part of the town's life their one or two Italian family businesses. Almost entirely self-employed and working in small service businesses, the Italians were unaffected by unemployment during the depression years, and most not only survived but prospered despite the economic difficulties around them.

Stabilisation and migration policy

As we have seen in Chapter 2, the Italian population of Britain had reached around 25,000 people by 1901. During the thirty years 1901 to 1931 the Italian Community stabilised around this number and even declined slightly. Table 3 gives these figures for Britain as a whole but also for England and Wales together, and Scotland. Scotland maintained a position of housing around 20 per cent of the Italian presence. It was in

71

Table Three

Italian-born population in Britain, 1911–31

Year	Great Britain	England & Wales	Scotland
1911	25,365	20,771 (81%)	4,594 (18%)
1921	26,055	20,401 (78%)	5,654 (22%)
1931	24,008	18,792 (78%)	5,216 (21%)

Source: British census 1911–31

fact during these two decades that the Scottish Italian contingent reached its most significant size as a proportion of the total Community.

As we already know, British census figures include only Italians born in Italy. We can therefore confidently assume that by 1931, including British-born second and even third-generation Italians, the overall size of the Community would have been of the order of 30,000 to 35,000. Indeed, Italian sources for 1927 quoted 29,880 Italians resident in Britain and, although this figure was probably an underestimate, since it enumerated only 20,951 as born in Italy and 8,829 as second generation, it does serve to give us an indication of the size of the British-born Italian contingent of this time.

By 1931 although the Community was still growing naturally from internal development, there was very little new immigration. There were two reasons why the Community had begun to stagnate. On the one hand, the number of Italian arrivals was affected by British immigration policy and, on the other, prospective emigrants were curtailed by Italian emigration policy.

In 1920 an Aliens Order (a refinement of the 1919 Aliens Act) was passed which restricted the entry of foreign workers to Britain. This Act of Parliament had substantially more impact than the 1905 Aliens Act in stemming the flow of Italians. The new legislation required, for the first time, that the immigrants have a work permit. Permits were only allocated where no local person could be found to carry out the job in question. Since by this time the majority of Italians were self-employed, in the catering industry or specialist trades, mostly in family businesses, few local non-Italians were interested in any positions on offer in these operations. Applications for work permits to bring over further relatives and *paesani* to help in these enterprises should therefore generally have been successful. There were, however, bureaucratic difficulties. It was

72

necessary to write to the Ministry of Labour explaining the position available and the person proposed to fill it. This was intimidating for many Italians who were limited in their writing skills and, of course, obliged to apply in English. The powers of the Minister to grant or refuse a permit were entirely discretionary and often no explanation was given why one person was given leave to enter and another refused. For example, in 1920, Biagio Candelini of Inverness applied to the Ministry of Labour 'to obtain the services of an alien' and received the following reply: '. . . in view of the serious unemployment at present existing in this country, permits in respect of aliens from abroad are now issued only in exceptional circumstances.' No explanation was given as to how the unemployment could directly impact on the position he wanted to offer to a person in his home town in Italy; it was unlikely a local person in Inverness would have been willing to work for an Italian. These, of course, were the days when an 'ethnic minority' did not question the British authorities. As 'aliens', the Italians simply accepted the decisions.

One way round the work permit problem was to bring relatives over from Italy while they were still of school age. In this way they were portrayed as dependents and not as potential workers. However, many young people between the ages of 12 and 14 were in fact sent to work. In 1920, Gino Guarnieri from *Lugagnano* (Pc) and two of his sisters were 'sent over' to a distant relative, Maria Gorolini, to work at her café in Orange Street near Piccadilly in London. They were aged 12, 13 and 14. The eldest of the three had to be 'sent back' since she was over school age and a work permit could not be secured for her.

In addition to these obstacles at the British end, Italy increasingly adopted a policy of restricted emigration as the 1920s passed. The fascists came to power in 1922 and initially accepted the phenomenon of emigration as a remedy to underdevelopment and unemployment, and continued the policy of previous governments in trying to help migrants and regulate the flow by providing instruction to candidates regarding travel and work permits, etc. Later, emigration for the masses was no longer considered desirable but, rather, a harmful element which would reduce the pool of available workers – especially for the large-scale land reclamation in the south of Italy and public works programmes. Certain travelling concessions were introduced for those who intended to return to Italy and only the more educated middle classes were allowed to leave since their presence abroad might serve to promote 'The New *Roma*'.

The period of the mid to late 1920s and 1930s became the period of the lowest emigration rates from Italy (apart from the two war periods themselves). Emigration declined from its peak of 600,000 a year, immediately before the First World War, to less than 50,000 in the late 1930s.

The Communities

Although, as we saw in Chapter 2, the Italians had already achieved a wide dispersal even before the First World War, it was in the 1920s and 1930s that this residential and business structure became a solidly established national network. The last traces of the itinerant element in the Community vanished and many of the young men who had arrived to staff businesses in the 1900s and 1910s now succeeded in opening their own businesses. The Italian café and fish restaurant became a facet of everyday life in all cities, towns and even small towns up and down the country.

The London area, however, still held around half of the British Italian Community. According to the Italian figures for 1927, the distribution of Italians for each of the consular areas was as in Table 4.

The Italian Consulates in this period were Glasgow, which covered the whole of Scotland; Liverpool which covered north and central England; Cardiff which covered Wales; and London for the south and east. Table 4 allows us at a glance to appreciate the relative sizes of the main Communities. The second-largest contingent outside London, the Scottish Community, accounted for fractionally over 20 per cent of the total. The Glasgow Colony itself had become the second-largest concentration of

Table Four

Distribution of Italians in Britain, 1927

Consular areas	Number	Percentage of total
London	14,800	50
Glasgow	6,092	20
Liverpool	6,000	20
Cardiff	2,238	7
Ireland	750	3
Total	29,880	100

Source: Italian consular figures.

Italians. If we make reference to the *Guida Generale della Comunità Italiana in Gran Bretagna*, a book which was published only twice, in 1933 and 1939, the distribution given for the Italians in Scotland was: Glasgow 4,000; Edinburgh 1,500; Dundee 1,000; and Aberdeen 1,000. These total 7,500, giving a more generous estimate, for just the four main Communities, than the official 1927 Italian figure for the whole of Scotland. The figures do, however, give us an interesting indication of the relative sizes of each of the main Scottish Communities. Within the two main Communities of Glasgow and Edinburgh, the Italians had now spread across the cities; the most normal pattern was to locate their homes and businesses on the main trunk routes and at busy crossroads locations. In Glasgow, Italian shops were spread along Maryhill Road, Rutherglen Road, Parliamentary Road, Dumbarton Road and Victoria Road. The Garnethill Colony was still there but only as a residential location. Many Italians who lived in this area of the city, perched on the famous Glaswegian drumlins, now had their businesses on the best shopping streets of the city: Argyll Street and Sauchiehall Street. In Edinburgh likewise, there was still quite a Colony in the Grassmarket, but Italian businesses had by this time permeated into the central business district of the city and the world famous Princes Street.

The Liverpool figure, similar to the Scottish total, as well as the contingent for Liverpool itself, included the cities of Manchester, Sheffield, Bradford and Newcastle, all of which had thriving little Italian Communities of their own. In Liverpool there was a Colony of *Siciliani* most of whom were importers of fruit and who lived near the docks. In Newcastle, a particularly well-known street of Italian settlement was Nalgo Place where, by all accounts, in the 1930s there was 'only one English family'.

In this period the Italian collectivity of Manchester declined by more than half from around 2,000 persons to 800. As we saw in Chapter 1, Manchester was a main centre for highly skilled craftsmen and artisans; this decline in the Community reflected the reduced demand for these skills by the 1920s. Also, Manchester's Ancoats had been host to a Colony of itinerants. As these people settled many moved from the city to the many smaller towns of the north-west conurbation. In Scotland, by contrast, where there had never been a tradition in the crafts nor indeed an early large transitory Community, the population remained more stable.

By the end of the 1930s, there were over 1,000 families in Wales. Like the Scottish Italian Community, this group had spread out in Wales across the valleys, every little town now hosting one or two Italian families. At this time the industrious small coal towns of the Rhondda valleys were at their peak and the Italian cafés became an institutionalised part of local life. However, no real 'Little Italy' had developed in the main Welsh cities of Cardiff or Swansea, to rival the Scottish Communities in Glasgow and Edinburgh. More than any other group of settlers, the Italians in Wales became geographically dispersed.

In London, the old Italian Community of Clerkenwell had partly dispersed northwards, although the area remained one of the two main foci of the Italian Community. In the 1920s and 1930s, Italian residency in Clerkenwell was centred on Victoria Dwellings (opposite the Italian School) where 200 Italian families lived, Cavendish Mansions and the Bourne Estate. Cavendish Mansions and Bourne Estate are still standing today and still house many of the older generations of Italians. It was in the 1920s and 1930s, however, that the Soho Colony grew and flourished. New immigrants who arrived in London in the 1920s came to Soho. The main streets of colonisation were around Newport Place. The occupants of Newport Dwellings and Newport Buildings were 80 per cent Italian.

Origins and their implications

In Chapter 2 we looked in outline at the geographical origins of the early Italian settlers. We are able now, through a stroke of good fortune, to review the origin composition of the Scottish Italian Community for the 1930s. A census of all Italians living abroad was conducted by the Italian fascist government under Mussolini in 1933. Unfortunately, only the figures for Scotland remain available today; these are still kept at the Italian Consulate General in Edinburgh. At the outbreak of the Second World War in 1939, and before the alignment of Italy with the axis powers in 1940, the consular authorities in England had much of their material and papers, including the 1933 census, sent back to Italy in their 'diplomatic bags'.[1] Thus, disappointingly, similar statistics are not available for England and Wales.

This 1933 census recorded the situation of the Italian Community, asking a range of questions mainly on origin, occupation and family. Out of a total of 1,216 heads of households enumerated, 70 per cent of the respondents came from central Italy (849); 18 per cent northern Italy (225) and 12 per cent the south (142).

The two main source regions were *Toscana* and *Lazio*, in fact the now familiar areas of the *Garfagnana* and the *Ciociaria*. The contingents of migrants from the north and 'deep south' of Italy were much smaller. The fact that 70 per cent of the Italians came broadly from central Italy does not, however, mean that there was a high degree of, or indeed any, similarity between them. *Toscana* and *Lazio* are more than 250 miles apart and the geographical, social and economic differences between the two regions were, and indeed still are, considerable. *Toscana*, closer to the north, and *Lazio*, debatably part of the south, gave to their emigrants very different heritages. These differences became obvious when the emigrants were thrown together in Scotland. Let us look closely at those origins.

The 1933 census figures show that, not only were the Italians in Scotland primarily from just two Italian regions, but further investigation revealed that in fact the majority came from just two provinces: *Lucca* in *Toscana*, which accounted for over a third of all Italians, and *Frosinone* in *Lazio* which accounted for a further quarter of the Community.

The main Scottish Italian Community of Glasgow broadly followed the national trend: over one-third of the Italians originated in *Lucca* and a quarter came from *Frosinone*. People from the small town of *Barga*, who accounted in overall terms for 13 per cent of the total Community, formed the heart for the *Lucchesi*, and Italians from *Picinisco*, who made up 9 per cent of the total Community, were the core for the *Frosinone* Italians. In addition the *Frosinone* group were migrants from the geographically and culturally similar *Isernia*, from villages like *Filignano, Venafro* and *Rocchetta al Volturno*. In numerical terms, the *Isernia* group formed the fourth-largest contingent in the city. With a similar background to the *Frosinone* group, these two sets of migrants easily interacted. The combined forces of the *Isernia* and *Frosinone* groups gave them a position of numerical superiority in Glasgow.

The result of this rather distinctive pattern of origin was that during the 1930s the Glasgow Italian Community comprised two main groups of Italians who came from very different backgrounds in Italy. On the one hand were the *Toscani*, nearly all of whom were *Lucchesi*, and on the other, the *Ciociari* from *Frosinone* to whom the *Isernia* group gravitated most naturally. This had the effect of splitting the Community into two distinct groups who avoided contact with each other where possible.

The *Lucchesi* considered themselves to be superior to the '*Napoletani*'. (In Glasgow, as in the early London Colony of the last century, the migrants from the *Ciociaria* were mistakenly called *Napoletani*.) One of the major differences between the two groups was linguistic. The *Lucchesi* spoke Italian or dialect very close to the language that was rapidly becoming the accepted standard Italian, and the *Ciociari* spoke dialects incomprehensible to the speaker of 'proper' Italian. As a result of this, communication between the two groups was limited, leading to further suspicion. The two groups even 'looked different'. Members of one could always identify, even at a glance, whether or not people belonged to their particular group. Surnames too were an indicator of origins. For example, it was common knowledge that the Coia families came from *Filignano* (Is), the Nardini and Biagi families (among many others) from *Barga* (Lu) and the Crolla families from *Picinisco* (Fr).

Their strong sense of *campanilismo* bound these groups together but, at the same time, kept them apart. As we know, the occupational structure, based on the small business, was dependent upon recruiting staff from source villages in Italy. By operating such a system, the proprietor knew all about his prospective employee's personal or family background. There was no question of trusting strangers from different villages, with different ways.

The second-generation Italians, who were born in the 1900s and 1910s and were young adults by the 1920s and 1930s, had a more relaxed attitude. This led to a merging of the two groups through inter-marriage, but also enhanced the existing tensions. For young people, it was sufficient to find an 'Italian' partner, which included persons of Italian origin. The parents of the couples in these 'mixed marriages', where one spouse in the union was *Lucchese* and the other *Ciociaro*, were usually bitterly disappointed, and many difficult inter-family negotiations occurred as a consequence. Protracted investigations were necessary by the parents to find out about the family history of their prospective in-laws, not personally known or known by any of the *paesani* group. Even today in Glasgow, people of this generation are always at pains to point out that 'She's from the south' or 'He's one of the *Toscani*'. These differences still count.

In total contrast to the Glasgow Italian Community, the Edinburgh Italians of the 1930s mostly originated from just one province: *Frosinone*, which accounted for 70 per cent of the total Community. People from the village of *Picinisco* in fact made up 32 per cent of the overall Community total. Further, there was no *Lucchesi* contingent worth mentioning in Edinburgh. The result of this was a more integrated Italian Community. Since the majority originated in the *comune* of *Picinisco*, nearly everyone knew, knew of, or could easily find out about, everyone else. The various families and their reputations could easily be assessed and the Community developed as a single entity rather than as two separate subgroups as in Glasgow.

The problem of inter-marriage with a different group of Italians did not arise in Edinburgh, but because of the smaller absolute size of the

Community compared with Glasgow, many more of the second-generation Edinburgh Italians were forced to marry out of the Italian Community altogether and to select spouses from the local Scottish population. An alternative was cousin marriage, a practice which had long been common in the tiny mountain hamlets that the migrants came from. In addition, there was cross marriage between the Edinburgh Italians and the Glasgow *Frosinone* contingent, as well as further partner selection from the ranks of the many Italian families sprinkled across the small towns of Fife, almost all of whom were also from *Frosinone*, although not from *Picinisco*. In Fife and further north in Dundee the main source of the Italians was *Belmonte Castello*.

The third largest group of Italians in Scotland were the *Spezzini* from the *Val di Vara*. Although pioneers had reached Scotland in the early 1900s such as Davide Rossi from *Padivarma*, Quaradeghini from *Stadomelli*, and Zavaroni from *Borghetto Vara*, the majority of *Spezzini* did not arrive until after the First World War. Almost all of them settled in the 1920s in Gourock, Port Glasgow, Greenock and the Clyde estuary islands. There they formed 'a little clique unto themselves'.

The current origin composition of the Scottish Communities mirrors strongly the early composition outlined above. As we shall see in Chapter 5, Scotland received very little 'new' immigration in the post-war era and the character of these 'old' Communities has remained unchanged.

Unfortunately, no comparable detailed statistics are available for the English Italian Communities in the 1930s. The widest range of origin was undoubtedly present in London, where almost all groups were represented. By the 1920s, the *Parmigiani* and *Piacentini* contingents were in strong predominance, although other small regionally and occupationally based groups were still recognisable and visible. Although there was undoubtedly origin-based division in the social and economic organisation of the Community, the fact that there were still two highly concentrated residential enclaves of Italians in London meant that 'Community spirit' was high. Indeed conversation with people who grew up in the Clerkenwell and Soho Colonies in these years reveals the existence of a tremendous feeling and sense of Community. The other side of this coin, however, was the difficulty experienced in London by the second generation in trying to secure employment outside the Italian Colony. The discrimination they experienced provided a bonding effect, in the face of adversity, within the Community as a whole. Soho and Clerkenwell were still very much 'face to face' Communities and, in Clerkenwell particularly, people still lived and worked within the Colony. Soho too was complete with its own range of services and facilities including an Italian chemist, G. Fortuna, at Frith Street. Although more men had to venture forth out of the Colony for employment, they often found themselves in kitchens exclusively staffed by other Italians. For the new arrivals this was a drawback since it reduced their opportunity for learning English.

Occupational structure

As well as stability in numbers, there were few changes in the occupational structure of the Italian Community during the inter-war years. Again it was a period of consolidation, especially within the catering sector, but it was also a time of terminal decline for the oldest of the Italian occupations. The decline in the number of street entertainers, which began at the end of the nineteenth century, as discussed in Chapter 2, continued steadily: organ-grinders in particular dropped from 1,119 in 1891 to only 97 in 1931 for the whole country.

In London, the Italians had come to occupy the dominant position in both of the main strands of the catering trade. By the 1920s there was a shift in economic status for the Soho caterers who began to move out of employment into self-employment. The further growth and establishment of small-time Clerkenwell caterers and the development of the Soho contingent into mainstream catering now assured the domination of both ends of the spectrum within the catering niche. Italians now spanned the range of occupations in the sector. There were still humble kitchen hands but Italians had become head waiters and chefs in prestigious hotels such as the Café Royal and the Criterion. These developments are reflected in the British census figures. In 1901 the British census recorded 298 Italian restaurant and café owners and 1,964 waiters. By 1931, there were still around 2,000 waiters but 1,183 Italians had become restaurant owners.

One side of development was in the snack bar and café–restaurant, where the business was based around serving food to working people. But, on the other side, the first Italian restaurants, which were grand and frequented by the upper echelons of society, began to emerge. Such restaurants – Gennaro's, Bianchi's, Isola Bella, Quaglino's, Bertorelli's and Leoni's Quo Vadis – were in Soho or Mayfair. Their interiors were dark and plush. Thick carpets and velvet drapes, linen tablecloths, napkins and silver cutlery were the order of the day. Men who were waiters at such establishments in the 1920s and 1930s describe with eloquence their days in the dining-rooms. The life was strenuous and the hours long with the exacting standards of formality of the day meaning only the very best could rise to the top. Gennaro's especially formed an exclusive international club in the 1930s and indeed as their advertising slogan said they were 'known throughout the whole world'. At this time there were few eating establishments at a middle level; the development of the *trattorie* did not occur until the 1960s, when the middle classes as well as the upper and lower classes began to 'eat out'.

Within the catering industry in general, different patterns began to develop across the country. Even if the majority of Italians were employed in the same sector, differences in organisation and specialisation became institutionalised at the local level in different locations. This was particularly the case with the ice-cream industry. Although the Italian Association of Ice-Cream Vendors had 4,200 members in 1933 with branches in London, Glasgow, Dundee, Edinburgh, Liverpool, Manchester, Leeds and the south of Wales, each of these geographical areas had in fact developed the ice-cream trade in a different way.

During the 1920s and 1930s, businesses called 'ice-cream parlours' grew up in coastal locations. By scanning through the pages of the *Guida Generale* of 1939, the enormous range of these Italian ice-cream parlours and their size and sumptuousness is striking. There were several large family chains, notably Notarianni Brothers who owned magnificent ice-cream parlours in Blackpool, Ramsgate, Eastbourne and Margate, and the Forte family who had similar businesses in Hove, Brighton, Weymouth, Exmouth, Bournemouth, Hastings and other locations. Indeed, it seems as if, in this era of day-trippers and holiday-making at seaside resorts, every thriving little coastal town had its equally thriving Italian ice-cream parlour. The Nardini family of Largs on the Clyde coast and the De Marco family of Portobello on the Forth estuary, both established in the 1920s, were the Scottish examples of this development.

These families who made ice-cream did so with original recipes which required fresh milk and in some cases other dairy products such as cream, butter and eggs. Many, however, used vegetable fats as well. It was not until after the Second World War that stabilisers, emulsifiers, and other chemicals and synthetics were introduced.

In order to service the ice-cream industry, considerable related activities grew up, particularly in the manufacture of wafers and cones and in the equipment for making the ice-cream. The machinery for producing the ice-cream was manufactured by Italians, notably Edoni and Lanni in Scotland, and Giusti, Marcantonio and Maiuri in London. Edoni in Glasgow and Giusti, now based in Northampton, are still in operation today. In Clerkenwell, the old-fashioned tubs for ice and hand-turning the ice-cream, used by people without machinery, were supplied by Dante Roberto & Son on Eyre Street Hill. Ice-cream barrows and carts were always made and decorated by the individuals themselves. In addition to the machinery and refrigeration manufacturers, there was also a plethora of ice-cream biscuit suppliers in each of the main centres. Many of these, now large, family concerns had been established in the early part of the century after the 'invention' of the ice-cream cone and wafer. The largest of these were Facchino in Birmingham, Valvona and Antonelli in Manchester, Askey (Tedeschi) in London and Glasgow, Greco in Middlesbrough, Zaccardelli & Cervi and Bonifacenda in Edinburgh. Of these, Antonelli, Greco and Zaccardelli & Cervi are still in operation today (1991).

Nearly every Italian family in Scotland and Wales by the 1930s owned at least one retailing business in either ice-cream, confectionary or fish frying. These enterprises were similar to, but not the same as, the café-restaurants in London. They often sold some food, snacks and hot drinks such as Bovril, Oxo and tea – drinking coffee had not yet become popular – but they also sold confectionary, cigarettes and ice-cream, unlike the café–restaurants in London (see Plate 7). Also they became as much social institutions in their local towns as they were retailing enterprises. In both Scotland and Wales, where there were strong temperance and anti-drinking lobbies, especially relating to the sale of alcohol on the sabbath, the Italian cafés and Bracchi's were able to promote themselves as respectable premises. Also, unlike the public houses, it became acceptable for women and children to enter. There were, however, in the 1920s and 1930s various lobbies over late opening hours and Sunday trading. The main commercial backbone of these shops was the range of items sold and the long hours they remained open.

The fish restaurants were more similar to the café–restaurants in London since they supplied fried food to the lower classes. In Scotland, particularly in this period, there was a tradition amongst the local population to buy 'fish suppers' when the pubs closed at 10 pm. These suppers were 'carried out' of the shop and eaten in the street. Bruno Sereni, who migrated from *Barga* to Glasgow as a young man in 1919, remembered the fights which occurred, particularly on Saturday nights, in his book *They Took The Low Road* (1974). The first words of English he learned to say were 'big fight in shop' when he was sent, as the 'boy', to fetch help from the police station. Normally people who made ice-cream sold cigarettes and confectionary, while the fish fryers, which often became fish restaurants, sold this and other deep-fried food and did not generally make ice-cream. There were in any case restrictions about frying food and making ice-cream on the same premises. It was not uncommon, however, for a family to own two separate businesses side by side.

Most Italians worked long hours and spent much of their time in their shops. The back shops became meeting points for the Community. A tradition of visiting friends and relatives on half days developed, and groups would gather informally and keep in touch in this way. Men enjoyed card games of *scopa* and *briscola* in the café back shops. Elpidio Rossi, now in his 70s and retired to Italy after a working life in Glasgow and London, described how his father would take him round 'visiting' *paesani*.[2] The visits always took place at the shop. His father was anxious for the son to meet and get to know the other people from their village present in the city. A whole way of life was thus conceived and organised around these family businesses. Although they separated people in geographic terms, they promoted strong bonds of common experience and similarity in life-style.

Connected to the catering trade were the *arrotini* who, unlike the 'ice men' who had almost disappeared by the 1930s due to the introduction of refrigeration and 'freezers' for ice-cream, continued to flourish. They had always been concentrated in London but a few families spread out to other urban centres where they largely became cutlery makers. Most notable amongst these were Caola in Bristol, Maturi in Birmingham and Leeds, and Tisi who established a firm in Southampton. The major ice firm of Gatti, which had long dominated the trade in London, although still in business by 1939, had declined, leaving the remainder of the trade to Perella of Eyre Street Hill in the Clerkenwell Colony, Bonvini, Biondino and Inzani nearby and then Assirati in Dean Street in the Soho Colony.

By the 1930s, the growth of Italian provisions shops and household supplies stores in the various Italian Communities was prolific. In Glasgow alone, for example, there were ten such businesses, dotted across the city, only one of which (Fazzi Bros) survives today. In London, there were several general stores in Soho, one of which survives today (Camisa), and several in Clerkenwell, two of which are still in business today (Terroni and Gazzano). See also Plate 16, Valvona & Crolla in Edinburgh. All of these surviving businesses are in their original premises. These shops were social centres of the Community; people met here and exchanged information and gossip. Apart from the Italian Church in London they were the most ethnically and culturally Italian places to gather: you could feel, taste and smell Italy in such premises. These images and smells are conjured up by the novelist Radclyffe Hall in her book set in the Soho Italian Colony of the 1920s:

83

The shop! All his life Gian Luca remembered those first impressions of the shop: the size of it, the smell of it, the dim mysterious gloom of it – but above all the smell, that wonderful smell that belongs to the salumeria. . . . The shop smelt of sawdust and cheeses and pickles and olives and sausages and garlic; the shop smelt of oil and cans and chianti and a little of split peas and lentils; the shop smelt of coffee and sour brown bread and very faintly of vanilla; the shop smelt of people; it also smelt of Old Compton Street. A dusty, adventurous smell. (1926, p.27)

The *Guida Generale* of 1939 lists no fewer than 1,029 Italian businesses in London connected with retailing and catering in one form or the other. There were, however, a number of other traditional occupations and activities still prevalent at this time.

Two of the semi-skilled crafts of the early Italian Community still survived. The statuette makers had disappeared in their itinerant form but several manufacturers had been established in London. Two of the largest firms, Pagliai and Orsi, were in Clerkenwell. Others such as Bastiani, Leonardi, Panichelli, Bonini, Carli, Cortesi and Giovannetti were dotted across the city, although Bastiani and Giovannetti were just outside the traditional Clerkenwell Colony. Elsewhere in the country the main statuette manufacturers were Baci & Baci in Manchester, Nieri Brothers also in Manchester, and Ranicoli in Birmingham. Surprisingly, although many of the original *figurinai* had settled in Scotland, there were no manufacturers in business by the 1930s.

There were, however, several specialist mosaic and *terrazzo* firms in Glasgow: De Cecco, Sidoli & Tat, Manzi & Bertoia. In addition there was one marble specialist: Capaldi in Renfield Street. Across England, especially in the cities of the north, such as Manchester, Liverpool, Newcastle upon Tyne, and Sheffield, there were numerous *terrazzo* and mosaic firms. There were also some firms to be found in Birmingham and Bristol, and one in Nottingham and one in Leicester.

In London there were still no fewer than 80 mosaic and *terrazzo* firms in the 1930s. Most of these were congregated geographically around the old Colony, especially just to the north in the Kings Cross area. At 48 Kings Cross Road, for example, no fewer than six skilled individual mosaic specialists were working from the same premises. At 46 Old Gloucester Street seven such men shared a common base from which they prepared their paints and materials for on-site work.

Mosaic workers were also still in great demand for public buildings – town halls and hospitals especially – in the 1920s and 1930s. From 1932 until the outbreak of war, for example, a large group of mosaic and *terrazzo* workers were employed at Senate House. As mentioned in Chapter 1, these men came almost exclusively from the region of *Friuli* and formed a closed society in occupational terms. Only *Friulani* were taken into this group for training, except in exceptional circumstances.

In the arts-related fields, in London there were 80 people still employed as sculptors, artists, teachers of music and art, etc. Of the oldest highly skilled crafts – the making of scientific instruments – only a few remained: one maker of clocks; one thermometer maker; two glass makers and one maker of artificial eyes.

A total of 70 people were now to be found in the professions; 26 were medical doctors. In a middle rung, however, only 70 people had entered white collar work in a clerical capacity.

In London there was a range of occupations and the beginnings of an internal economic structure within the Community. In Wales, by contrast, almost 100 per cent of the Italians listed in the *Guida Generale* were in small catering-related businesses. Scotland, while similar to Wales, had a slightly more diversified and developed occupational structure. It was in these decades that the first members of the second generation began to attend university and acquire degrees enabling them to enter the professions.

The biggest change in the Community in this era, however, was due to an entirely different development.

The rise of fascism

The major development within the British Italian Communities in the 1920s and more especially the 1930s was the rise of fascism. This new social and political force engulfed and encompassed all forms of activity within the Community. A number of factors contributed to its growth.

From the 1880s onwards the migrants who came to this country came primarily for economic reasons. When they left Italy, they were amongst the poorest sections of society. In addition, many were illiterate and few really knew much about 'Italy' beyond their own immediate geographical areas. Over the years, however, owing to Italian family tradition and increasing prosperity, contact with Italy was maintained. Although, for the majority, their migration had become a fact, with little hope of a permanent return, visits to the old country were not infrequent and indeed were perhaps increasing in frequency. Many had built splendid villas in their villages not only as a testimony to their success abroad, but also to their commitment to their origins. Despite this, however, there was still a sense of shame and even humiliation amongst the migrants because of their very humble origins, and the difficulty of reconciling this with their new found wealth – but continued lack of education and status – in their new country. In the immediate post-First World War period this situation was not helped by the limited interest shown by the Italian government and Italian authorities in the Italian Communities living abroad. There was a feeling of being abandoned by Italy, a feeling of existing in a no-man's land.

Apart from their families at home in Italy, the migrants had no real sense of belonging to the country of their origin – a country which they loved very much. This 'love' of their country can perhaps best be appreciated within the context of the way the Italians lived their lives. Although they were law-abiding citizens who had, as we have seen, by this time 'integrated' themselves into the economic and social structure of this country, there was little 'assimilation'. That is to say, as far as was possible, the Italians of this time clung to their traditional values and way of life as best as they could. Indeed, within the larger Italian Colonies of London, Manchester, Glasgow, and to a lesser extent Edinburgh, living in the old way was not as far-fetched as it might seem. Within the confines of the family, and indeed in many cases the family business, the traditional values and styles of living were easily upheld. Italian or Italian dialect was spoken at home and the food consumed was either Italian or at least cooked in the Italian way. Families were still large in this era and the extended family often formed a group of 40 to 50 people. In the larger Italian Communities, where numbers of *paesani* and members of the extended family were present, patterns of behaviour and attitude to life based on old-world traditions could easily be maintained. It must be remembered that, in any case, the hope of many Italians was still to return to Italy one day and for these people the notion of assimilation seemed absurd. There was ever present a *nostalgia*. Perhaps mythological by this time, but no less relevant and applicable, people cherished memories of Italy.

It was mentioned earlier (on page 73) that because of the rise of fascism in Italy it became increasingly difficult to emigrate. However, another side to this was that, in the 1920s, fascism began to politicise the phenomenon of emigration, or rather the existence of many Italians already abroad. The emigrant Communities were increasingly considered as part of an expanded Italy in a moral, political and economic sense. It was one of the aims of fascism to reunite into a brotherhood all the many sons of Italy living abroad under the Italian flag. The work of the *fasci* – fascist clubs – established in this era was to attempt to reduce the distance between the expatriates and *Roma* by encouraging full participation by the Italians in the Communities.

Mussolini was the first Italian leader to re-envelope, re-embrace the straggling international Communities of Italian emigrants into the Italian national fold. He was the first to give them the sense of belonging that they longed for. As an old Italian in London recently said 'He gave us back our dignity; we *were* Italian.'[3] The word *emigrante*, with all its negative connotations, was removed from Italian passports and replaced with *lavoratore Italiano all'estero*: Italian worker abroad. This gave a certain social redemption to the emigrant abroad. His national pride was restored and his Community was given *un certo senso dignitoso civismo* – a certain sense of civil dignity.

The role of the Italian Embassies and Consulates abroad increased. They were the vehicle by which Mussolini reached his emigrants. A turning point came in 1924 when, in *Roma*, an international conference on emigration was held, with delegates from 58 nations, including Britain. At this meeting many points regarding the condition of the migrant worker were established. Perhaps as a result of the conference, a number of bilateral agreements were struck amongst which, between Italy and Britain, there was in 1925 an agreement concerning professional reciprocality between doctors; in 1929 an agreement concerning documents and regulations of passenger ships; and in 1930 a convention for legal assistance in matters of civil and commercial law.

As we have seen in Chapter 2, the First World War had the effect of uniting the Italians in this country. Straggling and small Italian Communites, larger Communities split by internal schism, and groups simply apathetic towards politics were for the first time since emigration united into a common sense of purpose. This was the first time that Italy had fought as a nation state and it is from the First World War that Italian patriotism stems. After the War, this new-found patriotism did not dissipate and indeed it was the *ex combattenti*, who had returned to Italy to fight, who formed the group of patriots who laid the foundation for the growth of the fascist movement abroad. In fact fascism courted firstly these men who had fought for Italy in the Great War. Often, it was on the basis of the associations that they had formed on their return to Britain that the fascist movement grew.

There were a few anti-fascists, mostly intellectuals who were refugees from fascist oppression, living in London. Most notable was Luigi Sturzo, founder of the *Partito Popolare* which was reconstituted as the Christian Democrat Party after the fall of fascism, and has dominated Italian politics since 1945. Also the sons of Claudio Treves, one of the founders of the Italian Socialist Party, fled to Britain and with their cousin Uberto Limentani established the Italian League for the Rights of Man, continuing their struggle in exile. Gradually, however, the vast majority of the Italian Community in Britain embraced fascism in a whole-hearted manner. The basic principle of fascism – *Onore, Famiglia e Patria* (Honour, Family and Fatherland) – was, after all, the very principle by which most of them lived their lives and therefore a slogan and sentiment with which they could readily identify.

Most Italians in Britain today who lived through this period explain that fascism to them was a form of patriotism. They were not political and their involvement with the party was primarily due to an attachment to their country and an involvement in the Italian Community. Few probably fully understood either the events which were unfolding in Europe and the role Italy was playing, or indeed the full extent that the impact of dictatorship would have on their country. Many old Italians today still cling to the view that Mussolini did 'a lot of good for Italy'. Few understood what the loss of democracy would mean for their country in the future and all too few realised the full implication of the association with Hitler. The general attitude of Italians is summed up by Calisto Cavalli in his autobiography:

> *Several years before I joined, fascism had taken root in London and a large number of my fellow countrymen living there, including the best people in the Colony, had joined the Party. Others, even if they had not enrolled, were obviously sympathisers. Moreover, most Italians abroad had good reason to be grateful to the fascist government. Before fascism, all Italian governments cared little or nothing for the thousands of emigrants abroad: now things had changed. The fascist government genuinely helped fellow countrymen who had emigrated overseas and as far as possible promoted their well-being. (Cavalli, 1973, p.66)*

Indeed it was the policy of fascism to play on the nostalgia and simple patriotism of the expatriates. The Italian Community in Britain saw only the benefits of fascism. Amongst these were an Italian High School – *Scuola Media* – opened in 1935 at Hyde Park Gate. Attendance at this school enabled the London Italian children to enter Italian universities if they wished. There were also the holidays organised by the fascist party for the children of Italian migrants at seaside locations in Italy. Many of these children had never been to Italy and the opportunity was considered by their parents to be generous beyond belief. Indeed, much jockeying for the limited places took place in the various Italian Communities. Mother tongue language teaching to children was also seen as important throughout the Italian Community. Indeed, as Cavalli goes on to say, 'Thanks to the fascist government some ten evening schools had opened in London alone for the children of emigrants who had been born in London so that they could learn our mother tongue.'

In addition, there were the clubs, the *fasci*. These were often opened by the Italian government, and also existing clubs were expanded. These were primarily social clubs, and they formed the hearts and centres of the increasingly thriving Italian Communities. Many delegations from Italy were sent to Britain to enlist members for the fascist party and to help establish *fasci*. Most of the Italian adults of this period responded in a positive way to this courtship by the Italian Government. Many parents even called their daughters 'Italia'. When a long forgotten, isolated and totally abandoned Italian Community, such as the one in the north-east of Scotland, was visited in 1925 by three delegates from the Italian fascist party, who seemed to care about their Italian Community, it is little wonder that there was a high level of subscription and interest. Virtually all of the Italian men of Aberdeen, Fraserburgh, Stonehaven, Forres and Elgin turned out for this visitation which occurred at the historic centre of Aberdeen's Italian Community, the Market Square. The clubs gave the Italians a respectability; they could come out of their shops, back shops, kitchens, dining-rooms and salons, dress in their Sunday best and attend 'their' club – the Italian Club. There were more Italian clubs (*fasci*) all over the country in this era than in any other; all very active and flourishing. Kathleen Fusco, an old Italian lady in Portobello, Edinburgh, recently described her memories of attending the events at the *fascio* in Edinburgh as 'happy days'.[4] By the late 1930s the Italians in Britain were for the most part at least nominal members of the Italian fascist party.

The London *fascio*

The *fascio* in London was founded in 1921 and was one of the first to be set up outside Italy. The visit of Mussolini to London in 1922 gave enormous impetus to the development of fascism in this country amongst Italians. As the movement grew, so too did the range of social and cultural activities, all of which helped lead to the indoctrination of the Italians. The Italian Ambassador appointed to London was Count Dino Grandi, an ex-Foreign Minister, who became popular with the Italian Community. As a 'first hour' fascist and a callous squad leader in his youth, his mission was to turn the British Italian Community into a showpiece of fascist 'corporatist' theory. According to Dennis Mack Smith (1981), the well-known historian who specialises in Italian history, Grandi was no urbane career diplomat but a powerful figure in the Italian fascist party who had even been Mussolini's rival for leadership. It is significant that he was sent to London to promote fascist Italy through the manipulation of the Italian Community. He soon became popular amongst the Italian Community since, unlike his predecessors, he was often amongst the Italians.

The London *fascio* began in two little rooms in Great Russell Street, moved first to 37 Palace Court W2, then to 1a Devonshire Terrace W2, before arriving at 15 Greek Street W1, in the heart of the Soho Italian Community in 1932. Here at the *Club Cooperativo*, the *fascio* occupied the whole of the second floor, and was by this time fully integrated into the life of the Italian Community. By 1933 this club was directly under the control of the Italian authorities in London, and hence the *Movimento Nazionale del Fascismo*.

Gradually the movement swallowed up and incorporated virtually all of the other clubs and associations of the Community. Sooner or later they all became affiliated to fascism. The commodious meeting rooms of the *Club Cooperativo* already housed many of the associations. The *Mutuo Soccorso*, from which the *Club Cooperativo* had originally sprung, held its meetings at Greek Street. Other circles which used the Greek Street premises included the Association of Hairdressers, the *Associazione Nazionale Combattenti*, the *Alpini* and the two regionally based circles, *L'Unione Fubinese* and *La Famija Piemonteisa*. The Club premises attracted the London Italians with its billiards room, small theatre, bar and restaurant, and library of over 3,000 volumes. Naturally, when the Club was taken over by the fascist movement in 1932, so too were the other clubs and activities centred in its premises.

The *Associazione Nazionale Combattenti* had been founded in 1919 for Italian veterans of the First World War and from 1923 it became connected directly with the fascist movement. By the 1930s the association had divided into two sections: Soho under Francesco Tito, and Clerkenwell under Patroclo Rivaldi. The Clerkenwell branch had its office at the *Mazzini Garibaldi Club* and the Soho section was housed in the *fascio* at Greek Street. The overall president for most of this inter-war period was *Cav. Uff.* Rampagni. It was he who succeeded in establishing, again under the control of the *fascio*, a holiday house at Felixstowe for Italian children, a facility enormously appreciated by the Clerkenwell and Soho Italian Colonies, parents and children alike. The children of the Italian Colonies were encouraged to become involved in the activities organised for them by the *fasci* through the *Balilla*, members of which received annual Christmas presents. Most people in their 60s or 70s today remember not only the Italian language classes but singing *Giovinezza*, the fascist youth song, whilst saluting at special rallies.

Another semi-military group, the *Associazione Nazionale Alpini*, was also founded in this era. In fact the *Alpini* of London were the first section of the *Alpini* to be founded outside Italy in 1928. Each year, the *Alpini* of London would send a representative to their national gathering in Italy and they also organised a *Veglia Verde* in England. This event, according to the *Guida Generale* of 1933, became one of the most popular *feste* of the London Italian Community. Both the *Alpini* and another militaristic association, the *Associazione Nazionale Granatieri*, had their offices at the *fascio* in Greek Street.

Thus, by the mid 1930s, it can be clearly understood that the Greek Street *fascio* was a main centre of activity within the London Italian Community, for individuals and associations alike. It also produced its own newspaper, *L'Italia Nostra*.

At the end of 1936, the London *fascio* moved from Greek Street and the *Casa del Littorio* was founded at Charing Cross Road, WC2, in the very centre of London, just north of Trafalgar Square. This became the main London *fascio*, forming a very active and powerful nerve centre for the Community. This prestigious location – a building and club house on such a scale had never before been achieved by the British Italian Community – became a hive of activity. The main hall, the *Sala dell'Impero*, or Empire Room, was an enormous galleried chamber upon whose marble-clad walls were embossed a series of fascist slogans and achievements. Most noticeable amongst these was the *Credere, Obbedire, Combattere* – Believe, Obey, Fight – along the edge of the balcony. This chamber formed the focus for a vast range of activity, much of which reached cultural heights not previously experienced within the Community. An Italian orchestra, *La Società Sinfonica Italiana*, for example, was formed and gave ambitious concerts in the hall. Recitals were given by the Italian tenor, Beniamino Gigli, who was a regular visitor to the British Italian Community.

The spirit of the period was summed up by the Italian Ambassador, Dino Grandi, in his many speeches where he extolled the virtues of the high level of 'corporatism', and involvement which had been achieved by the Italian Community. Fascism had succeeded in its aim. The period up until the Second World War saw levels of activity and organisation within the Colonies across the country which had never previously been achieved nor indeed subsequently replicated. The London *fascio*, in the late 1930s, sponsored the following range of activities: firstly, it was the meeting-place of the majority of all associations and circles which existed amongst the Italians in the capital; secondly, it housed the administrative head-quarters for the teaching of Italian language at many schools throughout the city; thirdly, it held Italian classes itself; fourthly, it accommodated a school for young musicians, especially violinists; fifthly, it was the centre of the *dopolavoro*, after-work club; sixthly, it had a separate women's section; seventhly, it was the centre for several semi-militaristic associations as already mentioned; and eighthly, it hosted and organised a vast array of special events. The pull and allure of this club over the ordinary member of the Community is not difficult, therefore, to under-stand. The only complaint of some poorer members was that to attend frequently was a costly affair!

The Glasgow *fascio*

Outside London, the Glasgow *fascio*, or *Casa d'Italia*, as it was known, was the most important.

The *fascio* in Glasgow was founded in 1922 and, as in London, the growth and development of the movement was based initially on the *ex combattenti* of the First World War, and then on the range of social initia-tives and incentives that fascism offered. Indeed, apart from the *Mutuo Soccorso*, founded in 1891, there had been little corporative effort from within the Community and there certainly had been no external pressure put to bear on the Community by the Italian authorities to organise them-selves. By 1925 the evening school for the teaching of Italian language to children had been founded and by 1927 there were five classes operational. In the occupational sphere, again the *fascio* took the initiative and in 1928 the Union of Italian Traders was formed, an association which by 1939 had 1,000 members. The influence of this association on the general busi-ness development of the Italians in Glasgow was significant. It brought together for the first time all the little shop-keepers and small retailers into an occupational association.

In 1935 the *fascio* took over the newly established Club House, the *Casa d'Italia*, an enormously beautiful building in the prestigious location of

Park Circus, which had been acquired by the public subscription of the Glasgow Italian Community. Previously a private town house, the *Casa* required considerable renovation work which was done by skilled craftsmen from within the Community. Of note amongst these were: Jack Coia, architect; Giovanni Spinelli, painter; Alfonso Pacitti, woodworker and wood decorator; Vincenzo Di Mascio, electrician; and Pietro Zani who made the memorial plaque.

The *Casa d'Italia* soon became the nerve centre of the Italians in the city, and the range of its activity, like the London *fascio*, was enormous. Here under one roof the entire activity of the Glasgow Italian Colony took place – not only the *fascio* and the organisations directly dependent on this, such as the language schools, the *dopolavoro*, but also the sections of the *ex combattenti*, the *Nastro Azzuro*, the *Società Mutuo Soccorso*, the *Dante Alighieri Society*, the Scoto-Italian Society, the Scottish Italian Student Group, the Union of Italian Traders, as well as the College of Italian Hairdressers. The *dopolavoro* social club was very important in bringing people together and there was again a strong patriotic aspect to this. A popular activity organised by the *dopolavoro* was the showing of Italian films in theatres and cinemas in Glasgow, notably at Green's Playhouse.

In addition, the Glasgow *fascio* had a section in Stirling and, because of the scattered nature of the Colony, also appointed a number of district representatives in other places such as Coatbridge, Motherwell and Paisley. By 1939, the Glasgow *fascio* had 470 paid-up male members with a further 116 enrolled in the ladies section, and many more who used the *Casa* on a more casual basis. The 1933 census of Italians mentioned on page 76 also enumerated fascist party members. Almost 50 per cent of the respondents in Scotland were full members.

There were other *fasci* of note elsewhere in the country. The Edinburgh *fascio* of Picardy Place has already been mentioned. In addition there were *fasci* in Manchester at Thomas Street; Liverpool at Brunswick Street; Leeds at Grinston Street; Sheffield at Gibraltar Street; Cardiff at Church Street; Aberdeen at Crown Street; and in Dundee at Garland Place. In all of these locations the leaders and important people of the Community became actively involved in fascism. Before fascism, these men were activists in their Communities and most naturally became the organisers of the *fasci*. Virtually all of the well-known family names in Manchester, Glasgow, Edinburgh, Aberdeen, Cardiff and London could be mentioned in this context. Unfortunately, this involvement was, as we shall see in Chapter 4, to have devastating effects not only for the families of these men but also the Italian Communities.

Other institutions and clubs of the Community

Churches

In London, outside the fascist movement, and a supporter of it, the most important institution was undoubtedly St Peter's Italian Church, still in the 1920s and 1930s very much the emotional centre, particularly of the Clerkenwell Colony. However, although St Peter's continued to be an important and spiritual social centre for the London Italian Community, the growth of the secondary Italian concentration in Soho and also the dispersal of the Clerkenwell Community itself, led to two further churches also becoming of significance to London Italians.

The first was St Patrick's, Soho. By the 1920s, Soho was well established as an Italian Colony in its own right and St Patrick's of Soho Square became a centre for the Colony. There were services in Italian and *Dott. Don* Hughes, who had studied in Italy, became the first chaplain to the Italians. From 1931, an Italian priest, *Padre* Barbera, was attached to St Patrick's to minister to his fellow countrymen. He organised a mobile Italian library with over 2,000 volumes which came to the church every Saturday, a youth club and many other activities.

Secondly, with the continuing exodus of Italians from Clerkenwell, an Italian quarter began to spring up in the Southwark area of London, south of the River Thames. After St Peter's and St Patrick's, St George's Cathedral of Southwark became the most frequented religious centre. *Padre* Casimiro Liccioli was based here (1928–46) and was very active in making contact with the Italians and involving them in the various clubs and organisations that he founded around the church. For the men he set up *Una Congrega di San Giuseppe* and for women a Christian mother's union.

Elsewhere in the country, Italian chaplains were also attached to existing local churches in the manner described above for St Patrick's and St George's London. Most notable of these was perhaps *Padre* Gaetano Fracassi, attached to St Alban's in Manchester's Ancoats, who worked tirelessly throughout the 1920s and 1930s for the Italians of this city. In Glasgow there was *Don* Pietro Rota, who was attached to the Holy Redeemers in Clydebank, and from this base travelled around the Italians of the area. Canon Grant of St Mary's, Market Square, in Aberdeen was very active in helping the Italians of the north.

94

The Italian schools

Both the Italian authorities and the first generation of immigrants realised the importance of keeping the mother tongue and culture alive within their British-born offspring.

By 1933 there were seven schools in London offering tuition in Italian language. These classes came under the organisation of the *Direzione Didattica*, which was located at the Greek Street *fascio*. The seven schools had over 700 pupils under tuition. By 1939, the seven had increased to eleven schools with 1,300 students. The location of these schools reflected the geographical distribution of the Community. The largest school, which was also by this time a day school, under the local education authority, was St Peter's School on Little Saffron Hill (now Herbal Hill) in the heart of the Clerkenwell Colony (see Plate 8). The Italian children attended the school during the day with all other children of the neighbourhood, and in the evenings between 5.30 p.m. and 7.30 p.m. Italian language classes were held for 210 pupils, distributed between five classes.

St Patrick's School at Great Chapel Street in Soho was the second Italian school to be established and had the second-highest number of children attending (150 pupils in 1933), with lessons being held twice a week in the evenings. The lessons were given by the Italian sisters of Don Bosco whose convent, founded in 1930, was in Greek Street, near the *Club Cooperativo*. Also, at 49 Goodge Street, there was an Italian nursery under the direction of the Italian sisters.

The other schools which held classes were St George's in Southwark, which, although catering for only 120 pupils, had classes on four weekday evenings; King's Cross just north of Clerkenwell, with lessons three times a week for 100 pupils; Hackney School, E9, which held classes on Saturday mornings for 50 pupils; Marylebone School, NW1, with classes twice a week in the evenings for 45 pupils; and also Stratford School, E15, with classes for 45 pupils. With such a spread across London, it is clear that by this time Italians were resident in significant numbers outside the two traditional Colonies.

Elsewhere in the country, similar schools had also been established, the first in Manchester in 1919. By 1927, there were four in Glasgow, one in Liverpool and one in Cardiff with over 650 pupils between them.

Other clubs

By 1930 the *Mazzini Garibaldi Club* had moved from Laystall Street in Clerkenwell to 51 Red Lion Street in Bloomsbury, where it is still located today. This eastward move of the club indicated a geographical compromise between the two Italian Colonies of Clerkenwell and Soho. Although not entirely equidistant between the two, in Red Lion Street it was arguably a part of both Communities rather than distinctly a part of one or the other.

The new and spacious premises at Red Lion Street housed other associations: the Clerkenwell section of the *Associazione Nazionale Combattenti* and the Builders' Trade Workers Society which was composed mainly of mosaic workers. In this era the *Mazzini Garibaldi Club* became integrated within the fascist framework of the Community and came directly under the aegis of the London *fascio* from 1937. On the ground floor was a *dopolavoro* social club which organised family dinners and dances and, in summer, outings to the country. These *scampagnate*, or picnics, became extremely popular amongst the urbanised London Italian population. The membership in the 1930s was made up of Italians from practically every region of Italy and also included people from *Ticino*, the Italian canton of Switzerland, Corsica, Nice and Malta. Amongst the membership which, in 1931, numbered 400 people, there were artists and specialist craftsmen especially mosaic workers, asphalters, cabinet-makers, ice men, cooks and waiters; a complete cross-section of the Italian Community.

Not as grand or active as either the *Club Cooperativo* or the *Mazzini Garibaldi*, the *Unione Roma Club* in Clerkenwell had a similar range of activity but was more of a 'local' club for the Clerkenwell Italians. In 1933 with premises at 7 Little Bath Street, it had over 300 members, hosted the *Unione Trentina* and organised many social events for the local Italian Community.

In addition to the clubs mentioned above, there were many small private club houses, which were really drinking and gambling social clubs where the men of the Community could gather. One of the most notorious of these was the *Frattelanza Club* in Clerkenwell where the members of the 'racing fraternity' used to congregate. It was here that a 1920s-style gangster shoot-out took place between the Sabini gang and the Cortesi gang who controlled the then illegal race track gambling. In addition, men used to congregate in the barbers' shops which were popular as meeting places.

The women of the Colonies, both Clerkenwell and Soho, gathered at the public wash-houses to do laundry for their clients and exchange news and information in the same way as the men did in the barbers' shops and clubs. The Endell Street Baths, used by the women of Soho, are still there today as a public swimming pool.

The war in Abyssinia (Ethiopia)

When Mussolini began to pursue his imperalist activity in East Africa it quickly became clear that Britain would not tolerate this expansionism and in November 1935 economic sanctions were introduced against Italy. After fiascos in Ethiopia and Libya earlier in the century, Mussolini hoped to gain the respect of the world powers by his renewed attempts at empire building in Africa.

Whipped up into a frenzy of patriotism, as were the people at home in Italy, when war was declared, the blackshirts of the London *fascio* met to salute the legions leaving Italy for East Africa and as a gesture of support began a collection of money and gold for the cause. The other *fasci* throughout the country quickly followed suit and a general fund for contributions was opened. People handed in and sent in money, gold and silver, to the *fasci*. A service was held at St Peter's Italian Church in London, known as the *Giornata delle Fedi* – day of the wedding rings – in which the Italian women of the Colony swapped their gold wedding rings for metal ones. In addition to money, gold and silver, people sent insurance policies and war pensions to be cashed. By January 1936, the Consuls of London, Glasgow, Dublin, Liverpool and Cardiff and the secretaries of the various *fasci* presented themselves to the Italian Ambassador with money and gold to the value of £18,480. Over the next couple of months, a further £1,000 was collected. As well as this economic support for Italy, several young Italians from Britain looking for adventure volunteered for active service in Abyssinia, some of whom lost their lives. By May 1936, Italy was victorious and had entered Addis Ababa. The collections of money and gold were over.

Throughout this period there was an increasing hostility to the Italian population resident in Britain. It was during this time that many people began to realise the possible implications of fascism and Mussolini, not only for Italy, but for themselves as Italians living in Britain. Many Italians naturalised and became British citizens at this time.

The period of the 1920s and 1930s was a golden era for the Italians in Britain. The Community had made a significant degree of economic and social progess and had become an accepted minority, a position which was to change dramatically with the outbreak of the Second World War.

97

Chapter Four

The Second World War

Introduction

The effects of the Second World War on the British Italian Community were no less than devastating. Not many people outside the Italian Community realise this. The purpose of this chapter is to open up what has become a closed book, for British Italians and British people alike, for too long. The events of the last war and particularly the loss of life with the sinking of the *Arandora Star* affected the psyche of the 'old' British Italian Community in such a deep and fundamental way that it is only now, 50 years on, that the Community is beginning to come to terms with these events. There is a long-standing but muted grief and humiliation within the 'old' Community because of these events. This chapter offers an opportunity to explain this, and events in general, from the Italian point of view.

There are two main reasons why little is known about the experience of the Italians resident in this country during the last war. The first concerns the Italians themselves and the second concerns the British, in particular the British authorities. Italians – both the older generation, people now in their 70s and 80s, and the younger generation, people who were children during the war and are now in their 50s and 60s – do not like to talk about their experiences. Every single Italian family resident in this country experienced difficulty and hardship of an unprecedented nature. Many, in addition, also lost a loved member of the family other than through active military involvement and suffered a great deal of pain as a consequence. Within the 'old' Italian Community these difficulties and this suffering have become internalised. The old Italians have over the years tried to put the war behind them and to forget about it. It is only now, just past the symbolic fiftieth anniversary in 1990 of these events, that some of the survivors, particularly of the *Arandora Star* tragedy, are beginning to talk, beginning to open up. A few families who lost relatives

99

on that ship and who suffered in silence and ignominy for years are even now still reluctant to tell their stories. Also, there is no doubt that after the war the Italians were genuinely 'scared'. They did not know if they would be allowed to return to their businesses, or even allowed to continue their residence in this country. An awkward taboo surrounding all aspects of the war-time experience seemed to develop. Indeed, after the war many Italians who had been interned took out British citizenship.

Likewise, those who were children then and who remember the beatings, the hatred and the humiliation that were heaped upon them, do not want to be reminded or to remember. Carrying on and going to school was not easy and in fact the cultural identity of many people of this generation was so badly battered in these days that it is only in very recent times that this generation is proudly rediscovering its *italianità*.

The result of this silence is that even within the 'old' Community itself there is only a limited base of knowledge about what happened during the war. No real exchange of information has occurred. There has been no build-up of an 'oral history', no passing down the generations of personal accounts. Younger Italians of the third and fourth generation of the 'old' Community tend to be vague about what happened. Worst of all, though, there has been no documentation to make these events into proper history.

Perhaps one further reason for the reluctance to share the past on the part of the older generation was that the war affected the Italian Community in a number of different ways due in part to their own attitudes and responses. People's circumstances were very different and, as we have seen, so were their backgrounds in Italy. As a result, the Community became deeply split into the so-called 'good Italians' (the fascists) and 'bad Italians' (the others). A great deal of factionalism developed and the bitterness which surrounded this, and the consequences of it, can still be detected today in some sections of the 'old' Italian Community. The purpose of this chapter for British Italian readers is to draw together the various strands of information and give them a better sense of their own history.

The other reason for the ignorance surrounding the experience of British Italians during the Second World War was the attitude of the British authorities and the population at large. Mistakes are made during wartime by governments trying to protect their nation. It seems that in the general confusion, muddle and panic of May and June 1940, especially after Dunkirk (the evacuation began on 27 May and was completed on 3 June) when Britain was threatened with invasion, the steps taken to intern Italian 'enemy aliens' were, initially at least, excessive and

100

THE SECOND WORLD WAR

ill-conceived. As a result of this, much of the official documentary evidence has been kept under wraps until quite recently, and the most sensitive material will in fact remain closed until 2015, 75 years after the events. The few interested research workers who have made the attempt, have not yet been able to answer a number of outstanding questions with regard to internment in general.

In fact, the attempts which have been made to research this field are mainly concerned with the German and Austrian Jewish refugees who fled to this country from the rise of Naziism in the late 1930s and were then interned by the British authorities. No study has ever specifically focused on the Italians. Unlike the recently arrived Jewish refugees, the Italians, as we have seen in previous chapters, were by 1939 well integrated, respected and often prosperous members of British society. When Italy joined the war in 1940, shock waves went through the Italian Community when people realised the severity with which they were to be treated.

In addition, the reaction of local British people in many places was totally unexpected in the degree of its violence and viciousness. Apart from the official reluctance to expose the issues, there is also perhaps some embarrassment amongst the British when they remember their racialist attacks on their Italian neighbours. In any event, very few British people admit to knowing much about the internment of Italians during the war and even fewer have heard of the *Arandora Star*. For the British reader, the purpose of this chapter is simply to outline what happened and ask whether matters could have been better handled.

Fascism and the build up to war

As we have seen in Chapter 3, fascism for the average British Italian person was about patriotism. Within the Italian population, fascism was strongest and most prolific in the larger Communities where, quite simply, it was able to reinforce itself by association amongst large numbers of Italians. Geographically isolated families in Scotland, the north of England and Wales were, by definition, more socially isolated from the activity of the larger Italian Communities. The majority of such Italians were out of touch with politics and events in Italy. This is not to say that there were not hard-core fascists and supporters of Mussolini within the ranks of the Italian Community. But the majority were thankful for their progress in this country which had hosted them and their families for more than a generation, and did not wish to jeopardise this position. Most had no intention or possibility of returning to Italy. They simply wanted to keep their heads down and carry on working as best as they could.

Membership of the *fasci* in the cities consisted of two groups of people: the activists within their Italian Communities – organisers and leaders – who were in the minority; and the vast majority who were members taking advantage of all the social and cultural activities that the *fasci* offered for Italians. Many more people who were not actually *tesserati*, or full members of the *fasci*, certainly frequented the *fasci* and made use of the facilities. This is important to bear in mind.

Between 1939 and 1940, there had been much speculation, and various schemes had been discussed by the British government, concerning the fate of the resident Italian Community should Mussolini declare allegiance to the enemy. No clear plan, however, emerged from the many proposals and the tide of public and government opinion for blanket internment grew as events in Europe turned against the allies. A particularly virulent attack on the Italians was published in the *Daily Mirror* on 27 April 1940 demonstrating the xenophobia against Italians which was beginning to ferment in the country:

> *There are more than twenty thousand Italians in Great Britain. London alone shelters more than eleven thousand of them. The London Italian is an indigestible unit of population. He settles here more or less temporarily, working until he has enough money to buy himself a little land in Calabria, or Campagnia or Tuscany. He often avoids employing British labour. It is much cheaper to bring a few relations into England from the old home town. And so the boats unloaded all kinds of brown-eyed Francescas and Marias, beetle-browed Ginos, Titos and Marios. . . .*
>
> *Now every Italian colony in Great Britain and America is a seething cauldron of smoking Italian politics. Black fascism. Hot as hell. Even the peaceful, law-abiding proprietor of the back-street coffee shop bounces into a fine patriotic frenzy at the sound of Mussolini's name. . . .*
>
> *We are nicely honeycombed with little cells of potential betrayal. A storm is brewing in the Mediterranean. And we, in our droning, silly tolerance are helping it to gather force.*

Throughout 1939 and early 1940 the German and Austrian Jewish refugees, who were flooding into Britain in an attempt to escape Hitler's

Naziism, were being 'classified' by tribunals into 'A', 'B' or 'C' categories depending on the perceived level of threat to security, with 'A' being the most 'dangerous' group. From an administrative point of view, it was relatively straightforward for the British authorities to monitor the refugees as they entered the country. This was not the case with the Italians, many of whom had been settled in Britain since the nineteenth century. However, before June 1940 and the declaration of war by Italy, no screening process was inaugurated for the Italians. No attempt was made to sort out the fascists from the anti-fascists and, more importantly, from the innocuous or non-fascists, a term which best described the majority of Italians.

Despite the fact that the authorities took no action to assess the Italian population resident in Britain, they were concerned over the possibility of spies and fifth columnists. In a letter on 27 May 1940, Brigadier Harker, head of MI5, wrote:

> *We have reason to suppose that the first act of war on the part of Italy might be an attempt to use the Italian fascist organisation for attacks on key individuals and key points in this country by the employment of gangster methods. We are therefore anxious that our arrangements should be made so as to forestall such attempts if possible.*

These arrangements would entail arresting 'all known suspects as soon as instructions to that effect are issued by the Home Office'.[1] Without passing comment on the spectre of *Mafia* conjured up in this statement, the arrangement for the arrest of all known suspects referred to a list of 1,500 Italians compiled by MI5. These 1,500 were described as 'desperate' and 'dangerous characters' who would not hesitate to commit acts of sabotage and were to be arrested immediately if Italy declared war.

Somehow MI5 obtained the membership lists of the various *fasci* up and down the country. In addition, they most probably utilised the list of Italians published in the *Guida Generale degli Italiani in Gran Bretagna* of 1939. There is a suspicion that the 1933 Census of Italians Abroad may also have been acquired, perhaps most particularly the Scottish one since those detailed schedules remained in the Consulate then in Glasgow. As we saw in Chapter 3 the respondents were asked if they held *fascio* membership. To MI5, membership of the *fasci* became synonymous with 'professing fascism'. It would later, after tragic consequences, become apparent to the Home Office and Foreign Office alike that the MI5 list of 'dangerous characters' was fundamentally flawed and included not only many ordinary Italians but also several well-known anti-fascists.

In Cabinet meetings throughout May 1940, the discussion of internment, not only of the Italians but also of the German Jews, continued. It was around this time (May 1940) that Churchill was heard to remark that they should all be deported. So far only category 'A' of the Germans had been interned on mainland Britain and debate centred on the Italians and categories 'B' and 'C' of the Germans. The Home Secretary, Sir John Anderson, favoured a scheme which involved the immediate internment of the 1,500 Italians on the MI5 list when Italy declared war, followed by the selective internment of males between 17 and 60 years of age who had been resident in Britain for less than ten years. The Cabinet accepted these proposals except that the ten-year residency period was increased to 20. Only Italians resident from before 1919, therefore, were technically off the hook, assuming that is they had no contact with a *fascio*.

As the government grappled with these enormously complex issues and the different ministries – Home Office, Foreign Office, War Office – tried to agree briefs and responsibilities, life in the Italian Community continued under great stress. Already, British-born members of the second generation had been called up into the British forces – some to the Armed Forces and others, who felt they could not actually fight against Italy, to the 'Pioneer Corps'. With the outbreak of war in 1939, many entire families who were more recent arrivals, and therefore less settled, realised the way events might develop and returned to Italy. In other cases, wives and children returned to Italy, to safety as they saw it, leaving their husbands to carry on working. The period between 1939 and the summer of 1940 was very worrying for the Italians: they saw what was coming, knew that they were going to be caught between two countries and realised there was very little that they could do about it. Those who were able to 'go back' were the lucky ones; not everyone was in a position to do so. Many meetings and discussions took place in back shops, in the Italian clubs of Soho and in restaurant and café kitchens throughout the country. 'What was to be done?' 'What could be done?' 'What would happen, to us, to the businesses?' And so on, endlessly, until 10 June 1940.

The immediate consequences of Italy's declaration of war for the Italians resident in Britain were two-fold – arrest and anti-Italian rioting. Eloquently put by the historian David Ceserani, 'The ingredients of popular xenophobia, racism, political cynicism and press hysteria together culminated in Churchill's edict to "Collar the lot!".'[2] Churchill didn't bother about the complicated detail that the Cabinet had been considering for over a month, and previous government vacillation now coupled with panic produced the circumstances for this across-the-board internment. As we shall see, this decision led to serious practical problems as well as disaster and arguably even humiliation for the British government. We will return to the arrests and their consequences below.

The anti-Italian riots

The other consequence of Mussolini's declaration of war on the allies in his speech from the *Palazzo Vecchio* in *Roma* at 4 p.m. on 10 June 1940 was a night of terror for the Italian Community in Britain.

As darkness fell in Britain the mounting xenophobia reached fever pitch. Ransacking mobs attacked Italian property, mainly businesses, from Soho in London to Stonehaven in the north-east of Scotland. The fervour of hatred that was unleashed astonished most Italians and also many British people. Italian families in small towns who considered themselves well integrated into the local communities, and who had been there for decades, often generations, could not comprehend this violent reaction. Where they were known, respected and loved, so they thought, how could this happen? They were not the enemy after all, only compatriots of the enemy. Certainly in many cases the mobs that whipped themselves up into a frenzy were comprised of the local hooligan element, but this was not always the case. Across the country, a night of smashing, burning and looting ensued.

These anti-Italian riots were particularly widespread and vicious in Scotland due, perhaps, to the religious bigotry prevalent in that society. A long-standing hatred and fear of Catholics could well have been partly responsible for the violence vented on this night. In addition, it can be suggested that in the then infamous tough areas such as the Gorbals in Glasgow, and the heavy industrial towns of Greenock and Port Glasgow, this night presented an unprecedented crime opportunity.

A survey of the press, both local and national, for 11 and 12 June 1940 revealed the extent and location of these riots. On 11 June *The Times*, in an article headed 'Anti-Italian Demonstrations', mentioned trouble in Soho and Liverpool, and considerable damage in Glasgow and Edinburgh. Elsewhere, Cardiff and Belfast were also mentioned. By all accounts Edinburgh seems to have been the most affected city and, according to *The Times*, 'Several persons were injured and numerous arrests were made during serious anti-Italian demonstrations where police

105

made baton charges to check angry crowds'. In fact, if we turn to the local newspaper in Edinburgh, we find that the Edinburgh *Evening News* gave more graphic detail on these events and reported that:

> *The most riotous scenes occurred in Leith Street and Union Place which is contiguous. A crowd of over a thousand gathered, the great majority of them in the role of spectators. The trouble was due largely to irresponsible youths who started stone-throwing. There are numerous shops in the vicinity occupied by Italians and before police were able to get control of the mischief-makers many plate-glass windows were shattered. The police made a number of baton charges. Sections of the crowd showed hostility and, in the course of the skirmishes, policemen had their helmets knocked off. Stragglers lingered about in the streets till the early hours of the morning.*

Later in the report the *Evening News* went on to say that:

> *Leith Street and Leith Walk looked in places as if a series of heavy bombs had fallen. In Italian premises not a scrap of glass remained in single or double windows, furniture broken, window frames and dressing destroyed and the cigarette machines at the entrances damaged beyond repair.*

Apparently similar scenes of destruction were to be seen throughout the city along the major thoroughfares of Broughton Street and Gorgie Way. A shop in Antigua Street was smashed and the contents set on fire. Such was the extent of this general ransacking and unrest that more than a score of the mobsters were sufficiently injured to have been treated at Leith Hospital.

In Glasgow similar scenes occurred, especially in the Govan, Tradeston and Maryhill areas of the city. One Scottish lady, married to a Glasgow Italian, who lived in a tenement block on Parliamentary Road, witnessed a large mob working its way along the street systematically smashing, looting, and setting ablaze the Italian shops.[3] The *Glasgow Herald* (11 June 1940) described shops in Garscube Road, Paisley Road West and Maryhill Road which were looted and besieged by crowds of up to several hundred people. It told also of the many calls for help that the police received from Italian families who were locked inside their premises, usually above or behind their shops which were being attacked.

106

On the Clyde coast it appears that in Port Glasgow, Greenock and Gourock the scale of violence and damage approached the level reached in Edinburgh. The *Greenock Telegraph* declared on 11 June 1940 that:

> *Scenes unprecedented in Greenock and Port Glasgow took place late last night when gangs of infuriated persons gave vent to their feelings against local Italians following Mussolini's declaration of war on the Allies. The police had difficulty in coping adequately with the situation. Some of the most violent incidents took place in Ann Street, where shops owned by Italians were indiscriminately smashed.*

The *Greenock Telegraph* went on to say that all 17 of the Italian shops in the 'Port' were badly damaged and reported an eye witness account as saying that a positive orgy of wanton destruction had been indulged in by hooligan elements. The witness said:

> *In Princes Street I saw cash registers, pin tables, freezing machines and other articles being smashed to pieces on the pavement. In one or two cases it is no exaggeration to say that nothing but bare walls of the shops were left intact.*

Scanning the newspapers for 12 June 1940, we find that the Italians continued to be headline news. However, the articles turned their attention to the arrest of Italian men for internment. Only in the *Greenock Telegraph* is evidence found of a second night of rioting against the Italians, especially in Gourock:

> *From about 7 o'clock bands of youths arrived in the burgh* [from Greenock and Port Glasgow] *on foot, in buses and on cycles. They congregated near Pierhead. At 10 p.m. the gathering numbered several hundred.*

This was no spur-of-the-moment spontaneous gathering; its intent was clear. Apparently the police were able to keep this mob 'on the move' but nevertheless the image of such a large crowd – presumably making a considerable noise shouting anti-Italian slogans – moving through the streets of this small coastal town is terrifying to conjure up. There is no doubt that the Italians were indeed terrified. Most of the men had been removed by 11 June; only the women – wives, mothers and children – were left at home. Since the shops had been destroyed on the night of 10 June, the intent of the crowd was a frightening prospect for those huddled behind closed doors. The violence did, however, seem to be focused against property rather than individuals. Extreme physical violence against persons rather than property was rare, although not unknown. There are many stories of men, not yet arrested, being smuggled in, or out, of houses in the face of a belligerent crowd. Angry crowds also congregated at city police stations to boo, hiss, jeer and spit as the Italians were brought to the cells.

One of the difficulties in maintaining law and order on the night of 10 June 1940 was that the police were simultaneously conducting the across-the-board arrest of Italian males between the ages of 17 and 60. Police manpower was seriously stretched in this operation. This was particularly so in Glasgow and Edinburgh, both cities with large Italian Communities and wide-scale unrest. For example, according to the Edinburgh *Evening News* for 11 June, 'As soon as instructions [for the arrests] were received at police headquarters nearly 100 motor cars were brought into service and over 200 officers combed the city within the boundaries of Granton, Corstorphine and Portobello. The round-up continued all night, many of the Italians being called from their bed'. The police did, however, effect some arrests of mobsters and looters; the charges were usually for malicious damage and looting.

The round-up

The arrest of Italian males began a long catalogue of muddle and confusion. Differences, anomalies and idiosyncrasies abounded in the methods used and interpretations of the hastily compiled and unfinished sets of instructions. The discretionary elements which inevitably crept into procedures at this and every subsequent stage in the lengthy and complicated episode of internment would require not only access to many closed government files but also several doctoral theses to unravel.

Police were to arrest the 'dangerous characters' on the MI5 list, which we must assume had reached all the provincial Chief Constables, and all known Italians with less than 20 years residence in the age group 17 to 60. The reality was, however, that many men were arrested who should not have been and, secondly, that not all of those who should have been 'collared' were in fact arrested.

The first raids were made on the *fasci* in London, Glasgow and

Edinburgh at 6 p.m. on 10 June. Any Italians present were automatically arrested and documents and other articles were impounded. In London, 80 men had been arrested in this way within the first two hours of Mussolini's declaration. When the police entered the *fasci* and other Italian premises, such as the Italian Hospital and St Peter's Italian Church in London, the vast bulk of incriminating documentation had already been destroyed. Owing to fear of appearing on 'lists', almost all the copies of the 1939 *Guida Generale* had been destroyed. There are, as a result, sadly very few copies of this book still in private hands today.

The main arrests followed a different pattern across the country with the 'swoop' taking place in the middle of the night in Scotland and provincial England, and, in London, the majority being arrested between dawn and 8 a.m. on 11 June. Outside London the 'round-up' was a very much more detailed and thorough operation. This was particularly true for small towns with only a few Italian families where the local police knew the Italians and where to find them. Indeed, it appears that in the provinces 'the lot' were collared. Virtually all 'Italians' were arrested regardless of period of residence, political affiliations or nationality – many British-born and naturalised British subjects were arrested.

In the cities, but particularly London, the operation was more imprecise and, from the point of view of the British authorities, much more difficult. Reference to the press for the days of 10, 11 and 12 June confirms this and the words 'comb-out' of Italians crop up more than once, particularly with reference to the Italian Colonies of Soho and Clerkenwell. Also, in London, police were not simply picking up 'known Italians' but were in addition looking specifically for the 'dangerous characters' of the MI5 list, over half of whom lived in London. The 1931 census enumerated just under 10,000 Italians in London and the difficulty of such a scale of operation is not hard to imagine. The authorities took to publishing notices in the newspapers which announced that Italians should report to the police. The situation in London was quite simply that not all were 'collared' and many slipped through the net. Protestations about sons in the British Army and length of residence seemed to hold more sway with the police.

Once arrested, however, it proved enormously difficult for anti-fascists, British subjects, sympathisers and innocuous fascists, and men over 60 years of age alike to obtain release, and hundreds of entirely innocent civilians would soon perish as a result.

One group of Italians attempting to negotiate release were those nominated by the Italian Ambassador, Giuseppe Bastianini, to sail with him on the *Monarch of Bermuda*. This ship had been put at his disposal on 10 June 1940 by the British authorities as part of a pre-war negotiated arrangement for an exchange of diplomats between Britain and Italy. Of the 730 nominated by the Ambassador, many, including the Italian Consuls in Cardiff and Liverpool, were found languishing in police cells. Eventually these diplomats and 49 other men who had been arrested in London managed to secure their release. Others decided that they did not want to return to Italy and chose to remain with their compatriots, even if this meant internment. In the end the ship left from Glasgow with 629 Italians on board who were exchanged at Lisbon for a British party which had left Italy on the SS *Conte Rosso*.

The procedure of the actual arrests is something which still rankles with many 'old' Italians today. Often the process was amicable enough with the police politely explaining their orders and asking the Italians quickly and quietly to accompany them down to the local police station. In other cases, however, witnessed by the entire family which had naturally been aroused, fairly unpleasant scenes ensued with police searching for 'enemy propaganda' and evidence. This sort of behaviour was especially difficult for the Italians to understand where the arresting officers were local bobbies, well-known men, who for years had frequented shops and cafés on a daily basis when on their beat. Obviously, not all arrests were conducted in an unpleasant way: a range of stories regarding this are available and assuredly the circumstances would vary according to the individuals involved. Certainly, in the vast majority of cases the Italians went quietly and with no trouble.

The officers did not really seem to know much about the destination and fate of their prisoners or for how long they would be gone. In many cases, the Italians were told to take very little with them, just a change of underwear, since they would not be away for long. Most men packed a small suitcase and those with foresight concealed valuables, especially money and gold, amongst their possessions. In general, however, the arrests were very rushed and there was little time for considering which, if any, items would be needed.

The grief and fear of wives and especially children who watched their fathers, elder brothers and uncles being taken away on this night should not be underestimated. Owing to the blackout, sometimes the whole ghastly affair was conducted in darkness, adding to the drama of the situation. For children who were old enough to remember that night, and their fear and confusion for their fathers and themselves, the effect was traumatic.

The next morning, the children faced agonising taunting at school. 'You're father's been taken to a concentration camp', and so on. One lady, now in her early 60s, told of how her mother explained to her that her father had been 'interned' and that he was in an 'internment', not a 'concentration', camp. She had no idea what the difference was. Her brother, who was a little younger, was regularly beaten at school and picked upon as a 'Tally Bastard', 'Wog', 'Ay-tie'.[4] It was in this way a generation of British Italians learned that it was not a good thing to be Italian and how it was better to 'assimilate' or de-Italianise themselves. This night, and the months and often years of internment which followed, left an indelible mark on the minds and psyche of the second-generation British Italian Community.

Across the country many adult British-born second-generation or naturalised British members of the Italian Community who had escaped internment found that they too were considered the 'enemy' and treated as such by local populations. They too tried to de-Italianise themselves in order to survive. According to the *Daily Express* newspaper on 12 June: 'A rush of new posters has come out overnight in Soho shop and café windows. Italian provisions stores, tightly packed with spaghetti, chianti and olive oil with names such as Gennari Limited or Brega and Rossi, now bear the announcements "This firm is entirely British".' Reports confirmed that even the obviously named 'Spaghetti House' in Old Compton Street, Soho, put up a notice declaring itself to be 'A British Restaurant'. The well-known Bianchi's in Frith Street is actually on a BBC documentary film taking down its 'Italian Restaurant' sign and replacing this with a 'Swiss Restaurant' sign over its door. The *Daily Express* went on to tell that, in Charlotte Street, *Signor* Bertorelli pinned up a poster on the wall of his restaurant which read 'The proprietors of this restaurant are British subjects and have sons serving in the British Army'. A similar plea for peace was being made nationwide with shopkeepers in Greenock flying Union Jacks to show their allegiance. In Gourock the owner of the Continental Café, Mr R. Toma, the descendants of whom are still in business in the town today, actually handed over his café to the authorities with the words 'If there is to be any looting, I would prefer the stock to be given to the soldiers'. Finally, the *Daily Herald* of 12 June 1940 reported an organ-grinder, one of the last of his kind, in Leeds who had a notice on his organ which said 'I'm British and the monkey is from India'.

There were, however, many British-born Italians who were determined to go with 'the Italians' and to remain united with their roots and their

111

Community. As well as the difficulties of internment which followed, the 'Community' and every family was placed in a situation which began to weaken the entire family-based structure. The schism within a single family can be imagined. There were numerous cases where a father was interned and his son served in the British forces. The British-born second-generation men divided into three distinct groups:

(a) those who were interned with their fathers and who were therefore normally classified under defence regulation 18(b), in other words members of the *fascio* and as such a threat to national security;

(b) those who were not interned and who were prepared to 'help' the British war effort, but not in an active way, who joined the special unit based at Slough, the '270 Aliens Corps', known as the 'Pioneer Corps';

(c) those who served in active service in the British Armed Forces.

The first generation was not uniform either in its treatment and experience. In London, many men were not arrested or interned, even on a short-term basis, simply because the authorities were unable to cope with the large numbers and were therefore more lenient. As we shall see below, those who were interned were subsequently sorted into three groups:

(1) those who were shipped to the Isle of Man;
(2) those who were deported to Canada;
(3) those who ended up in Australia.

This seemingly harmless geographical classification had more significant implications.

Internment

The initial phase

The men who were arrested on 10 June usually spent the first few nights at a local police station with subsequent transferral to 'collecting points' throughout the country. In London, the initial detention of the 'dangerous characters' was at Brompton Oratory School. From here the men were transferred to a camp at Lingfield racecourse in Surrey. Already it was becoming obvious to the authorities that they were not dealing with professing fascists but harmless caterers. From the Scottish police stations, the internees were moved to Maryhill Army Barracks in Glasgow and to a camp set up at Milton Bridge near Edinburgh.

In each of these locations varying periods of time up to two weeks were spent before transferral to Warth Mills, near Bury, in Lancashire. This was the final gathering station for all Italians from throughout Britain. Warth Mills, a cotton mill which closed down many years before the war, was a huge rectangular building, three or four storeys high with regular rows of large windows. It had been left untouched from the day it closed and, with the passage of time, had deteriorated enormously. All the windows were smashed as well as many of the panes in the glass roof, and the pitted factory floors were covered with oil and grease. The original machinery was still in place. Conditions were abysmal: only a few taps of cold water, minimal sanitation, straw palliasses to sleep on and appalling food rations, irregularly dished out. It was here, for the first time, that all geographical and socio-economic sections of the British Italian Community met: the young, the old, the fascists, the innocuous or non-fascists, the anti-fascists, the upper crust from London, the shopkeepers, the artists, the musicians, those from the north of Italy and those from the south of Italy. It was a most extraordinary gathering. Around 4,200 Italians had been arrested in two weeks, 300 of whom were British-born.

It is an interesting and curious thought that, here at Warth Mills, in these desperate circumstances in this desolate location, a large section of the British Italian male population was assembled. Two things happened. Firstly, the British authorities supposedly began to sort out the active fascists from the ordinary Italians and, secondly, various groups within this all-male community begin to organise and sort themselves out. By natural laws, various types were attracted to each other and the large group-name tags of 'Scottish', 'English' and 'Welsh' Italians emerged.

During this period, the British Government attempted to finalise its plans for the internees and selections began amidst the abominable conditions. The Italians could not understand the basis upon which these selections were made. Officially, the 'professing fascists' on the MI5 list were to be deported and after much persuasion Canada had reluctantly agreed to take them. By the end of June the Foreign Office was becoming suspicious of the Security Services' assumptions and tactics. This is revealed in a Foreign Office memo of 22 June 1940:

MI5's criteria for judging whether or not a person was a 'desperate character' more often than not resolved itself into

113

mere membership of the Fascio. *On it being pointed out that membership of the* Fascio *was to all intents and purposes obligatory on any Italian resident abroad who desired to have any sort of claim to diplomatic or consular protection, they relented somewhat and limited their objection to Fascists of military age and special ardour . . . As the discussion with MI5 proceeded there grew up a strong suspicion that in actual fact they had little or no information, let alone evidence, in regard to more than a fraction of the persons they had led the Home Secretary to describe to the Cabinet as 'desperate characters'.*[5]

Nevertheless, on 21 June 'the list' had been sent to Warth Mills and to five other smaller camps around the country where Italians were still being held. Commandants were instructed to mark for deportation any persons named on the list. Only 700 of the 1,500 could be identified. A rather pathetic range of excuses was given by MI5 for this, including the complete inexactitude that Italian names have a number of alternative spellings. The majority of the internees were destined for internment on the Isle of Man. To the Italians it seemed as if the selections were done on an entirely random basis. Many old Italians describe being lined up and simply divided on the basis of 'You, this side. You, that side', and so on.

Rando Bertoia of Glasgow, a survivor of the *Arandora Star*, said recently:

It will always remain a mystery to me how I was picked for the Arandora Star. *We were just picked at random. Some were very old men and they were taken away. They should have been left to go to the Isle of Man. My father was left. But other old men came with me. At that time Britain was in turmoil, a panic and all the rest of it. So I think they just grabbed some here and some there. Probably they took the names if people were* fascisti. *But they were just picked at random, I wasn't in the* fascisti *or anything. I was nothing. I wasn't registered anywhere and I hadn't joined anything. As a matter of fact some of the real* fascisti *remained out.*[6]

The men found it difficult to comprehend the separation of fathers, sons and brothers. Often since fathers were old – many men in their 60s and 70s had been arrested – sons were extremely reticent to be separated from them. Thus it happened that people began to swap papers if they were nominated for a batch that would have separated them from their kin. This was to have tragic consequences for the Community.

The first group of men left and word filtered back to Warth Mills that they had been shipped to the Isle of Man. On 30th June another selection of men was made and transported to Liverpool docks. When the men saw the size of the ship that they were to board, some began to realise that they were destined for considerably further afield than the Isle of Man. The ship was the SS *Arandora Star*, destined for Canada.

The *Arandora Star*

The 1,500 ton *Arandora Star* set sail from Liverpool bound for Canada early on 1 July 1940. On 2 July at 7 a.m. the ship was torpedoed 125 miles west of Ireland by the German U Boat, *U47*, under the command of Gunther Prien – a man known in Germany as the 'Bull of Scapa Flow'. The *Arandora Star* sank within 30 minutes, with a loss of over 700 lives.

The sinking of the *Arandora Star* was, and still is, the most tragic event in the history of the Italian Community. It also makes the British Italian Community unique in global terms: no other Italian Community in the world has suffered such a blow. When news of the event came out and families tried to find out if they had lost a loved one, the shock and horror was beyond all preconceived ideas of the meaning of internment. How could such a tragedy have occurred?

The *Arandora Star* left Liverpool unescorted and was an easy target for the enemy. Despite the fact that she flew a swastika, indicating that the ship carried German prisoners of war, this did not dissuade Captain Prien from taking a shot with his last torpedo. The ship also carried British soldiers and had anti-submarine guns visible on the decks. As well as the German PoWs there were German Jewish refugees, and the Italian internees. Should such an incompatible mixture ever have been crammed on the same ship? The *Arandora Star* sustained a direct hit on her starboard side which wrecked the engine room. Both she and many of her passengers had no chance of survival. Many of the Italians had been allocated to the 'A' or bottom deck cabins. This group sustained the highest casualty level. The ship was immediately plunged into darkness and the possibility of finding a route up to safety in the pitch black through a maze of narrow corridors was virtually nil. Others who had been quartered in the ballroom and mess-decks were more fortunate and stood a better chance of survival. A number of factors, however, such as barbed wire at strategic points on the ship, an insufficient number of lifeboats, in addition to several being unsuccessfully launched, and confusion because there had been no emergency drill, all contributed to the horrendously high death rate.

Accounts of (surviving) survivors help illustrate these points. According to Nicola Cua of London:

> The main cause of the high death toll was that there were not enough lifeboats. Also, we didn't have any boat drill whatsoever and the ship went down in 20 or 30 minutes. The Germans were all merchant seamen and they were all young; they knew exactly what to do. We didn't know anything at all. We had cork life-jackets but they are the worst things you can have unless you know how to use them. Because the way that a life-jacket is tied, if you don't jump in [to the water] properly it can come up and knock you out.[7]

Romolo Chiocconi of Glasgow also believes that the Italians were at a disadvantage:

> There was no panic as such but the officers made no attempt to co-ordinate things. I must say they didn't try to organise any-thing and I think if there had been a leader who took charge not so many people would have died. In fact, some of the Germans tried to organise the release of lifeboats. But there weren't enough lifeboats anyway. The poor Italians, they were trying to undo the ropes and one thing or another and they didn't know what to do. One of the lifeboats got filled up and then they let her down. It fell at an angle and hit off the side of the ship . . . everybody down one on top of each other. And most of them did not know how to swim.[8]

Because there was not enough space in the lifeboats for everybody, some had to resort to desperate measures to make sure that the lifeboats that were launched did not become overloaded. According to Gino Guarnieri:

> There were about 20 of us in the lifeboat. There was an officer, he had a small hatchet in his hand and he cut the rope. He said, 'Come on all of you start rowing.' We said, 'Why row, there are still a lot of people on top of the boat, let them come down.' Mostly they were old people, well over 50. He said, 'I've got no time to argue with you. If any one of you disobeys my orders,

I'll chop your head off. Start rowing.' We rowed about 200 yards. Then he said, 'Now we stop.' He said, 'Now I'll tell you why I did this. If we had stayed there every one of us would have gone down with the ship any minute. If we had stopped there we wouldn't have saved them and we would have drowned ourselves.'[9]

Enrico Casci of Falkirk described further scenes of chaos especially for those unable to find a place in one of the lifeboats:

We were dressed wrongly, with all our clothes on, an overcoat and everything. The German boys were just as they had been brought into the world, stark naked. If you're going to hit the water, you have more of a fighting chance that way. With clothes on you become saturated with water. It is absolutely no use that way. There weren't enough lifeboats for everyone. Definitely not. But mind you, there were rafts tied to the railings and hatchets to get them out. People were throwing everything that could float into the water. I saw some big tanks, big empty barrels being thrown over the side, but there were a lot of poor lads down there whose heads were getting split open. No matter how far you tried to jump out, away from the ship, the ship was at least 50 feet high, so you are not going to jump out very far.[10]

When news broke of the sinking of *Arandora Star*, the British press tried to blame the high death toll on fighting and panic amongst the internees. Increasingly, however, the true nature of the tragedy came to the attention of MPs who raised questions in the House of Commons, especially with regard to some of the individuals who were on board. Despite all the evidence and individual cases coming to light, the Secretary of State for War, Anthony Eden, was still maintaining at the end of July 1940 that all the people on board the *Arandora Star* had been Italian fascists and German Nazis. No government department knew the correct story and journalists and relatives alike were being referred from the Home Office to the War Office and then to the Ministry of Information. It was a chaotic nightmare.

Owing to the chaotic muddle in which the selection of men took place and the rushed nature of the departure, it has never been conclusively established exactly how many men were on board the *Arandora Star* and how many were lost at sea. No proper embarkation list was compiled.

Certainly, if there was one, it went down with the ship – no record was left with the Port Authority. Available documentation at the Public Records Office, Kew – Foreign Office, Home Office and War Office files – all give differing figures[11]. Naturally, had the *Arandora Star* reached her destination, the question of the number and identity of internees on board would not have arisen since the Canadian authorities could simply have undertaken their own count and compiled a roll call when the ship docked.

The best estimate is that 1,564 men were on board. Of these, between 712 and 734 were Italians. The rest were either German (Jewish refugees as well as Nazis) and British servicemen. For the Italians, only two figures can be conclusively established. Firstly, the number who are known to have lost their lives was 446. Secondly, the group of survivors fit enough to be subsequently shipped to Australia numbered 200 men. A further group of survivors, between 64 and 88 men, were injured and sent to hospitals in Scotland. Around 40 of these then joined their compatriots interned on the Isle of Man; others seem to have been released. The Italian survivors therefore numbered between 266 and 288. Suffice it to say that around 60 per cent of all those on board lost their lives.

The confusion of the whole disaster was compounded by the fact that some Italians had swapped papers to ensure kin groupings remained intact. The example of Giuseppe Gazzano, whose family have had a provisions shop on Farringdon Road in Clerkenwell since 1901, is mentioned by Elena Salvoni (1990, p.46) in her autobiography. Gazzano told her that he 'was interned in 1940 and had been allocated a ticket on the *Arandora Star* but gave it up to a man he knew whose 16-year-old son was sailing on it and who asked him to swap places so he could be with his boy'. Both father and son were lost and Giuseppe Gazzano survives to this day. In addition to the fact that the authorities had no embarkation list, the consequence of this swapping was that, when the ship went down, it took months before it was conclusively established who had been lost and who had been saved.

The list compiled by the Foreign Office was the one published after the tragedy. Many people who had been saved were reported as drowned and vice versa. This obviously caused much anguish within the Italian Community. The Home Office list of the missing which was compiled between November 1940 and April 1941, and is the most accurate, was the final account of those who lost their lives – 446 men.[12] This list is printed in full, for the first time since 1940, in Appendix 3. Most of the bodies were never recovered although many were washed up on the shores of Ireland and western Scotland, where they were buried in local cemeteries.

The average age of the 446 men was just under 50 and 10 per cent of the men (44) were actually over 60 years of age. One wonders how much of a threat so many elderly men could have posed to national security, even assuming that was their intention. Survivors of the *Arandora Star* dismayingly tell how many middle-aged men simply stood on the decks as the ship went down, resigned to their fate. Old and unable to swim (remember many were from mountain communities in Italy where they had no contact with the sea), they knew their chances of survival were next to nil as they witnessed the harrowing scenes of struggle and squabble for the all too few places in the lifeboats. Without any prior screening of the Italians, why were so many old men randomly chosen for deportation?

Mostly the men came from London, Glasgow, Edinburgh or Manchester. Arguably, these men were from the large Italian Communities where there was fascist activity. However, over one-third of the total who were lost came from small towns throughout the country where in many cases they would have been the solitary male from the one Italian family in the town. Often these places were remote, in Scotland and the north of England, where the men would have had no or little contact with fascism within the Italian Communities. Some small but tightly knit Italian Communities were very badly affected by the loss of life. This was particularly true for the Welsh Valley Italian Communities where the relative loss of life was colossal. Bearing in mind the notion of 'chain migration' and that most of the Italians in Wales originated in the *comune* of *Bardi* (Pr), two sets of relatives in fact were devastated by this loss of life: those in Wales, and those at home in Italy. A total of 48 men from the *Bardi* area were lost on the *Arandora Star*. Not only does a street in the main section of the village – *Via Vittime Arandora Star* – bear their name, but a chapel was erected to their memory in the village cemetery in 1969 (see Plate 9). Another example of high loss of life from a small Italian Community was Ayr on the west coast of Scotland, from where ten men were lost, almost one from every Italian family resident in the town.

The range of occupation amongst the missing men was fairly predictable. From London most men had been cooks, waiters and catering assistants. Amongst the Scottish and Welsh contingent, most had been shopkeepers, refreshment house owners, café and ice-cream shop workers and proprietors. Mixed in with this group were also remnants of the old traditional occupations with one or two mosaic and *terrazzo* workers. The arts too were still represented: opera singers, a violinist, artists and sculptors were also present.

There were also two priests lost. One of these, *Padre* Gaetano Fracassi from Manchester was 64 years of age and had dedicated his life to the Manchester Italian Community. The Bishop of Salford had tried to expedite his release but to no avail. His loss is still talked about today in the 'old' Italian group of the city. A number of cases soon came to light of men who were obviously utterly harmless and by no means 'dangerous' and who should not have been on board. Gaetano Pacitto, a naturalised British subject from Hull, 65 years of age, was one clear example. The case of Francesco D'Ambrosio, confectioner and restaurateur from Hamilton, who had lived in Scotland for 42 years, had applied for naturalisation and had two sons in the British Army, was first cited by Professor Françoise Lafitte in 1940. We now know in addition from the Home Office list that D'Ambrosio was also the oldest Italian on board the *Arandora Star*. Born in *Picinisco* (Fr) in 1872, he was 68 years of age. Sir Robert Mark, in his autobiography (1978), describes how, as a young constable in Manchester, he was sent to arrest Ernani Landucci who had been a waiter at a hotel in Manchester for nearly 30 years. Landucci readily admitted that he was a member of the *fascio* in Manchester but he said that it meant nothing. He owned a small piece of land in the south of Italy and therefore was required to pay his taxes, 2/6d annually, through the Italian Consulate. This was the limit of his subversive activities. On being arrested he opened a bottle of wine and gave the toast, 'Bugger the *Fascio*!'. Four days later he drowned when the *Arandora Star* was torpedoed.

Decio Anzani was perhaps the best-known example of an anti-fascist from London who lost his life. He had lived in Britain for 31 years and was secretary to the League for the Rights of Man: an anti-fascist organisation. Other well-known anti-fascists such as Uberto Limentani and Paolo Treves had also been on board but had saved themselves.

Few of the men who were on board the *Arandora Star* were committed to Mussolini's militaristic cause. There were fascists on board, but there were also many fascists who were not selected for the *Arandora Star*, nor indeed for the *Ettrick* which was also destined for Canada, and who spent the entire War on the Isle of Man. There was no proper selection process before embarkation – how could there have been? There had been no prior screening of the internees.

On 19 July 1940, Sir John Anderson, the Home Secretary, wrote the following letter to Lord Halifax, the Foreign Secretary, in which he made it clear that he realised mistakes had been made in selecting Italians for the *Arandora Star*:

. . . it appears that the 734 Italians who were sent to Canada on the Arandora Star *were selected by MI5 as persons they wished to get rid of from this country on the grounds that they were potentially dangerous . . . I agree with your views that the arrangements for dealing with these Italian fascists have been most unsatisfactory. I am inclined to think that one, and possibly the main source of the trouble, is that there has been no sifting of the Italians resident in this country such as has taken place in the case of Germans and Austrians. In these circumstances there was no alternative but to rely on the opinion of the Security Services as to the potential danger of the Italians who had been interned and as to the desirability of sending them overseas.*[13]

Lord Snell was charged with conducting a government inquiry into the tragedy.[14] He recognised that the method for selecting 'dangerous' Italians was not satisfactory and the result was that among those earmarked for deportation were a number of non-fascists and people whose sympathies lay with Britain. He admitted that there were mistakes in the compilation of the MI5 list. Many of the Italians on board the *Arandora Star* had no fascist connections. The report was a whitewash, however, concluding that there were only about a dozen errors in selection and that Lord Snell did not consider this number of errors to be cause for serious criticism. Its results were never published due presumably to government fear of stirring up the issues again.

Perhaps as deplorable as the mismanagement of selection for the *Arandora Star* was the treatment of the survivors of the tragedy.

Survivors

The survivors were picked up on the afternoon of 2 July by the Canadian destroyer the *St Laurent* and were taken to Greenock. The irony of this for Amilcare Cima, the oldest surviving survivor (90) of the *Arandora Star* at the time of writing, was two-fold. Firstly, 2 July was his birthday and secondly, as he described in 1990:

At 4.15 the H83, St Laurent *destroyer, came for us, picked us up and took us back to Greenock – the very place from which I had come in the first place! My sister came down to where they had us. She brought some bread and a few other items with her,*

121

but they wouldn't let her in in order to give these things to me.
Eventually she made contact with a local lawyer who arranged
for some clothes to be brought to me.[15]

The men were not even given the opportunity to contact relatives. Between 66 and 88 men were badly injured and sent to Scottish hospitals, mostly to Mearns Kirk, the majority of whom subsequently joined the internees on the Isle of Man. The other 200 were at sea again on 10 July, this time on board the HMT *Dunera*, and bound for internment in Australia. In the only written account by any of the Italian *Arandora Star* survivors, Vittorio Tolaini set the scene for the nightmare which was to follow:

> *On reaching the dockside, we found a large contingent of*
> *soldiers who were to act as escort to us on the forthcoming*
> *voyage. They assisted our boarding with punches, kicks and*
> *painful prods with their rifle butts, along with an assault of*
> *disgusting language . . . As I stepped on board the suitcase,*
> *which contained the clothes my brother had brought me, was*
> *snatched away and ripped with a bayonet. A pyjama jacket was*
> *taken out and thrown at me, the suitcase was then tossed on to*
> *a huge pile of cases on the deck. The suitcases belonged to the*
> *two thousand Jews already on board. . . . Ahead of me, one*
> *Luigi Beschizza, was searched and a gold Hunter watch and*
> *chain was forcibly taken from him. His anger at this abuse*
> *became uncontrollable. Throwing down a penny which he found*
> *in his pocket, he yelled with emotion, 'You have taken my watch,*
> *so you might as well take every bloody thing.' The soldiers*
> *ordered him to pick it up. He refused. For his show of defiance*
> *he was brutally struck across the mouth and pushed down the*
> *steps below with a rifle butt against his back. Next to be searched*
> *was me. Finding nothing, the soldiers struck me in the spine with*
> *a rifle and pushed me below to join Luigi Beschizza. In this way,*
> *we were all herded below like animals. (Tolaini, 1982)*

One might expect that, given the traumatic episode of the *Arandora Star*, the passengers of the *Dunera* would have been treated at least to Geneva Convention standards for PoWs by the British. Not only were the conditions gruesome and deteriorating as the journey proceeded, but the continual beatings, threats and searches meted out by the guards were almost inhumane. According to Stent (1980, p.114) nothing else occurred during the internment period which remotely touched the stark, almost unreal horror of the journey of His Majesty's troopship *Dunera* from Liverpool to Australia. The passage lasted from 10 July 1940 to 7 September – 55 days of hell on the high seas. Only by a hair's breadth did the *Dunera* avoid sharing the fate of the *Arandora Star*. In the Bay of Biscay a torpedo missed her by 100–200 metres and the internees, locked below deck, heard the explosion and tried to get out. The doors were kept locked and shots were fired through them to settle the internees. According to Luigi Beschizza, one of the survivors, it was a miracle no one was injured.[16]

By the time the starving, unshaven, scantily clad, dysentery infected 200 reached port in South Australia they had been stripped of every possession they had salvaged from the *Arandora Star*. Gradually all the hiding places that the men ingeniously invented were discovered by the guards who searched rigorously and ruthlessly every day while the men conducted their (compulsory) exercise period on deck. All valuables as well as sentimental trinkets were removed. Cigarettes became an obsession with the smokers and one man, still alive at the time of writing, swapped a South African gold Krugerrand for a packet of cigarettes from a guard. Only one man, Carlo Notarianni, managed to conceal a hundred pound note until his arrival in Australia. This he did by placing the paper note inside his artifical hand; the one item which the guards never thought to remove.

It was some considerable time before news of the *Dunera* began to leak out in Britain. Letters about the atrocities of the journey filtered through towards the end of the year. It was not until the beginning of 1941 that the *Dunera* began to attract attention in Parliament along with claims for compensation from the internees. Eventually several members of the crew were court-martialled but no enquiry was ever held and the affair was hushed up.

The men who were interned in Australia passed the war years in relative tranquillity. Despite permission to return to England after their tribunals, conducted by a Major Layton, most were too scared to risk another sea voyage. From 1940 until December 1941 they were imprisoned at Tatura Internment Camp in Victoria. When Japan entered the war in 1941, they were transferred to Loveday Camp in South Australia, near the Murray River, where many worked as lumberjacks. From 1942 until the end of the war they again spent their internment at Tatura. Most took up work within the camp itself running their own facilities, or helped the war effort on the outside. There was, however, a group of hard-core fascists who made life difficult for the more apathetic, but generally a process of self-selection operated where the men organised themselves into 'like' groups. The younger men played football and were taught in a school set up by the more educated and intellectual internees like Gaetano Zezi, the doctor, and Giovanni Baldelli, the poet. They also built a chapel known as *La Nostra Chiesetta* and the well-known painter Francesco Matania designed the altar-piece. Although there were several deaths during the period of internment, the vast majority returned home to Britain in 1945.

Of the original *Arandora Star* survivors only 21 men are still alive. In 1990, on the fiftieth anniversary of the sinking of the *Arandora Star*, these men were awarded the prestigious civic title of *Cavaliere al Merito della Repubblica Italiana* by President Cossiga of Italy.

Canada

On 3 July 1940, another ship, the SS *Ettrick*, set sail from Liverpool also bound for Canada. There were 407 Italians on board and, this time, after a voyage of ten days, the *Ettrick*, which was accompanied by a destroyer escort, reached its destination safely. One man, Bartolomeo Gazzi from *Bardi* (Pr), died during the journey; survivors say that he committed suicide. Similar to the voyage of the *Dunera*, this was a thoroughly unpleasant experience for the internees who were badly treated by the British soldiers, in overcrowded and sordid conditions. The real trouble began, however, when the ship docked at Quebec and the men were kept aboard ship, on deck, for 12 hours before receiving any food. They were then taken ashore where they stood around on the quayside for a further six hours. During this time they were systematically robbed of their possessions. The 406 Italian men who reached Canada were interned at a camp near Montreal on St Helen's Isle, where an old fort had been sited. Like the internees in Australia, virtually all spent the next five years here; some taking up jobs in lumberjacking in the last year or so. Unlike in Australia the main problems for the men to contend with were intense cold and snow rather than extreme heat and dust.

During this time a certain Home Office commissioner, Alexander Paterson, was sent to review cases and assess whether individuals could be released. In his reports he stated that he was surprised to find that many of the internees had strong Scottish accents and concluded that the Scottish police had interpreted their instructions more vigorously than in England.[17] He found that the majority of men were eligible to return –

many under a clause introduced subsequent to internment which applied to internees who had lived continuously or almost continuously in the United Kingdom since childhood. Very few men chose to return; many who had lost fathers and brothers on the *Arandora Star* were implored by their families to remain in safety until the war was over.

The Isle of Man

The internment camps on the Isle of Man by and large consisted of terraced streets of peace-time boarding-houses and mansion blocks surrounded by barbed wire fences. These had been commandeered by the War Office and fenced in to serve as internment camps. Conditions here were, on the whole, better than in the purpose-built camps in the Dominions.

The main camps at which the Italians were held were: Metropole for the fascists and PoWs who were mainly merchant seamen; Onchan where the 'aristocrats' – the wholesalers, hotel and restaurant proprietors and other 'Sohoites' – were held; and Ramsey which accommodated the ice-cream men and fish and chip shop proprietors, owners of small cafés, etc. There was another large camp at Palace and a smaller one at Granville. A special kind of camp culture developed in all of them almost at once.

In July of 1940 Sir Percy Lorraine, an ex-British Ambassador to *Roma* was appointed by the Home Office to head a committee which would conduct tribunals to assess and classify the Italians. It had by now been recognised by both the Home Office and the Foreign Office that mistakes had been made in the internment and deportation of Italians. In his letter of 19 July to the Foreign Secretary, Sir John Anderson, stated that he proposed to 'appoint a Committee of enquiry to visit the camps in which Italians are detained and to classify them on some systematic basis'.[18] The Lorraine Committee had enormous difficulty in defining what constituted a 'true fascist' and MI5 were reluctantly forced to accept that membership of a *fascio* did not automatically disqualify individuals for release. Monsignor Gaetano Rossi (1990) described the process of the tribunals in his memoirs. The Italians:

> . . . *were asked if they were prepared to collaborate with the British authorities. Some of them agreed, but many internees were not disposed to go against their own country to help Britain. It was not a question of being fascists or anti-fascist, it was a question that we were Italian, the largest number of the*

internees were not prepared to go against their own country; this refusal was not a proof of supporting the fascist movement but simply a question of national feelings, but this aspect was continually ignored by the authorities.

The length of imprisonment in the camps depended upon the willingness of the internee to help the British war effort. When released, therefore, the men were not generally allowed to return to their businesses, but were allocated jobs in industry, agriculture and other sectors.

By November 1940, the first group of 410 internees who were willing to help with the British war effort had been released. Many joined the Pioneer Corps and others were allocated to jobs of national usefulness, in agriculture and industry. In London the men were often assigned to bomb damage clearance. Both the Soho and Clerkenwell Italian Colonies of London sustained considerable bomb damage during the war. Newport Dwellings in Soho, whose inhabitants were 80 per cent Italian, was hit directly by a mine which dropped steadily and visibly in broad daylight, supported by a parachute. Many were killed since, until it was too late, the spectators thought it was an airman parachuting down.

Tribunals were held at regular intervals to assess the willingness of the internees to disown Italy and help the British war effort. Many men could not agree to this, even after 1943 and Italy's capitulation, and they therefore remained behind barbed wire until 1945 when most were allowed to return to their homes (see Plate 10). It was a wrenchingly difficult decision for many, especially those who had fought for Italy during the First World War. Group pressure amongst the internees encouraged the individual to remain a 'good Italian', which meant to stay in. However, often families on the mainland were experiencing enormous hardships and many men felt that their place was at home with their wives and children. Inevitably, among this generation of the Italian Community, factions formed in these difficult times, some of which exist to this day.

The women at home

Wives and mothers were left at home to carry on as best they could. With the breadwinners removed many were reduced to relying on charity from the Italian Community as well as the population at large. Those who had businesses fared better, but often, however, these had to be closed down. If a shop was in a 'restricted zone', which meant one of particular military significance, relatives were not allowed to carry on with the business and in some cases mothers with children were forced to move out of the area altogether, with little alternative means of making a living. Many women, who were suddenly thrust into the throes of 'running a business' rather than just serving behind the counter, had never really been involved in the management and organisation or staffing side of a shop, café or restaurant before. Linguistic and business skills often fell short of the mark. Countless women, however, determinedly closed ranks in family groups and fought to keep their shops open for fear of losing them. Sisters, wives, sisters-in-law, and mothers worked in co-operation in this period in a way unprecedented in the competitive Italian small business environment. When a family concern was given over to an uninterned male to run, distant relative or otherwise, the chances of the owning family reacquiring the business were slim. This applied particularly in London where most properties were rented, and many families 'lost' their shops in this way.

In addition there were the complications of the war-time economy. The black market proved too much for many women, given their inexperience, and many shops closed down. Serving horse meat led to many convictions in the London restaurants. Others, unable to cope, took in 'managers' from the local communities – a relationship which often proved extremely fraught and tension-ridden. Again shops were lost in this way. In London many of the top Italian restaurants were taken over by the Custodian of Enemy Property.

For the Scottish Italian and other ice-cream makers the biggest problem was rationing which, of course, meant no ice-cream since sugar and, to a lesser extent, milk were rationed. Shops were kept open, just selling cigarettes and soft drinks, as there were few confectionery items either. The allocated quota of cigarettes depended on pre-war sales but this was never enough and people had to turn to the black market to try to fill their shelves. It is well known within the Italian Community that many families made their fortunes in this period since they were able to control the black market for their own people – the Italians. But this was the exception, not the rule, and most families struggled badly.

There was of course in many localities a good deal of on-going racism which had to be faced by the women and children on a day to day basis. Most were shunned by locals as 'enemy aliens' and, where good relations had previously existed, all pretence at tolerance disappeared. Most of the businesses that folded did so because local people refused to use the service they provided. Furthermore, supplies and stock from regular sources also became problematic, hence reliance on the black market. Suppliers of soft drinks, ingredients for hot drinks and many other staple items, particularly of the Scottish Italian concerns, often became unsure about supplying the 'enemy'. Where good trading connections had been built up over many years, these attitudes were little understood by the Italians, especially the ones whose survival depended upon it. Wives were able to visit husbands interned on the Isle of Man and most managed at least one visit a year for the long-term internees. Sometimes, when they sought accommodation in transit they were refused and experienced hostility from the local people. Marion Sarti, a Scottish woman who had had to register as an alien, slept in a field near Carlisle with her daughter in 1941 when no one in the town would give her accommodation as she travelled to the Isle of Man to visit her Italian husband, Amadeo.

The prisoners of war

Although Italian prisoners of war were not part of the British Italian Community as such, a final mention should be given to this group of men, some of whom remained in this country after the war ended.

By 1945, there were no fewer than 140,000 Italian PoWs stationed at camps around the country. Indeed, more Italian PoWs were accommodated in Britain than in any other European nation or in the United States. Perhaps the best-known PoW camp was Camp 60 on Lambholm Island, Orkney. Captured during the North African campaign, several hundred Italian PoWs were sent there to work on the Churchill Barrier, a massive series of concrete causeways which seal the eastern approaches to Scapa Flow. Debatably this was using them in the British war effort which contravened the Geneva Convention on PoWs.

Under the direction of one of the prisoners, Domenico Chiocchetti, the area of the camp was transformed by laying paths, planting shrubs and flowers, and, most importantly, building a chapel. This chapel, which still stands today, and forms a tourist attraction on the otherwise rather bleak island, was constructed in 1943 by joining two Nissen huts together. On the interior, the corrugated iron was hidden by decorated plaster board. Chiocchetti was aided by a small band of helpers which included Bruttapasta, a cement worker; Palumbo, a smith; Primavera and Micheloni, electricians; Barcaglioni; Battato; Devitto; Fornasier; Pennisi; Sporza and others. In 1960, Chicocchetti (who is still alive at the time of writing) returned to Orkney from his native *Moena* (Tn) to restore the chapel, where it remains today as a testimony not only to the faith of these men in adversity but also to the Italian love of the creation of beauty. Other chapels were also built at the different PoW camps throughout the country; for example, at Slough. These did not survive, however, and the Italian Chapel on Orkney has become a living symbol of the Italian PoWs in this country.

Another important memorial to the Italian PoWs is the Military Cemetery of Brookwood in Sussex. Here, 346 of the PoWs who died while prisoners in this country are buried. From the 1960s a remembrance service has been held here, for them and also the men who lost their lives on the *Arandora Star*, every November by the Italian military, consular and religious authorities. The service is held out of doors, and the attendance gathered from Italian Communities in the south-east usually runs to several hundred people. The main Italian Communities and associations send delegates and in general terms this ceremony has come to represent the equivalent of 'Remembrance Sunday' for the Italian Community. The event has also come to symbolise a pilgrimage representing the effect of the war on the Community.

From 1943 onwards, after Italy's capitulation, the position of the PoWs became unclear. Britain continued to use them despite complaints from the Badoglio government in Italy. In December 1945 the repatriation of the Italian PoWs began and by mid 1946 only 1,500 who had been given employment in the agricultural sector remained. Finally, and completing our picture of the Second World War on the eve of the new era, 841 Italian women came to Britain after the war as 'war brides' married to British soldiers who had been in the Armed Forces serving in Italy.

PART TWO:

1945 ONWARDS

Chapter Five

Settlement and occupation

Introduction

With the ending of hostilities in 1945, the last of the internees from the Isle of Man, Australia and Canada returned to their families. Indeed, two of the *Arandora Star* survivors, Luigi Beschizza and Vittorio Tolaini, brought back with them to London Australian Italian brides. The experience had been traumatic for the Italians and, as we shall see in this chapter, the reconstruction of the business Community was piecemeal. Later, in Chapter 7, when we look at the Italian family, we shall learn that the Italians were deeply affected in a number of different ways by the war. Indeed, it is fair to say that it cast a long shadow over the 'old' Community.

However, the ending of the war constituted another landmark in British Italian history. A new era was about to dawn for the British Italian Community in which its overall size, shape and structure would be fundamentally altered. In addition to a reactivation of the old chains of migration, there was shortly to be a 'mass' influx of southern Italian migrant workers leading to the creation of entirely 'new' Italian Communities, and causing in addition considerable growth and change in some of the 'old' Italian Communities.

This chapter moves our story forward by bringing the occupational development of the 'old' Italian Communities up to date, and, by introducing the 'new', impersonally recruited migrants of the late 1940s and 1950s, and the industries they came to serve.

Post-war migration

The new migrations were due both to a 'push' factor leading to a mass emigration, particularly from the south of Italy, and a 'pull' factor caused by restructuring and expansion of the British economy in the post-war period.

133

Emigration

The restrictions placed on emigration from Italy in the 1930s and the upheaval caused by the Second World War created an enormous pool of aspirant migrants, particularly in the south of Italy. The mass out-flowing of people from the *Mezzogiorno* which resulted in the post-war era was so enormous it has been described as the 'haemorrhage of the south'. Conditions had become desperate. People were literally starving, and there seemed no hope of improvement. Poverty, unemployment and social distress were widespread. For many the only hope, not only for progression but survival, was emigration. Two fundamental and inter-related structural aspects were responsible for this: pressure of an increasing population combined with an inefficient and overburdened agricultural economy. If the inefficient economic, political and social structure of southern agriculture, upon which most people were dependent, is also taken into consideration, the 'push' forces that produced the massive depopulation of the countryside can be readily understood.

As was the case with the emigrants from Italy in the nineteenth century, few of the southern Italian immigrants to reach Britain in the 1950s actively 'chose' to come to this country. That large numbers of these migrants arrived here was often, from their individual point of view, mere chance. They had applied to their local employment offices for work opportunities anywhere in the world. Southern Italians who emigrated in the 1950s tend to express the view that they 'had to emigrate' and that they had 'no choice' in the matter. It was a question of waiting for an opportunity. That they were allocated to the coal mines, the brickyards or the tin and steel industries of England and Wales, was simply the luck of the draw.

Immigration

In 1947 only 350 Italians entered Britain, but by 1949 the figure had risen to over 6,500. As we shall see below, these first arrivals were of the old variety and were chain dependent. The new emigration from the south of Italy was, however, by this time gaining momentum. In fact, the broad pattern of Italian immigration to England in the 1950s and 1960s mirrored the general trend of emigration from the south of Italy which peaked at around 200,000 in 1951, in 1956 and again in 1960. Between 1950 and 1960 Italian immigration to Britain averaged around 8,000 per annum; 1956 formed the peak year when 11,520 Italian migrants entered Britain. After another peak in 1960–1, there was a fairly steady downward trend.

In total, between 1948 and 1968, 148,140 Italians came to this country. This is over five times the number who had settled over the entire period of immigration up until the Second World War. Indeed, during each of the two peak three-year periods of 1955–7 and 1960–2, more arrived (32,515 and 30,028 respectively) than had settled during the whole of the previous period, until 1939.

However, not all of these new immigrants settled permanently in Britain, and over the period 20 per cent of the inward flow returned to Italy. In fact, by 1969, more Italians were leaving Britain than entering, and the 1970s became known as the period of 'return migration'. Nevertheless, between 1948 and 1968 a net immigration of 118,558 Italians had been absorbed and in just 20 years the British Italian Community had not only quadrupled in size, but, as we shall see below, had changed completely in character.

Community size

Table 5 gives the British census figures for 1951, 1961 and 1971 indicating the rapid growth of the Community over the period. By 1971, return migration had taken hold and the size of the Community had declined from its all time high in the late 1960s, but stabilised at almost 110,000 Italian-born persons. (The 1931 figure for Italian-born was 24,008.) The size of the Community was, of course, very much greater than the 108,930 Italian-born in 1971. If we consider also second-generation, British-born, children as well as descendants of 'old' immigrants, the Community was in fact almost double this size. Indeed Italian sources for 1972 quote 213,500 Italians resident in Britain.

In Table 5 the broad pattern of geographical distribution is clearly seen: by 1971 the Italian presence in Scotland had dwindled to only 5 per cent

Table Five

Italian-born population in Britain, 1951–71

Year	Great Britain	England & Wales	Scotland
1951	38,427	33,159 (86%)	5,268 (14%)
1961	87,250	81,330 (93%)	5,920 (7%)
1971	108,930	103,510 (95%)	5,420 (5%)

Source: British census 1951–71.

135

of the national total. In 1931 over 20 per cent of all Italians were resident in Scotland but, as we shall learn below, Scotland received very little 'new' immigration in the post-war period. As a result the balance of the Community shifted overwhelmingly to England.

We are ready now to examine the new immigrants in detail and most importantly how they were able to arrive in Britain in such massed numbers. Then, at the end of the chapter, to complete the post-war migratory picture, we will consider briefly the phenomenon of return migration.

The new arrivals

As we first noted in Chapter 1 when looking at the early Italian immigrants of the nineteenth century, there is normally a relationship between the time of arrival, the occupation, and the area of origin in Italy of the different groups of migrants. Although the new arrivals of this post-Second World War period were not as diversified as the various groups of nineteenth-century immigrants, these same guidelines hold true and help in our understanding of the new immigrations. On this basis, and following the same structure as Chapter 1, the three new groups of Italian immigrants to arrive in Britain after the war, in chronological order of first arrival, were as follows:

(1) the prisoners of war;
(2) the caterers;
(3) the industrial workers.

The Italian prisoners of war who remained in Britain after the war were by definition the first group to 'arrive'. They were quickly followed, however, by a reactivation of the old migratory chains and an inflow of people from the old source villages to the well-established 'old' Italian Communities. The third group, the most important for our study, were the unskilled industrial workers who flooded into England, especially in the 1950s. These were the migrants who founded 'new' Italian Communities and who were responsible for the complete change in the structure and orientation of the Italian presence in Britain.

Let us consider each of the three categories of new arrivals in turn. The migration to the county town of Bedford is then discussed in more detail as a case study of the industrial workers, as Bedford has one of the largest and most interesting southern Italian Communities to have grown up in this period.

The prisoners of war

As we have seen in Chapter 4, Italian prisoners of war were held in this country during the Second World War. Camps near to Italian Communities, for example at High Barnet just north of London and Mugdock just outside Glasgow, received regular visits from the British Italians who would bring *salami*, Italian bread and *prosciutto* to the PoWs. Also those men who were working in agriculture gravitated naturally to making 'friends' with any locally based Italian families who would invite them for meals. Many of these men chose to remain in this country, often because they had met and fallen in love with local Italian girls and decided to marry. Initially they were able to do so by continuing in agriculture but they soon merged into the ranks of the 'old' Italian Communities, and normally became incorporated into traditional family businesses.

There was another set of men who had developed no connections with the Italian Communities but who also decided to stay. We saw in Chapter 4 that by the end of 1946 there were still 1,500 Italian PoWs present in Britain who had been given employment in the agricultural sector. These men, like the rest of the PoWs, had been intended for repatriation but were granted permission to remain as 'civilian workers' with annually renewable contracts which obliged them to stay in the service of the farm proprietors with whom they were already employed. Around 1,100 accepted such contracts, and many subsequently transferred to the four-year contracts in agriculture which became available to PoWs and European Voluntary Workers (most of whom were stateless refugees from Eastern Europe). The Italian PoWs saw these contracts as an opportunity, realising the difficulties that might await them in seeking work at home in Italy, especially the south.

After the end of the four years the men were free to move elsewhere in the country and to seek other employment. It was thus in the late 1940s that many provincial towns, particularly in mid and southern England, received their first Italian immigrants, who were seeking regular employment, for which work permits were available, in light and heavy industry.

It was not long after the war, however, that waves of new immigrants began to arrive. The first consisted of our familiar friends who arrived again at the request of, and with the aid of, relatives and *paesani* already established.

The caterers

The expansion of the service sector and especially the catering trade in this post-war era, with its explosion of cafés, coffee, milk and sandwich bars and later *spaghetti* houses and *trattorie* sparked off an influx of Italians to the traditional locations and the traditional catering-based occupations. Many of the 'old' chains of migration, which had lain dormant for a decade, or even two, were thus revitalised. New migrants from old sources – the *Val Taro*, the *Val Ceno*, the *Garfagnana* and the *Ciociaria* – began to swell the numbers of the pre-war Italian Communities, especially in London, but also to a lesser extent in Glasgow, Edinburgh and Manchester. (See Plate 11.) Their arrival was a continuation of precisely the type of migration which had prevailed before the war. People were again being 'called for' and 'brought over' by their relatives, and there was no shortage of willing hands looking for opportunities. *Padroni* of a familiar type, indeed often the same men, re-emerged and, as restaurant chains became common, they again played an important role in the transferral of relatively large numbers of young men and women from their villages.

But let us pause to take stock for a moment. It was mentioned in Chapter 4 that many, if not the vast majority, of Italian businesses had been badly affected by the Second World war. Some were taken over by the Custodian of Enemy Property and some closed down, simply unable to survive in the face of local racism, trading difficulties and sheer lack of profits.

Although many men were released from internment before the end of the war, unless their business activity was classified as being useful to the nation, they were required to take up other occupations, either in agriculture or industry. Large Italian manufacturing operations particularly in the ice-cream wafer industry fared well since they were able to switch their operations quickly to making biscuits for national food consumption. Antonelli in Manchester and many others followed this path on release from internment. Bakeries too, for example Renucci in Glasgow, were of course able to carry on providing their staple products. The majority of small shops, owned and run by individual proprietors, struggled enormously to maintain a foothold in their local economy. This applied for several years after the war since both rationing and local resentment did not end with the cessation of hostilities.

Rebuilding the position of strength and economic well-being of the 'golden era' was, for many, an uphill battle in the 1950s. For example,

Calisto Cavalli of London, who spent five years on the Isle of Man, latterly as camp leader of Onchan, devoted much more of his time to the Italian Community on his release than to developing his business. Many small-time entrepreneurs had been 'broken' by the experience of the war. They lost not only the will but the confidence to rebuild their little empires and live the good life in this country. They indeed felt as, and perhaps behaved as, 'enemy aliens' for the rest of their lives.

It was in the 1950s that many Italians of the 'old' Communities became naturalised British subjects since they were fearful of drawing further attention to themselves as aliens. Gone were the grandiose clubs in which they could strut proudly as Italians. In the business sphere many men, who dreamed of, and perhaps succeeded in, expanding in the 'golden era', now became content to lead a quiet life, scared of petty officialdom, and reduced to hiding behind their counters. Looking through trade directories for the pre- and post-war periods, one is immediately struck by the number of Italian businesses which simply disappeared during the war. Although new outlets did open up in profusion as the 1950s progressed, the immediate impression gained is of the number which simply did not survive the war years. In the 1920s and 1930s, the most common practice was to place, proudly, the name of the café or restaurant proprietor above the door. Also popular were catchy and short Italian place-names such as 'Roma', 'Barga' or 'Isola Bella'. After the war business names became distinctly Anglicised and 'Criterion Café', 'Premier Café' and the 'Cosy Corner' began to predominate.

However, not all businessmen were ruined or debilitated as a result of the war. Many younger men were able to make good progress again after the war – the most outstanding example being Charles (now Lord) Forte, who had also been interned on the Isle of Man. Many of the grand old Italian restaurants of Soho which had been established in the 1920s and 1930s reopened after the war when their owners claimed back their properties from the Custodian of Enemy Property. Leoni, for example, claimed back his Quo Vadis in Dean Street, Soho, which had been let to citizens of the British Commonwealth who had neglected the premises and damaged the fittings. He proceeded to restore the restaurant to its former state, and later expanded it until, in the 1950s, it became one of the most celebrated and popular restaurants in London patronised by the British upper classes – an achievement for a boy who had left his village *Cannero* (No) at 12 and worked his way up the catering ranks.

There were two main factors which led to the regeneration of the catering industry, most especially in London, in the 1950s. Firstly, there was a downward spread of affluence which encouraged more and more people to eat out on a regular basis. Young people became an independent group in their own right for the first time, with spending power of their own. In the catering industry it was this period which, more than any other, led to a massive expansion in the numbers of small owner-run businesses, particularly in London. The second factor, dependent on the first, was the inflow of migrants from Italy who brought new ideas with them.

The 1920 Aliens Order remained the controlling legislation for immigration, and entry to Britain was gained by presentation of a work permit issued by the Ministry of Labour. It was the employer who applied to the Ministry of Labour for a work permit which he then sent to the prospective employee. Once granted, the permit was for four years and the employee was not allowed to change jobs. He was, however, allowed to bring his family over if he could guarantee lodgings and maintenance. After four years he gained residence permission and was allowed to change jobs, which in catering usually meant the start of the climb to self-employment. It was not unknown in this period for the unscrupulous *padrone* to deduct a commission from employees' wages on the basis that he had been required to pay a fee to obtain the work permit. Work permits were not issued where local people could have filled the vacancy but, in the family businesses of the now Italian-dominated catering sector, local competition for jobs was rarely a problem. Sometimes, however, when a permit was not immediately forthcoming, an individual might, if still interested in coming to Britain, take up an agricultural or industrial contract, fulfil the four-year requirement attached, and then change to the originally intended, family-connected occupation. The result of the new injection of blood, however, was the range of new ideas and new developments that it brought from Italy with it.

From the old style café–restaurant in London serving basic food to working men and women, the first new development was the 'coffee bar'. Apart from the high-class Italian restaurants, these were the first attempt to sell 'Italianness', in the form of new concepts imported from Italy, to the population at large. The now ubiquitous *espresso* coffee machines were invented by Gaggia of *Milano* in 1946, a triumph for Italian design, style and innovation. It was not long before the new immigrants called to the catering trade realised the potential of coffee, and these machines which served *espresso* and *cappuccino* were introduced to London. The coffee is made very strong, by a process of infusion rather than percolation. *Espresso* is served black, in little cups. *Cappuccino*, which takes its name from the brown and cream habits of the Cappuccino friars, consists of a measure of *espresso* in a large cup of milk which has been heated by having steam passed through it, thus giving the beverage its distinctive 'head' of foam. The technology and ritual of preparing the two kinds of coffee are decidedly conspicuous allowing a high degree of 'Italian factor'. Each cup is made individually, with the aid of the large, heavily chromed machines which splutter and hiss. A little knock-drawer under the machine made of wood and lined with metal paper, conspicuously opened and closed for every cup, holds the discarded coffee. Skill and technique in making coffee is a matter of pride to the Italians. Coffee bars became very popular and fashionable with the young, especially in the 'swinging sixties'.

Increasingly it became a social motivation, rather than a thirst for coffee, that drew people to the coffee bars. Consequently, they were prepared to spend longer there and the proprietors began to offer simple Italian dishes which soon became very popular. These consisted of *spaghetti bolognese*, *ravioli*, *pizza*, *minestrone* and other regional, everyday specialities. On this basis, it was not long before Italian entrepreneurs introduced another new form of retail catering outlet, the *trattoria*.

The *trattoria* bears the same relationship to the *ristorante*, or formal restaurant, as the *pensione* does to the *albergo*, or hotel. Its market is not the businessman or the wealthy, and it does not cater for 'special occasions'. Similar to their counterparts in Italy, the *trattorie* do not offer elaborate menus or use expensive ingredients; they offer a high standard of cooking at modest prices. In the 1950s the little *trattoria*, run by an Italian family in an informal way, was something new in London. These establishments had checkered tablecloths, a *chianti* bottle on each table with a candle stuck in it, crudely painted scenes of Italy on the walls, more *chianti* bottles dangling from overhead trellises bestrewn with artificial vine leaves, and served simple pasta dishes and a limited range of chicken and veal main dishes, with mandolin strumming in the background. The *trattorie* became extremely popular with the newly affluent classes for whom a meal at Quo Vadis, Bianchi's or Quaglino's was financially out of the question.

Unlike the café–restaurants which, as we have seen, assumed English names and continued to sell food to the working classes, with no Italian factor involved, the *trattorie*, like the coffee bars, sold Italianness. Their names reflected this and again, 'Sorrento', 'Canasta', 'Napoli' and 'Il Grotto Blu', became part of the scene.

Trattorie, of the kind just described, had their heyday in the 1950s and early 1960s, although some like them still existed in the provinces until the early 1980s. Just as the *trattorie* tended to replace the coffee bars, in turn a new style of *trattoria* replaced the little place with the murals and the *chianti* bottles. A stylistic revolution led by three remarkable innovators, Mario Cassandro and Francesco Lagattola (the famous Mario & Franco partnership) in catering, and Enzo Apicella in design, opened another new phase. The new development, in fact, covered both ends of the retail catering market and became a competitor of the high-class Italian restaurants as well as replacing the chianti bottle *trattorie*. Flexibility in concept allowed a remarkable longevity which has currency even in the 1990s.

The innovatory design of Apicella is now copied everywhere but, in the 1960s, interior design for restaurants which emphasised space and light, when hitherto restaurants had generally been crowded, dark and plush, was a revolutionary concept. The three men opened *trattorie* where the walls, inside and out, were of white *stucco*, the windows were large so the interior was light and could be viewed from outside by passers-by. Mirrors were introduced to reflect light. The floors were covered with hand-made tiles rather than thick carpets. The chairs were mock-peasant, with rush seats, rather than velvet upholstered formal dining chairs. The colour schemes were warm yellows and oranges, and indoor plants were introduced. Spotlights were used to draw attention to the innovatory features. In sum, Apicella introduced to the London restaurant scene the elements which post-war Mediterranean leaders of taste had introduced into their homes and holiday villas in exclusive locations such as the islands of *Capri* and *Ischia*.

There was also a large increase in the demand for Italian waiters with this *trattoria* and restaurant expansion, a demand which out-stripped supply, and the hotels and clubs of the West End were forced to hire other European, Filipino and South American staff, who were looking for work in general and did not have the connection with catering, or ambition within it, of the Italians.

Another development in London was that of the sandwich bar which tended to evolve naturally from the café–restaurant, but moved up-market and up-town in the sense that it catered exclusively to white-collar workers. The old style café–restaurants are today found mainly in the inner London suburbs where they still trade with working men. As well as this traditional side of catering, Italians were to be found in all other aspects of the service and food industry. The growth of the Forte empire at an international level was the most outstanding business success of the Italian Community in the 1970s. In addition there was, of course, a plethora of businesses which served the needs of the Italian Community itself, notably the Italian provisions shops. These too are now also frequented by the local populations who tend to call them delicatessen.

The culmination of the *trattoria* and restaurant movement was the leading fashionable and chic restaurant of the 1970s – La Merdiana. Founded by Alvaro who had been a waiter with Mario & Franco, La Meridiana became a favourite place with the glitterati, a true 'faces' place, for almost a decade. Enzo Apicella again designed this restaurant and had an interest in it. By the mid-1980s, however, the leaders of taste had tired of these 'bright lights' and incredibly noisy restaurants and La Meridiana and many others like it closed their doors. At the top end of the catering industry there was a move back to the grander, more comfortable style of restaurants. In 1981 Pino Bassanini and his father, of Meridiana fame, had taken over L'Escargot in Soho. This and Quo Vadis (although no longer owned by the Leoni family) have made a remarkable 'comeback'.

The most prolific growth in catering has, however, not been led by Italians, and has been at the bottom end of the market with 'fast food'. Children now form part of the market which 'eats out', mainly in American outlets. By the late 1980s, McDonalds had dispersed north-wards from London and, with Pizza Hut, had reached Scotland.

There have also been innovative developments by Italians in traditional sectors. The chain of Costa Coffee bars at principal railway stations throughout the country, opened in the 1980s, are a superb example of up-to-date Italian-style retail catering.

In general terms in the 'old' Italian Communities of Glasgow and Edinburgh there has been a decline in the number of Italians in the traditional forms of catering but the standards of those still involved has risen enormously. In the second, third and fourth generations, there was large-scale movement to the professions. The small independent café owned by a single family, particularly in Scotland and Wales, is very much a phenomenon of the past, although many splendid examples exist in a fossilised state, exactly the way they did many decades ago.

While the flurry of post-war development was occurring in the catering industry, by the late 1940s negotiations were under way for an influx of a completely new type of Italian immigrant. Completely new geographical origins and new occupations, as well as new mechanisms of transferral, were to characterise the mass influx from the south of Italy.

143

The industrial workers

The reconstruction of Britain after the War required an abundance of labour resources not available in this country. Foreign labour had to be imported and Italians formed part of this much needed workforce. In the late 1940s agreements were struck between the British Ministry of Labour and the Italian government *Ministero del Lavoro* for the recruitment of Italian labour, particularly to fill shortages in the industrial sector. Large batches of workers, up to 2,000 at a time, were designated to specific industries. Agreements were reached for 2,000 Italian women in textiles and 2,800 Italian men in foundries.

Resistance from trades unions and public opinion led to the suspension of these official inter-governmental schemes in favour of a more *laissez-faire* system (for all nationalities of immigrant workers). From 1951 the recruitment schemes were devolved to individual employers and interested firms who operated under the Aliens Order of 1920 with requests to the Ministry of Labour for a given number of work permits. Negotiations between the firms and the Italian authorities in Britain then began for the required number of workers. This was the 'pull' force or 'trigger' for the mass immigration.

The large inflow of Italian migrants who arrived in England in the post-war period therefore did so by an entirely new migratory mechanism: that of 'impersonal recruitment schemes'. Unlike the old system of chain migration, the recruits of these new schemes had no prior personal contacts at their proposed destination and all arrangements were made 'impersonally' by total strangers. The new system took two forms: 'bulk recruitment' and 'group recruitment'. For clarity, we will look at each type separately in order to distinguish the two. By the mid 1950s, as we shall see, the 'bulk' schemes began to merge into the 'group' schemes. Later still, the group schemes merged into a new wave of chain migration which developed dependent on the newly recruited workers.

Recruitment brought workers to locations and industries where there was a labour shortage and demand outstripped the local supply of workers. As this was seldom the case in Scotland, where unemployment has generally been higher than the Scots would like, only a small number of migrants arrived by group recruitment, mostly to agriculture, in the 1950s and 1960s, and there were no bulk schemes at all to Scotland.

One of the main outcomes of this large-scale recruitment of Italians into British industry was that, unlike the old chain migration which produced connections between certain source villages and specific destinations, the new type of migrants originated from every single province in the south of Italy and from literally thousands of little *paesi*. Each bulk group of men, collected together at *Napoli* or *Roma* for transportation to specific industries in Britain, was very amorphous. They had in common their youth and health and unmarried status, but they represented a vast range of geographical and hence social origins. Although small family and village groups often emigrated together, in general terms the migrants were a heterogeneous cross-section of the Italian population. One similarity, however, was that they were mostly *contadini* about to become industrial workers in urban environments, thus undergoing a dramatic change in their way of life.

Due to the nature of the social structure in the south of Italy and the phenomenon of *campanilismo*, family and *paesani* groups stuck together and were suspicious of others during their train journeys through Italy and France to the first disembarkation point at London's Victoria station. For example, six *paesani* left *Busso* (Cb) together making the journey to *Napoli*. On assembling there with a large group of 200 or 300 other Italian men, all impersonally recruited through agencies working on behalf of industrial clients, they kept themselves to themselves, avoiding contact with others unless absolutely necessary. This kind of behaviour had important implications for the subsequent development of the 'new' Italian Colonies.

Bulk recruitment

The 'bulk recruitment schemes', as the name suggests, brought workers in large batches. It was this recruitment which, in the 1950s, led to the rapid growth of entirely new Italian Communities. The largest of these were in Bedford and Peterborough, and, in the 1960s, Nottingham.

Women
In 1949 the pioneers of this 'new' immigration from Italy to Britain were women. The first of the official inter-governmental bulk recruitment schemes permitted the entry of 2,000 Italian women between the ages of 18 and 40 who were destined primarily for the textile, rubber and ceramics industries of central and northern England. Many, however, were allocated service-sector contracts as domestic servants and hospital orderlies and maids. The vast majority were single and in their early twenties. By 1950, there were large contingents of Italian women working in Norwich, Coventry, Wolverhampton and in the textile towns of Lancashire,

Cheshire, Derbyshire and Yorkshire. As a result of this scheme, in the immediate post-war period, Italian female immigration considerably outnumbered male immigration. Although many of these women remained only on a temporary basis, completing between one and four years of their contracts, hundreds settled.

In the textile industry, the women were initially housed in purpose-built hostels. By today's standards their living and working conditions were stark. As in many other industries, which were also recruiting workers in this period, the hostels were organised by the 'National Service Hostels'. Two of the largest were at Glen Mill, Oldham, and Inskip, near Preston. The May Field Hostel at Keighley also became home for considerable numbers of these young girls. Cavernous, badly heated, basic dormitory-style huts became home to these *signorine* who had left Italy seeking work and perhaps a little adventure. The reality of their new lives was somewhat different.

The girls, who had come from all over Italy, experienced considerable homesickness and isolation at leaving their family-centred way of life behind. The majority were *contadine* and they found adaptation to the factory environment very hard. Disconcertingly alone, except for each other, in an alien environment, they received little social or welfare help from the Italian or British authorities. Because of the shortage of Italian men at that time, their search for spouses led to much inter-marriage, not with locals, by whom they were positively shunned, but with other ethnic groups. This was particularly true for the women who reached the cotton mills and lace factories of Bradford, Shipley, Halifax and Keighley: many still living there today are married to Polish, Yugoslavian, Ukrainian and Latvian European Voluntary Workers who had arrived in these localities at the same time and under similar work schemes. These 'mixed marriages' have not always been problem free.

In the early period of settlement one of the main difficulties for the women was in finding rented accommodation which would allow them to move out of the hostels. One example of two sisters who moved 12 times in three years will illustrate this point. From *Vobarno* in *Brescia*, Verginia and Sofia Bonetti (pseudonyms), aged 20 and 21, arrived in England on 16 March 1950. They were housed at the National Service Hostel, Inskip, near Preston, and employed by S. W. Highley Ltd, Halifax. By 24 May, the sisters had moved out of the hostel and were sharing a small bedsit at Trinity Place, Halifax. Astonishingly, but not atypically, only three months after arrival in England, on 5 June 1950, Verginia married a Latvian refugee and moved with him to Haughshaw Road. It is inconceivable that such a hasty marriage would have taken place had elder members of her family been present to advise. Sofia quickly followed suit and, by the autumn of 1950, she too had married – in her case a Yugoslavian. A sequence of residential moves in Halifax followed, on average four a year, until both couples transferred to Bedford in 1953 where their husbands found work in the brickyards. The sisters remain in Bedford today but, like many of their contemporaries in the north of England, rather regret their youthful rush to marry men from a different culture. They feel trapped since they are unable to return to Italy with their 'foreign' spouses and they suffer considerable isolation from their families in Italy. Like their 'sisters' in Yorkshire and Lancashire, the women regret their emigration and feel a little bitter about the way they were treated and abandoned for use as work machines without any guidance or help.

Foundry workers

The other inter-governmental scheme was that for foundry workers. An agreement for 2,800 workers had been struck although the numbers recruited fell short of this mark. These men were distributed to foundries throughout the country. A marked concentration developed in the 1950s around the South Wales steelworks and foundries where in some factories up to a quarter of the production workers were Italian. Later these schemes continued with workers being recruited directly. Independent firms, such as Stanton & Staveley in Ilkeston near Nottingham, Britannia Iron and Steel in Bedford (both now part of British Steel), and Coalite in Chesterfield all contracted hundreds of Italian workers.

The most significant of these employers was the Stanton & Staveley foundry at Ilkeston which first brought over workers in the early to mid 1950s. Also in the 1950s Beeston Boiler Company brought migrants to Nottingham. In the 1960s, however, Stanton & Staveley became highly active and imported over 1,300 Italian labourers in three batches of 450 men in 1964, 1965 and 1966. By the 1960s the period of hostel accommodation was over, Britain having come under a good deal of criticism from the United Nations for abusive practices, and all of these workers had to be found accommodation in the town. Local Italian Community leaders and priests worked tirelessly to insert new arrivals into Italian families in rented accommodation. The last group to arrive in 1966 proved to be the most problematic, many of the workers having been rejected by other countries, and there were a number of social and welfare problems within the Community. They could not settle, and not many remained in Nottingham.

147

Miners

One of the most interesting of the bulk recruitment schemes, initiated by the National Coal Board, was the importation of Italian men to work in coal mines throughout England and Wales. Over the period 1951 to 1955, when the contracts all but ceased owing to hostility from the National Union of Mineworkers, almost 2,000 were recruited. The majority arrived between 1951 and 1952 and, although these workers came from all over Italy and even included one or two people from 'old' sources, a large proportion were *Siciliani* who came from the province of *Agrigento*, and particularly from the villages of *Favara*, *Canicattì* and *Cianciana*.

Initially these men were housed in special hostels constructed near the pits, although most sought alternative rented accommodation in the nearby towns quite quickly. Many of these migrants returned to Italy or transferred to coal mines in Belgium before their four-year contracts were finished, unable to tolerate the combination of working and living conditions. Vindictiveness of locals and trade union members alike was often staggering by today's standards. However, a surprising number persevered and later moved into other jobs when their restricted period was over. From over 750 records kept on file at the Italian Consulate in Manchester on these miners, only a handful of men were still in contact with the Consulate in 1991. The vast majority had either moved to other areas or, as is mostly now the case, retired to Italy. A few men, especially in Wales, worked in coal mining for 30 years, until retirement in the mid 1980s.

Tin-plate workers

Meetings were held in July 1950 between the Ministry of Labour, the Italian Embassy and the Council for the Welsh Tin Industry to reach agreement on a scheme, which was to last seven years, for the employment of Italians. The Italians began to arrive in August, having been recruited in *Napoli*, and by the end of 1950 a total of 317 were in the employment of tin manufacturers in west Wales. All men were at first housed in the Industrial Hostel at Morriston, Swansea. Initially there was trouble with the Polish workers already present and quite a number of Italians returned to Italy. By the end of 1952 a total of 857 men had been imported from Italy and 85 had been transferred from the large number of Italians in Yorkshire and South Wales with whom the British coal miners had refused to work. The recruiting missions went to several National Coal Board hostels to interview men, but their transferral was not always a straightforward process since the Mineworkers Union was against other industries also employing foreign labour.

There was a short-lived recession in the tin-plate industry in 1953 and over 300 Italians were made redundant. Recruitment began again towards the end of 1953 and by the end of 1956 the number of Italians brought into the industry was 2,259. Of the 1,054 who remained in employment at that time, 355 had reached the higher grades: 5 were rollermen, 115 were doublers, 36 were furnacemen and 199 were first helpers.

In the early days, the availability of hostel accommodation determined the number of Italians to be recruited into the industry and the works at which they could be employed. For some time the number of vacancies at the Morriston Hostel controlled the rate of intake, but the enterprise of individual managements and the Italians themselves in finding private lodgings not only effected a marked improvement in this respect, but contributed substantially to the Italians settling down more happily. Indeed, as the years progressed, the length of stay at the hostel for the vast majority of newcomers declined and they easily secured accommodation nearer their places of employment. Without the advantage of hostel accommodation the works east of Port Talbot had not taken immediate advantage of the opportunity to recruit Italians, but after a cautious start they, too, found that securing private lodgings was less of a problem than they had anticipated and were able to recruit up to the level of their requirements.

From 1957 onwards, with the closure of the tin mills and the total demise of the industry, employment was found in various parts of England and Wales for all those Italians who wanted to remain in this country. For example, early in 1958, 14 men were transferred to the Bedfordshire brickyards. Around 60 men preferred to return to Italy.

Brickworkers
It was as a result of the demand for bricks for rebuilding British cities in the post-war period, and hence for brickmakers, that the largest number of bulk recruits arrived. First employed in 1951 by the Marston Brick Company, between mid 1951 and early 1952, over 700 arrived. Through subsequent application for more work permits, the various brick companies of the Bedfordshire clay belt were able to import more labour, leading to the single largest flow of migrants from Italy. (See Plate 12.) In total, in the 1950s and early 1960s around 15,000 Italians were recruited into the brick industry. Over half of these settled in Bedford, the rest in other brick-making towns like Peterborough, Bletchley, Loughborough and, to a lesser extent, Nottingham. Thus were founded the 'new' Italian Communities. We will return in more detail to the migration to Bedford later.

149

Group recruitment

Group recruitment, as the name suggests, brought workers from Italy 'in groups' throughout the 1950s and more particularly the 1960s. Again this labour was mainly for the industrial sectors of the economy, both heavy and light. It was not exclusively large firms who needed workers during the 1950s and 1960s; unskilled, but reliable and hardworking, men and women were also required by many smaller firms. Group recruitment was used to meet their needs, as well as the needs of many industries which had already recruited Italian workers in 'bulk' but sought 'top up' groups, particularly when the market for their particular activity was buoyant.

Although this 'group' migration did not lead to the dramatic and sudden emergence of 'new' Italian Communities, a slow and steady build-up throughout the period led to the development of further 'new' Italian Communities especially in Hertfordshire and Surrey. An Italian Community of mostly *Siciliani* from *Mussomeli* and *Acquaviva Platani* (Cl) grew up in the Lee Valley north of London based on the horticultural and market gardening industry. A very similar Community also from *Mussomeli* and *Acquaviva Platini* grew up in Surrey employed in a range of factory work.

Apart from these two examples of 'new' Communities, based initially on group recruitment, the main effect of this process was that, on the one hand, it cast its net far and wide in Italy for workers, and that, on the other hand, it deposited its catch across the whole of England and Wales in small groups. Three examples of Italians impersonally recruited in groups will illustrate the very wide-ranging and diversified nature of this phenomenon.

Firstly, in 1952 the Duke of Argyll made a request through the Italian Consulate in Glasgow to the *comune* of *Barga* (Lu) for a group of 50 lumberjacks. (As we saw in Chapter 3 one of the main Glasgow Italian connections was with the *Barga* area.) Men from the wooded mountain hamlets around *Barga* were well suited to this work and the group was recruited without undue difficulty. The men were housed in purpose-built cabins on the Duke's estates, near his feudal town of Inveraray. Conditions were rather harsh, and the men were very isolated in this remote area, although most had relatives and friends in Glasgow. Indeed, most moved to Glasgow and entered the ranks of the traditional catering occupations when their four-year contracts finished.

Secondly, small groups of men, 10 or 20 at a time, were recruited from the *Bergamo*, *Trento* and *Brescia* areas to work in the expansion of the national electricity grid. Because of their Alpine origins, these men possessed a knowledge of electricity was based on hydro-electric power. Their contracts were for transmission lines and pylon constructors. One group of 17 men was housed in a small hostel on the Isle of Ely in 1964. Another smaller group was employed by Balfour Beatty near Nottingham for similar work. Injury levels were high amongst these men and few settled.

Thirdly, some of the newly arrived, but immediately redundant, mineworkers of South Wales, were re-recruited by the tin mines of Cornwall, especially Killerton mine. The men were housed in a hostel and worked in shifts. Although never subsequently recruited in large numbers, a little Community of around 40 Italian families grew up at St Just, near Land's End. The men were recruited in just one or two groups and most came from *Copertino* (Le) and *Francavilla* (Br). In 1955 15 men were recruited together from these two villages, but it is a moot point as to whether this was 'group recruitment' or plain old-fashioned 'chain migration'.

The development of chain migration

Just as bulk recruitment gave way to group recruitment, the group movement in turn led to a development of chain migration amongst the 'new' settlers. This occurred in the following way. For example, a firm in Derby would secure the necessary work permits to employ Italians from the Ministry of Labour. Then, through the Italian Consulate, it would make an application for a group of, say 20, workers from Italy. The Consulate would process the request back to Italy, and the Italian Ministry of Labour would notify the local employment exchanges. This typically resulted in random take-up from across the south of Italy, perhaps with a slight over-representation of one or two villages if several male members of a family, or even several *paesani*, decided to leave together. On moving to Derby in the 1950s to take up their four-year contracts, if the work conditions proved acceptable, these men would inevitably send for their wives and children – the first link in the chain. Assuming the firm was pleased with their work, as the firm itself expanded, it might well decide to take on further Italian workmen. Before going to the Consulate to ask for more impersonally recruited workers, it was logical to ask the Italian men already in its employ if they had any relatives or friends (*paesani*) who might be interested in the available jobs. The men would appreciate being consulted and would be likely to get on well with any new arrivals – also in everyone's interest. A new group of 30 would then arrive from the same sources as the first group, clearly recruited as a group, but not entirely impersonally. The blurring effect between the two mechanisms can therefore be appreciated.

Of course, in addition to making up groups of workers at employers' requests, once settled and established, the new migrants also began, in that time honoured way, to 'call for' their families and *paesani*. For them, however, this was, initially at least, a more complex and more difficult process than it was for the members of the 'old' catering-based Communities. Jobs had to be located in the market place and in competition with all other workers. This was not straightforward and inevitably, since a high level of English language was needed to conduct the necessary negotiations, intermediaries were required. Enter a new type of *padrone*. These new-style *padroni* were therefore similar to the 'labour boss' *padroni* of the American immigration of the nineteenth century, as described in Chapter 1, in that they procured workers for another employer, and did not themselves have jobs to offer.

Individuals from the ranks of the 'new' migrants, perhaps better educated, more ambitious or just more orientated towards 'helping' their compatriots would take on the role of arranging matters in a satisfactory way. This involved locating job vacancies and co-ordinating between employers, the Italian and English authorities and of course the Italians themselves who were under pressure from their relatives still at home in Italy to be 'brought over'. Naturally an 'arrangement fee' for clients and another from employers was usually part of the process which involved considerable amounts of bureaucratic work on the part of the *padrone*. Many men in the new and growing Italian Communities took on this role, became 'important' and often profited accordingly. Gradually, however, as the 'new' immigrants themselves began to settle in, learn the language and how to operate in urban Britain, many people were able to arrange matters by themselves on behalf of their aspirant relatives, thus 'cutting out the middle man'. A further method employed by prospective migrants was to write to the Italian missionary priests who were present in most of the 'new' Italian Communities from the mid 1950s. These men were recognised as 'leaders' and organisers by both the Italians and employers alike and their welfare role in this early period often far outweighed their spiritual role.

More and more, however, chain migration without 'intermediaries' became normal and by the 1960s this was again the dominant means by which Italians were transferring from Italy to this country. We can clearly see this development in the following case study for the Bedford migration.

The Bedford brickworkers: a case study

During the 1950s, Britain witnessed the development of the first true 'Little Italy', since the growth of the Clerkenwell Colony in the mid nineteenth century, in the English county town of Bedford. The number of Italians grew dramatically in the early and mid 1950s and a Community formed which has no parallel in the country today, in terms of its size, range of institutions or way of life.

Bedford had no previous connection with Italians and, apart from a small number of prisoners of war who worked on the farms and then remained to take up the first contracts at the brickyards, the first batch of 200 men to arrive in the summer of 1951 heralded a new connection. The availability of brickyard labouring contracts provided the 'trigger' which led to a mass migration from the south of Italy to Bedford: Britain's 'brick capital'. (See Plate 12.) An article in *New Society* aptly described the 'pull' in the following way:

> *Happily faced with the insatiable demands of the post-war building boom, and unhappily faced with a desperate shortage of English labourers willing, in a time of affluence, to do the tough dirty work of the brickfields, Bedford's major brick-works, launched their 'bulk recruitment scheme' to lure underpaid, underemployed (often totally unemployed) Campanians and Calabrians from their homes 1,000 miles north from Italy's toe with promises and realities golden to them: steady, well paid, secure jobs. (Barr 1964, p.7)*

The southern Italians who arrived in Bedford in this way during the 1950s were followed by a steady, more chain-dependent, flow throughout the late 1950s and 1960s. The pattern of migration to Bedford followed the national trend of Italian immigration to England, reaching its peak between 1955 and 1956. Figures 1, 2 and 3 give an indication of arrival in Bedford from 1952 to 1979.[1] From the 1955 peak, the number of arrivals fell continuously with a particularly sharp drop in the number of male migrants between 1955 and 1958. A much reduced, but steady, trickle of migrants was, however, maintained in the early 1960s and it was only in the late 1960s and early 1970s that the migration ceased almost completely.

The initial phase of migration consisted almost exclusively of men (90 per cent) through the bulk recruitment mechanism of transferral.

153

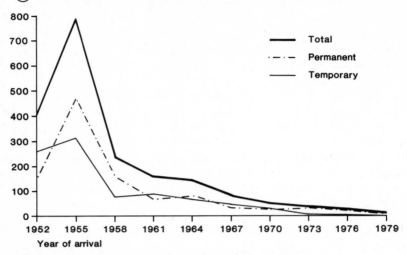

① PERMANENT AND TEMPORARY MIGRATION TO BEDFORD

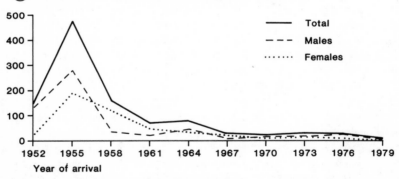

② MIGRATION TO BEDFORD:PERMANENT MIGRANTS

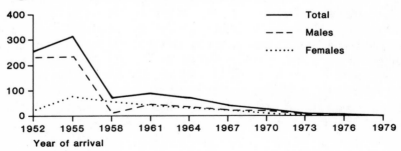

③ MIGRATION TO BEDFORD:TEMPORARY MIGRANTS

In 1952 all (except one) of the 411 male migrants who entered Bedford did so with contracts arranged by the recruiting agencies of the brick companies, who had set up offices in *Napoli*. However, of this initial intake, only 153 men settled in Bedford – over 60 per cent of the first arrivals returned to Italy within one to four years. The early 'Community' was thus characterised by a high level of transitoriness; new workers coming and going and also, as the workers moved out of the brickyard hostels and sought rented accommodation in the town, by a high level of internal mobility as people moved often to try to improve their accommodation.

The majority of the men who came on the brickyard contracts were for the first time in steady full-time employment with a regular and fixed income. They lived a most frugal and thrifty existence. All first-generation migrants in Bedford today claim, when summarising their years abroad, with particular reference to the earlier phase, that they have made nothing but *'sacrifici'*. Early first-generation male migrants, single and perhaps especially married, made the most sacrifices. The factors involved in adaptation, even on a day-to-day basis, working at the brickyards and living in the hostels at Ampthill, Roundhouse Brogborough, Church Farm, Coronation and Kempston Hardwick were colossal for these southern Italian land peasants, who for the most part knew nothing other than life in the village in which they and their forefathers had been born. Chadwick-Jones (1965), in a study of a steel factory in Swansea, where a quarter of the process workers were Italian, mentioned a similar difficulty in adapting to the rigorous regime of industrial work teams. To be in this completely alien environment carrying out heavy industrial labour in adverse climatic conditions, without even the food that they were accustomed to, was for many an intolerable level of *sacrifici*. In this context the high level of return to Italy before the completion of the four-year contract is easily understood.

A further element of *sacrifici* related to the obligation of the migrant to provide financial support for his wife, children, and often parents at home in Italy. The women of the family were able to carry on working the land but this was often no more than subsistence agriculture and anything other than barely subsistence survival was thus funded from abroad, including such items as clothing, medicine and doctors' bills and, above all, money and goods necessary for participation in the all-pervasive system of *raccomandazione*.

The women at home in Italy too made *sacrifici* since, apart from the struggle to survive, they were bereft, often for many years, of their menfolk. Even girls who had married by proxy, after their fiancés had

155

emigrated, sometimes had to wait up to four years before being able to join their 'husbands' in Bedford. Married women could only join their husbands in Bedford by leaving one, perhaps two, of their children behind with their *nonni*. The trauma and the drama of emigration in the 1950s from the south of Italy to England was probably no less intense than that experienced by their northern compatriots who established the 'old' Communities across the country more than half a century before.

By 1955, although 92 per cent of male migrants arrived on brickwork contracts, some had been personally encouraged and sponsored by men already working at the brickyards. The vast majority of arrivals were still housed initially at the hostels but they were able more quickly to move to the town since many now had relatives and *paesani* already there. In this short period of time, just three or four years, the Bedford Italian Community had become established and the temporary aspect of the all-male worker population had declined. From the total of 783 male migrants who arrived in 1955, 468 (60 per cent) stayed permanently.

Also, the flow of women began to increase. In fact, amongst permanent migrants of 1955, women formed 40 per cent (189) of the total. By 1958, three and a half times as many women as men arrived in the town, representing a backlog of spouse arrival. Indeed, 85 per cent of the women who arrived were married and came to the town to join their husbands. Many of these wives arrived with children and the Community was then not only firmly established, but set for further internal growth. By 1958 the sex structure had become balanced and there were almost equal numbers of men and women. These were mostly married couples since single female migration to Bedford was not a major feature of the migration. During the phase of bulk recruitment, married males who intended to settle sent for their wives within three to four years.

Single men nearly all married during the course of the 1950s. In the absence of a large pool of *signorine* they achieved this by a number of methods. Large numbers married by proxy, tying the knot with girls known before emigration. Others returned to their villages to choose wives and married there. A few found spouses amongst the ranks of the many contracted domestic servants in London and in the hospitals of the Home Counties. Very few of the first-generation male immigrants who were single on arrival in Bedford married local English girls. Most men were anxious not only to find an Italian spouse, but to marry a *paesana*.

The period of bulk recruitment schemes to the brickyards came to an end in 1956. Throughout the period of bulk importation, in addition to the opposition of the trades unions, there had been disapproval from

Bedford Town Council who were concerned about over-crowding and bad housing conditions in the town centre. Although Italian labour at the brickyards built up until 1959, the years of bulk recruitment were limited to the five-year period 1951–6 and in 1959 the borough prohibited the brickyards from further bulk importation of labour. Recruitment of men on an individual basis was, however, still permitted. In 1960 the brick companies were anxious to restart the bulk recruitment schemes because of a mini-boom in the industry, but the Town Council voted unanimously against it. This restrictive policy of the Town Council, coupled with the declining demand for bricks in the mid to late 1960s, led to a change in the character of the migration to Bedford.

While the early migrants had relied almost exclusively on impersonal recruitment and mass sponsorship for their arrival, already by 1955 other types of more personal recruitment had begun to influence the composition of the workforce who arrived. The year 1961, in fact, formed a watershed in the type of migration to Bedford: after this date the only mechanism was classical chain migration with migrants relying on relatives and contacts already in the town. These people came to employment other than at the brickyards, and were received by their friends and relatives into a thriving Italian Community. It was possible in the fairly stable economic climate of the early 1960s for those migrants already established with local knowledge to find the necessary employment opportunities for kin and *paesani* who wanted to come to Bedford. In the mid 1960s the chain was at its most effective, since the jobs were not only found by a *paesano*, but sometimes the employer himself was a *paesano*. If work could not immediately be found in the town, relatives sometimes took up contracts elsewhere in England, where available, and later transferred to Bedford when a job could be found.

Men and women alike, even those who settled in Bedford, all harboured the hope of returning to Italy. It had never been their intention to stay for more than a few years, work hard, save and return home. A number of factors compounded to make this an impossible dream. Firstly, was the availability of plentiful work in the town for women as well as men. On first arrival, married women were precluded from taking up employment but successfully had this restriction removed from their residence permit. The single largest employer of Italian women in Bedford throughout the 1950s, 1960s and 1970s was the Meltis factory (later taken over by Tobler Suchard) and still known affectionately within the Community as '*O Meltis*'.

It is difficult to gain an accurate picture of size of the Italian Community in Bedford during the 1950s, not least because of the high level of movement into and out of the town by Italians and the overall transitory nature of the Community within Bedford. Different writers have quoted different figures. Sibley (1962) has stated that in 1954 there were 1,075 Italians in Bedford. Brown (1970) has said that by the end of 1955 there were 1,414 adults and 285 children under twelve years old living in multiple-occupation accommodation and the west-central area of the town was virtually a 'colony of Italians'. King and King (1977) give a figure of 2,405 Italian adults living in multiple-occupation in 1956. By the end of 1958 there were 3,131 Italians in multiple-occupation according to Brown (1970). By 1961 the Bedford southern Italian Community had been firmly established; the British census enumerated 3,323 people of Italian birth in Bedford.

From 1970 onwards, as reference to Figures 1, 2 and 3 shows, the migratory flow to Bedford contained no more than a handful of people, the majority of whom where either old relatives or young single people from a very changed Italy, who were coming to 'visit' relatives or to learn English and had very different intentions about their stay. In fact, throughout the 1970s, the flow of return migrants to Italy from Bedford exceeded the flow of new immigration. The 1980s saw a stable Community which had reached maturity and, with the passing away of many of the first generation of migrants, the adult second generation is now in predominance. This we will return to in Chapter 7.

The 'old' and the 'new' Communities

With such a massive influx of immigrants in the 1950s and 1960s, especially to a new sector of the economy, it is not surprising that the distribution and structure of the Italian Community was fundamentally altered. The most significant changes were the demise of the Scottish Italian Community as a national presence; the creation of 'new' Communities; the takeover of 'old' Italian Communities by 'new' migrants and the development of 'mixed' Italian Communities, where the notion of Communities within Communities can be applied.

The two types of migrants described in the preceding sections, the caterers and the industrial workers, arrived simultaneously over the period 1945 to 1969 and often to similar destinations. Obviously, where 'new' Communities formed, only the industrial workers were present.

The 'new' Communities are composed of immigrants almost exclusively from the south of Italy and, as we will see in Chapter 7, this led to a

158

Plate One *Surveying instrument made by Casartelli, Manchester, c1830*
Credit: Manchester Museum of Science and Industry

Plate Two *Organ-grinder with monkey, Bradford, c1890*
Credit: Bradford Heritage Unit

Plate Three *Monument to the* Figurinai, *Coreglia Antelminelli, Lucca*
Credit: T. Colpi

Plate Four *Monument to the* Arrotini, *Pinzolo, Trento*
Credit: A. Collini

Plate Five Gelataio Garfagnino – *an ice-cream man from the* Garfagnana, *Scotland* c*1905 Credit: P. Cresci*

Plate Six *Dorà Provisions Shop, Rindley Road, Pimlico, London,* c*1905 Credit: M. Dorà*

Plate Seven *The Premier Café, Glasgow, 1920s*
Credit: People's Palace Museum

Plate Eight *Sister Agnes with the girls class, St Peter's School,*
Clerkenwell, 1930s Credit: Finsbury Public Library

Plate Nine *Chapel dedicated to the men lost on the* Arandora Star, *Bardi Credit: T. Colpi*

Plate Ten *The last of the Glasgow Italian men are released from the Isle of Man Credit: People's Palace Museum*

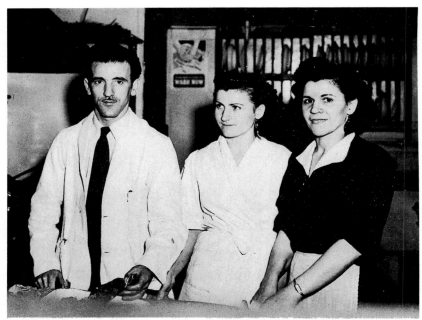

Plate Eleven *Gino Guarnieri with his sisters at his café-restaurant, London, 1956 Credit: G. Guarnieri*

Plate Twelve *Bedfordshire Brickyards, 1950s Credit:* La Voce

Plate Thirteen *The Italian Youth Club in Bedford is opened, 1966*
Credit: La Voce

Plate Fourteen *Three gradations of* bomboniere *Credit: A. Bavaro*

Plate Fifteen *The committee of the* Associazione Parmigiani Valtaro, *London, 1991 Credit: T. Colpi*

Plate Sixteen *Valvona & Crolla, Edinburgh, 1991 Credit: P. Contini*

completely new way of life and the creation of entirely new social patterns from the ones prevalent in the 'old' Communities by the 1950s and 1960s. The new migrants came from a much greater variety of geographical sources than those who had been recruited through chain migration. One of the major differences between the 'old' and the 'new' Italian Communities is still that the 'old', chain-dependent, Communities are composed of predominant origin and social groups whereas the 'new' Communities are often wide and varied in their origins. The fact that chain migration was later operational alongside the impersonal recruitment schemes has, as we will see in Chapter 6, sometimes led to the pre-eminence of certain village groupings within the 'new' Communities – but not always.

Where the 'old' Italian Communities received a new injection of migrants through chain migration, who were thus absorbed into the old, normally catering, occupations the Communities simply grew, prospered and changed little in their socio-economic patterns. This was the case in Scotland. The new migrants were of an 'old' type and did not therefore rock the status quo of the Community.

More often, however, particularly in central and northern England, the industrial workers reached destinations where 'old' Italian Communities already existed. These became 'mixed' Communities. In such 'mixed' Communities where the 'old' met with the 'new' industrial workers, especially when this second group were in large numbers, the result was two distinct subgroups within the so-called Italian 'Community' – Communities within Communities. There was very little social interaction between the two, especially where the 'old' felt overwhelmed. This was the situation particularly in east and west Midlands, the north of England and South Wales where the cumulative impact of steady industrial recruitment throughout the 1950s and 1960s was greatest and the 'new' immigrants soon outnumbered the 'old' Italians. Only now is social interaction between the two groups occurring.

In the 'mixed' Communities, 'old' source predominances have often been lost. One of the most obvious examples is the Manchester Italian Community which, up until the Second World War, originated predominantly in the province of *Frosinone*. This character has now been, if not lost, certainly masked, by the large influx of 'new' migrants from the 'deep south'. Today, the structure of the Manchester Italian Community owes its origin to no particular group.

By the 1960s many of the industrial workers and more particularly their children, the second generation, had begun to realise the economic advantages of trying to enter the traditional catering sphere of activity of the 'old' Italians. However, the development of traditional style occupations amongst the 'new' immigrants has been slow and piecemeal. This is not surprising. As we have seen in Chapters 1 and 2, the evolution into the catering trade took perhaps 50 years and then took another 50 to develop to a level of national penetration by the time of the outbreak of the Second World War. *Contadini* of the 1950s, who then became industrial workers, have had an uphill struggle to break into the realms of the 'old' Italian Community for two reasons.

Firstly, the 'knowledge' and background for catering and service industries was lacking, and secondly the 'old' Communities were not about to welcome with open arms these new-found competitors. The so-called 'Ice-cream Wars' of the late 1970s and early 1980s amply illustrate this point. Antony Rea of the Manchester Italian Community explained that when the 'Neapolitans' and 'Sicilians' arrived and tried to invade the trade, the 'old' families all had their own territories.[2] The demarcation battles had been fought decades before and there was therefore no direct competition in the trade. The arrival of the 'young pretenders' led to a tremendous upheaval and a not inconsiderable amount of industrial violence. Inevitably, new territories, agreements and alliances were forged over a period of several years of hostility, and the industry has settled to a period of relative calm again.

In the 'new' Communities, entry into the traditional sectors of activity has been more successful since there was little competition from 'old' Italian families. For example, in Bedford, first-generation members, former brickworkers, established in the 1950s food provisions stores and bakeries serving the Italian Community. One of these firms still trades and has become a wholesaler, now importing not just for Italian shops in Bedford but for the whole country. Second-generation business activity, unlike that of the first generation which serves only the ethnic Community, has tended to branch out, still most often trading on ethnicity, but serving the local population rather than the Italians. *Pizzerie*, Italian shoe shops and hairdressing have been popular ventures.

The Italian factor in British society thus changed dramatically and rapidly in the years following the War. The 'new' immigrants and their descendants now form at least 70 per cent of the total Community. In today's terminology, they form an 'ethnic group'. Very different from the 'old' Italian presence, the 'new' immigrants are now integrated but little assimilated into British society. Consequently, their distinctive approach to life is largely maintained and its study is both fascinating and important. Since the 'new' Communities and the new type of migrants represent a significant proportion of the Italians in Britain today, a large part of the remainder of our story is dedicated to describing their contribution. Naturally, the 'old' immigrants and their descendants, whilst perhaps no longer numerically dominant, are in many localities still highly visible and dynamic. They will not be ignored in the ensuing pages.

Return migration

The 1970s saw a net outflow of Italians from Britain; that is to say, more left the country than entered. The majority, in fact, returned home to Italy. The aim of the immigrants of the 1950s and 1960s, regardless of the mechanisms of migration which brought them here, had, for most, been to work hard for some years and return to Italy with their savings. Having left in poverty and having, in the case particularly of the southern migrants, left poverty behind them, to be able to return home in a condition of economic respectability, and in many cases economic success, clearly gave a well-deserved sense of accomplishment.

Throughout Italy, both north and south, and from the old *emigrazione* as well as the more recent period, the building of villas by migrants has always been a feature of village life. The house, or *casa*, is very important to Italians since it is the physical centre of that all-important unit – the family. Villas, often used only on a seasonal basis by people who remain abroad, are a testimony to the success of a family and they have become a status symbol within the village of origin. Emigrants are anxious for their *paesani* at home to see just how well they are doing abroad. Unfinished villas can often be seen dotted around the outskirts of villages since there is a tendency, especially in the south, to build a little at a time and not everyone who starts building succeeds in completing the project. Refurbishment of old houses in village centres where property has been in a family for years or generations is also common. Premises which look modest on the outside have interiors full of the brightest, cleanest and newest technology in kitchens, bathrooms and home entertainment.

In the 1970s not all of the migrants who returned to Italy on a permanent basis went back to live in their native villages. In the more rural areas there was little more opportunity for employment than there had been in the 1950s and 1960s. During the phase of mass emigration in the 1950s and early 1960s the majority of emigrants had sought and found opportunities abroad. By the mid 1960s, however, there had been substantial internal migration within Italy itself. Increasing industrialisation and prosperity in the north induced migrants from the south to relocate within their own country rather than move abroad. Fiat and related industries in *Torino* became a prodigious employer of *Meridionali*. Other opportunities in light industries sprung up all around the country.

One interesting result of this development in Italian migration, as far as the British Italian Community was concerned, was that migrants who were thinking of returning home in the late 1960s often had *paesani* established in little niches in particular locations in Italy. They could, therefore, negotiate their return in the time-tested way – through chain migration, albeit in a new form – to the locations where new opportunities now lay.

For example, many migrants who came from *Buonvicino* (Cs) to Bedford and Bletchley in the 1950s and early 1960s were able in the 1970s to return to *Roma*. Younger siblings and family members had migrated to *Roma* in the late 1960s. They had established themselves in market gardening in the *Fiumicino* area, near the airport. After 1973 and the economic recession in Britain when unskilled jobs became more difficult to hold onto and when, by the late 1970s, there were the beginnings of mass redundancies at the brickyards, people from *Buonvicino* in Bedford and Bletchley were able to secure jobs and accommodation in the new enclave of family and friends at *Fiumicino*. The main catalyst was the Magurno family who, collectively, were able to build an apartment block to house the returnees.

However, in a not insignificant number of cases, individuals did return to their villages. These consisted of two main types. The first were almost pioneers of sorts; innovators at least. In *Campania, Molise, Calabria* and *Sicilia*, villages which had connections with England received return migrants who had emigrated as *contadini* and came back to join the class of the local petty bourgeoisie. They opened small bars and cafés, hairdressing shops, motor mechanic garages, bakeries, butcher shops, etc. with skills and capital acquired in England. It is not uncommon either to see English Italian ice-cream vans from the 1970s still in operation in Italy or kept as 'souvenirs'. The second type were those who returned to live in their villages, but became 'commuters'. They found jobs in nearby towns and provincial capitals, and took up the way of life now followed by their *paesani*. By the 1970s, agriculture had been abandoned and people commuted to nearby towns for work.

The few Italian immigrants who did reach Britain in the 1970s were of a completely new genre. Young, with very different intentions about their stay and from a very much changed Italy, they came as students and temporary workers. Most viewed their stay as short term and experiential. The prime motivation was often to learn English, and with Britain's accession to the European Economic Community (now EC) in 1973 there was no longer any restriction on work permits and temporary residence. It is interesting that, while the free market in labour across Europe has been one of the best-known facts about British membership, there is little conscious recognition of the way this has facilitated migration from Italy, the one member country with such a large number of nationals already here.

After 1973, therefore, employment could easily be found, particularly on a black economy basis since no work visa was required, especially in the catering industry of London. This was the favourite destination although Italian Communities, large and small, 'old' and 'new', received these 'visitor migrants' of the 1970s. Inevitably not all returned to Italy; many stayed and merged into the ranks of the Community.

Chapter Six

Composition of the Community

Introduction

In Chapter 5 the various types of migrants who entered Britain in the 1950s and 1960s were introduced. Building on this framework, in addition to the framework given in Chapters 1–3 for the 'old' Communities, we are now in a position to survey the composition of the present-day Italian Community. This chapter takes up the discussion at the broadest level and introduces the total Community: its size and geographical distribution in Britain, and its origin in Italy. The most reliable and up-to-date information currently available is used to present as clear, accurate and informative a picture as possible. Given the disparity of sources, this is not always easy!

A secondary theme of the chapter, and the remaining chapters of the book, is how the Italians lead their lives and the way their Communities are organised. The importance of origins in Italy has been stressed elsewhere as relevant to the 'old' Communities. Here, the notion of *campanilismo* as a dynamic force within the present-day Italian Communities is further developed. Origin-based networks are especially important in the 'new' Communities, but also retain a forceful applicability in the 'old' Communities.

Size and distribution of the total Community

As indicated in the Introduction to the book, and as we have seen at various points in the history of the Community, it is difficult to estimate accurately the size of the Italian population living in Britain. Nowadays, this difficulty is even more pronounced because of the length of Italian presence and the several generations present.

The British census continues to enumerate only those people born in Italy. The 1981 census gave 97,848 people born in Italy as resident in this country. Not all of these people are necessarily Italian citizens, since the census no longer makes a distinction between birthplace and nationality. That is to say, we cannot subtract from the 97,848 any British and other nationals who were born in Italy. In any event it is clear that there has been a decline in the number of Italian-born since 1971 when, as we saw in Chapter 5, the figure stood at 108,930. (The 1991 census figures were not available at the time of writing.)

Italian sources, it will be remembered, also take account of people with Italian parentage. The Italian Ministry of Foreign Affairs in *Roma* estimates that there are now 196,000 people either Italian-born or of Italian origin living in Britain. This total is based on estimates submitted by each of the Italian Consulates to the Ministry. These in turn are calculated by the Consulates as multiples of the number of family files and individual records in their archives. Now that the computerisation of the Consulates has been completed in both Edinburgh and Manchester, and is under way in London, data collection should not only become a more accurate process but one which should also in the future allow more detailed statistics to be published.

In Chapter 5 we saw the Italian sources for 1972 quoted 213,500 Italians resident in Britain. By 1980, this figure had risen to 220,000 but in 1983 it fell to 196,000. This decline was due primarily to an overestimate of the effects of return migration in the 1970s on the size of the British Italian Community in the 1980s. We know from the 1981 British census that the Italian-born population stood at 97,848. If we estimate that the British-born second and subsequent generations of Italians are at least equal in number to the Italian-born, it is unlikely that the Italian Community would be less than 200,000 and, as indicated in the Introduction, and justified shortly, the preferred estimate of *The Italian Factor* is 250,000.

Let us now turn our attention to the broad geographical distribution of the Italians, using both British and Italian statistics. Table 6 gives the country breakdown for the British census. The geographical distribution of Italians in Britain has altered little since accommodation of the 'mass' immigration in the 1950s and 1960s. The Scottish and Welsh Italian Communities remain small in comparison with the English contingent. The greatest concentration of Italians is in the South East which had 62 per cent of the national total. Greater London alone had 30,752 in 1981 – 31 per cent of all Italian-born. In London, the major concentrations were in the central and northern boroughs. The largest number lived in Enfield

Table Six

Italian-born population in Britain, 1981

Country	Total	Percentage of total
England	89,085	91
Scotland	4,789	5
Wales	3,974	4
Great Britain	97,848	100

Source: British census 1981.

in north London (2,595) and both Haringey and Barnet also had large numbers (1,945 and 2,273 respectively). Islington (2,159) and Westminster (1,922), in the centre of London, still contained concentrations of Italians, mostly in the traditional areas of residence. The boroughs of Islington and Camden (1,709), especially, still held much of the 'old' Community who had moved northwards from the Clerkenwell Colony in the 1920s and 1930s, and after bomb damage during the War. The Italians were, however, by this date spread throughout the entire metropolis area.

Elsewhere in the country, other areas and counties with large concentrations of Italian-born were Bedfordshire with 4,642; Hertfordshire with 4,374; South and West Yorkshire together with 3,462; Surrey with 3,261; Greater Manchester with 3,170 and West Midlands with 3,097. All other counties had less than 3,000 Italian-born population. In Scotland only the Glasgow area rose above 2,000 and in Wales no county had more than 750 Italian Italians present. Not only did Bedfordshire hold the largest number of Italians outside London, in terms of proportional densities of Italians relative to the local population, it stood out as having several times the national ratio of Italian to British population.

Having briefly reviewed the Italian-born position, let us turn now to the assessment of total Community size. For this, and all subsequent information, we are reliant principally on the Italian statistics. Table 7 gives the division by consular area of the latest official estimate of 196,000 Italians in Britain in 1984. The Edinburgh figure is for the whole of Scotland, the Bedford total for the three counties of Bedfordshire, Northamptonshire and Cambridgeshire, the London consular jurisdiction includes mid and South Wales and covers as far north as Wolverhampton, while Manchester includes North Wales and the whole of the rest of England from the West Midlands to the Scottish border.[1]

Table Seven

Distribution of Italians in Britain

Consular area	Number	Percentage of total
London	100,000	51
Bedford	30,000	15
Manchester	43,000	22
Edinburgh	23,000	12
Total	196,000	100

Source: *Aspetti e Problemi dell'Emigrazione Italiana all'Estero*, MAE 1984.

It is interesting to compare these figures with the British census data on Italian-born Italians analysed by consular jurisdiction. We find that the Manchester figure of 43,000 Italians is about 2.5 times the census figure of 18,700 Italian-born and the Bedford figure of 30,000 Italians is about 3.3 times the census figure of 9,000 Italian-born. Both these figures are realistic given the inclusion of second and third-generation Italians.[2] The Edinburgh figure at 23,000 is nearly five times the British census figure of 4,800 for Scotland, but this is not entirely unreasonable when we remember the depth of the history of the Scottish Italian Community and the many generations now present. However, the London figure of 100,000 is only about 1.5 times the census figure of 65,300 Italian-born. This is surprisingly low and merits closer examination.

A more realistic figure for the London consular area, taking account of second and subsequent generations, should be about 2.5 times the Italian-born at 160,000, given the ratios for the three other parts of the country. Furthermore, the presence of at least 100,000 records on individuals within the Consulate and, given none of these are over ten years old, as the Consulate lost all its records in a fire in 1980, indicates that 100,000 has to be the smallest possible figure for the jurisdiction area rather than a likely estimate. Therefore the assumption made in presenting a figure of 250,000 for the British Italian Community as a whole is that approximately 150,000 are in the London jurisdiction, not 100,000 as claimed in the official estimates.

The aggregate figures of Table 7 give us no indication of more specific towns and areas of concentration. For this we must look to the records held by each of the Consulates.[3] These are therefore minimum numbers of active Italians and total approximately 150,000. All subsequent analyses of presence within Britain is based on this core number of confirmed, identified Italians, rather than on the broader estimate (250,000) of the likely total Community. For clarity, the various Community size estimates are summarised in Table 8.

Table Eight

Size of the Italian Community

Consular area	Author's estimate	Official estimate	Consular records	Italian-born
London	154,000	100,000	100,000	65,300
Bedford	30,000	30,000	17,700	9,000
Manchester	43,000	43,000	24,000	18,700
Edinburgh	23,000	23,000	8,300	4,800
Total	250,000	196,000	150,000	97,800

Source: MAE, Italian Consulates, British census.

Although there are several large Italian Communities in Britain today, over half of all Italians live in small Communities where they represent a tiny percentage of the total urban population. Map Three locates Communities with 500 and more identified Italians. As a general rule, people of the 'old' phase of immigration are now dispersed widely within their towns and cities, normally in the residential suburbs, whereas 'new' immigrants are often still concentrated in central urban areas, where they settled in the 1950s and 1960s.

Scotland

All records held at the Italian Consulate General in Edinburgh are now completely and efficiently computerised. In May 1991 a total of 8,298 people had been enumerated, both Italian-born and of Italian origin, representing therefore more than one-third of the Consulate's own estimate of the number of Italians resident in Scotland.[4] From a survey of these identified Italians, we find that over 40 per cent (3,492) live in the Glasgow area including Hamilton and Motherwell with a further 9 per cent in the Kilmarnock and coastal areas, south and south-west of Glasgow. Thus around 50 per cent of the Community live on the west side

MAP THREE: ITALIAN COMMUNITIES IN GREAT BRITAIN

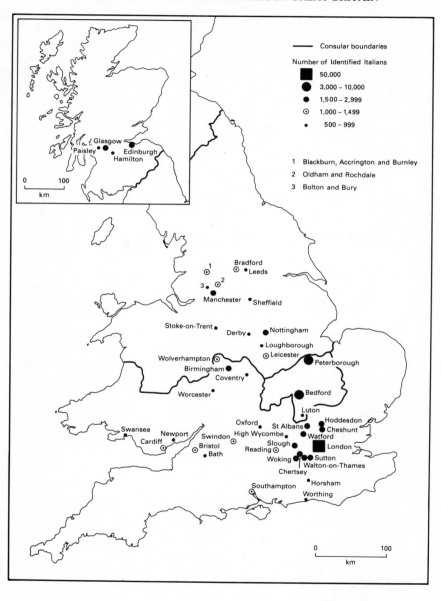

Consular boundaries

Number of Identified Italians

■	50,000
●	3,000 – 10,000
●	1,500 – 2,999
⊙	1,000 – 1,499
•	500 – 999

1 Blackburn, Accrington and Burnley
2 Oldham and Rochdale
3 Bolton and Bury

Glasgow
Paisley   Edinburgh
Hamilton

0   100
km

Bradford
Leeds
1
3   2
Manchester   Sheffield
Stoke-on-Trent   Derby   Nottingham
Loughborough
Wolverhampton   Leicester
Birmingham   Peterborough
Coventry
Worcester   Bedford
Luton
Oxford   St Albans   Hoddesdon
Swansea   High Wycombe   Cheshunt
Cardiff   Newport   Swindon   Watford
Bristol   Slough   London
Bath   Reading   Sutton
Woking   Walton-on-Thames
Chertsey
Horsham
Southampton   Worthing

0   100
km

of the country. The Edinburgh Community (2,200) is around two-thirds the size of that in Glasgow and is more geographically concentrated in the city of Edinburgh itself. There are not the same number of off-shoot Communities around Edinburgh as there are on the west side of the country in places like Paisley and the Clyde ports and resorts. A small Community of 300 Italians is located in Falkirk, however, which is closer to Edinburgh than Glasgow.

In the north, Aberdeen registers an Italian Community of around 300 people and Dundee one of 400. Perth and Stirling host smaller contingents of around 150 Italians. The rest of the Italian population is dotted around Scotland with 100 or so Italians resident in small towns of the Highlands, a similar number in the Dumfries area and again in the Borders. A more substantial group of 345 people is located in Fife. In total 17 per cent of the Italian Community in Scotland live in small towns as opposed to cities or the central lowlands conurbation.

The north of England

As in Edinburgh, by 1991, all personal files held at the Manchester Consulate, almost 24,000, had been efficiently computerised, representing, therefore, just over half of the Consulate's own figure for the potential Italian population in their jurisdiction area.

The counties of Lancashire (4,304), West Yorkshire (3,438), Nottinghamshire (2,271), Cheshire (1,938), and Leicestershire (1,906), have the largest concentrations of identified or known Italians. Within Lancashire the largest Community of Italians, 1,300 people, is centred on the Blackburn, Burnley, Accrington conurbation, with the Rochdale, Oldham concentration second in size with over 1,000 Italians. Bolton and Bury have a significant contingent too at around 700, and the Preston area has almost 500. The second-largest county contingent of Italians is West Yorkshire (3,438), which contains several sizeable Italian Communities. The most notable of these is Bradford where over 1,000 Italians live. Secondly, the Community in Leeds reaches around 900 people and the smaller towns of Keighley, Huddersfield and Halifax all have medium-sized Italian Communities of around 300 to 500 people. Sheffield in South Yorkshire has well over 500 Italian residents.

Nottinghamshire (2,271) is host to one main Italian Community in Nottingham itself which is in fact the largest Italian Community of the East Midlands area, with 2,000 members. Many Italians live in the Lenton and Bakersfield areas. Lenton had been the initial area of settlement in the 1950s but had been demolished by compulsory purchase in the late 1960s. Many Italians lost their homes although compensation became available through appeals, and new houses were built. New Lenton, as it is now known, remains an area of Italian concentration.

Greater Manchester still retains over 1,500 Italians, although Cheshire (1,938) holds many Manchester Italians who have moved south to the city's better residential suburbs which are in the county of Cheshire. The Leicestershire county total of 1,906 is made up of two Italian Communities, the larger in Leicester itself of just over 1,000 and the smaller in Loughborough with 650 Italians. The next largest county total is Staffordshire (1,182) which is dominated by one Italian Community, that in Stoke on Trent, which numbers around 900 people. The Italians of Derbyshire (1,327) are mostly in Derby which hosts around 40 per cent of the county total with 500 Italians, but other places too such as Chester-field, Matlock and Buxton all have Italian presences.

As will be remembered from Chapter 5, much of the bulk recruitment, and more especially the impersonal group recruitment, of the 1950s and 1960s arrived to central and northern England. In many cases the Communities of Italians which grew up in this period were superimposed on smaller 'old' Communities who were overwhelmed by the mass migration in this post-war era, but many 'new' (or almost new) Communities also grew up, the most exceptional examples of which are Nottingham and to a lesser extent Loughborough. The small Italian Communities from the previous era in places of the north such as Carlisle and Newcastle, and also Bradford and Sheffield, and Leicester in the East Midlands, are all now predominantly 'new' Communities.

The south of England

One of the reasons the estimated figures of the Consulate General in London appear flawed is that this Consulate, despite an early lead in the mid 1980s, has been slowest to computerise. In 1991 a total of 40,740 records had been computerised out of an estimated 100,000 records accumulated in the Consulate since 1980. However, there is no reason to believe that this 40 per cent is unrepresentative of the total and consequently figures are presented in this section as a proportion of the 100,000 Italians known to the Consulate.

Before the post-war immigrations there were few localities in the south of England, outside London, where there were sizeable concentrations of Italians. It was the south, perhaps more than anywhere, especially the

Home Counties, which experienced the rapid growth of 'new' Italian Communities, especially in the 1960s. Although there are more Italians in Bedford and Peterborough than in other towns, the combined concentration of Italians in locations such as St Albans, Watford, Hoddesdon, Cheshunt and Waltham Abbey in south Hertfordshire is almost as great; 7,500 (7.5 per cent) of the area's 100,000 Italians live in Hertfordshire. There are also significant 'new' Communities in Chertsey, Woking, Walton on Thames and Sutton, accounting for over 9 per cent of the area total (9,250 people). These Communities grew up firstly from various impersonal recruitment schemes, such as railway and factory workers in Surrey and market gardeners in Hertfordshire. All, however, blossomed as a result of chain migration throughout the 1960s.

The other Home Counties of Kent, Berkshire and Essex similarly have substantial Italian presences. Kent has an Italian population of around 3,400, fairly spread across the county. Berkshire has over 4,000, two-thirds of whom are concentrated in Slough and one-third in the Reading area.

The 'old' London Italian Community was supplemented by 'new' migrants throughout the 1950s, 1960s and to a lesser extent the 1970s. In addition, as we shall see in the concluding chapter of the book, it was the only Community in the country to receive any further Italian immigration in the 1980s. The size of the Italian presence in the capital is the most difficult to estimate but accounts for just over 50 per cent of records held – an estimated Community size of at least 50,750 people.

The other sizeable concentration of Italians in the London consular area are: Southampton (1,250); Birmingham (2,300); Wolverhampton (1,400); Coventry (900); Swindon (1,250); Bristol (1,500) and Cardiff (1,250).

Wales

The Italian consular jurisdictions of London and Manchester bisect Wales. Combining the available figures of identified Italians, the Welsh Italian Community is 5,000 – only slightly greater than the British census total of Italian-born at 3,974. A good number of the 'old' Welsh Italian Community has long since merged into the Welsh community and become British, thus no longer featuring in the consular records. Most are now British passport holders. More than two-thirds of the Welsh Italian Community is congregated in the south of Wales, in the counties of South and West Glamorgan, Gwent and south Dyfed. As we saw in Chapter 3, the 'old' Welsh Italian Community had been geographically dispersed and not particularly concentrated in any of the towns and cities. The 'new' migration, which brought the industrial workers, led to the formation of Communities centred on Cardiff (1,250), Swansea and Newport, both with around 750 Italians, and to a lesser extent Milford Haven where there were no particular concentrations in the pre-war era. Today, apart from the Welsh valleys of Mid Glamorgan, where remnants of the 'old' Community still survive and indeed retain their former pre-eminence, the Welsh Italian Community, like the rest of England, is composed of an industrial workforce.

Bedford

In 1983 a complete survey of Italian passports issued at the Vice-Consulate revealed a total of 4,622 current passport holders with a further 852 people whose passports were out of date, but who were probably still resident in the town, giving a total of 5,474.[5] Of these, between 20 and 30 per cent were second-generation members, either born in Italy and brought to Bedford with their migrating parents or born in Bedford. This figure does not, however, include children under 16 who do not possess a passport. On this basis, the Community in Bedford is estimated at 10,000, forming the largest proportionate concentration of Italians in Britain today. (The local population of Bedford is 95,000). Luton in south Bedfordshire also has a smaller Community of around 700 Italians. The Peterborough Community is just over half the size of the Italian presence in Bedford, at around 6,000 people, and also forms a sizeable presence.

In both towns, although the Italians have become increasingly dispersed, residential enclaves are still apparent. In Bedford this is especially true of the Queen's Park and Castle Road areas and in Peterborough around Gladstone Street, in Stanground and in the Fletton area south of the River Nene.

Origins of the total Community

It is now time to turn to the geographical origins in Italy of the current British Italian population. For this, we must rely on Italian sources. As can be seen, these indicate 110,500 Italian-born living in Britain, about 13 per cent higher than the 97,800 figure enumerated by the British census. Table 9 and Map 4 give the regional origins for the Community as a whole. They indicate that the overall composition of the Italian Community in Britain today is heavily weighted towards southern Italy, with the *Siciliano* contingent being particularly strong. In fact, 80 per cent of the

COMPOSITION OF THE COMMUNITY

Table Nine

Regional origin of British Italian Community

Region	Total	Percentage of total Italian-born
Sicilia	38,400	35
Campania	22,000	20
Calabria	10,000	9
Emilia-Romagna	8,500	7
Puglia	5,500	5
Toscana	4,000	4
Abruzzo	4,000	4
Basilicata	4,000	4
Lazio	4,000	4
Veneto	3,500	3
Molise	3,000	2
Sardegna	1,000	1
All other regions	2,600	2
Italian-born total	110,500	100
Born in Britain or elsewhere abroad	85,500	
	196,000	

Source: *Aspetti e Problemi dell'Emigrazione Italiana all'Estero*, MAE 1984.

total originated in southern Italy; 35 per cent in *Sicilia*. This demonstrates clearly how the character of the Italian Community changed as a result of the 'new' immigration. This may seem surprising, particularly to readers resident in localities where the 'old' Italian Communities, with origins in northern and central Italy, still retain dominance or at least a high profile and whose residents may retain the impression that their Italian Communities are typical and similar to those elsewhere in the country. The British Italian Community today is primarily a southern Italian Community.

This composition does not, however, have an even or entirely random distribution across Britain. As a result of chain migration there are often concentrations and pockets of different regional groups. For example, the 8,500 *Emiliani*, who are the fourth-largest regional group, are mainly from the two provinces of *Parma* and *Piacenza*, live in London and work in the catering niche. The *Siciliani* are represented in most English counties but

175

MAP FOUR: REGIONAL ORIGIN OF BRITISH ITALIAN COMMUNITY

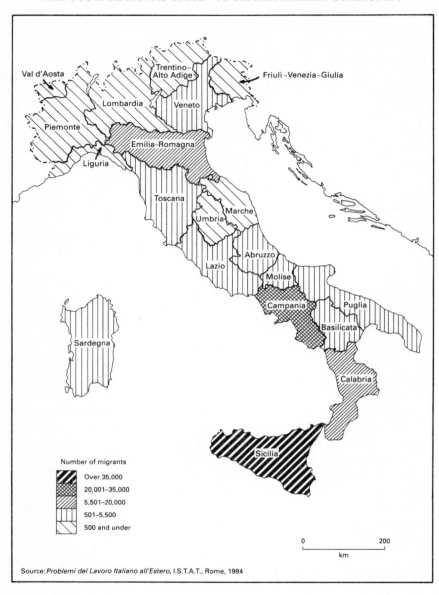

Val d'Aosta

Piemonte

Lombardia

Trentino-Alto Adige

Veneto

Friuli-Venezia-Giulia

Liguria

Emilia-Romagna

Toscana

Umbria

Marche

Lazio

Abruzzo

Molise

Campania

Puglia

Basilicata

Sardegna

Calabria

Sicilia

Number of migrants

Over 35,000
20,001–35,000
5,501–20,000
501–5,500
500 and under

0   200
km

Source: *Problemi del Lavoro Italiano all'Estero*, I.S.T.A.T., Rome, 1984

these Communities are characterised by certain provincial and even village concentrations in different towns. It is the uneven distribution of the various origin groups which gives rise to Italian Communities different in nature and structure.

The fact that the vast majority of the Italians in Britain come from the south of Italy means that there are a number of predominant themes which are relevant in our study. One of the most important of these is the notion of *campanilismo*, based on the geographical origins in Italy. Not new to the discussion, *campanilismo* was, and still is, relevant to the older, pre-war Italian Communities. Before considering the specific origins of the different Italian Communities, let us begin with a discussion of *campanilismo*. On initial meeting, the first question Italians always ask each other is 'Where are you from?' The answer tells them everything they need to know.

Origins and *campanilismo*

First mentioned in Chapter 2, *campanilismo* remains a potent force today both in Italy and the migrant communities abroad.

In Italy

The extraordinary regionalism of Italy was a particular characteristic of the *Mezzogiorno* in the 1950s and 1960s when the 'new' wave of immigrants left to come to Britain. As a social process, *campanilismo* came to denote a certain narrow-minded fanaticism which sees no further than the interests of its own Community. The notion encompasses all forms of parochialism and exaggerated local pride and thus has the effect of a permanent bonding between people who share the same village of birth. People from neighbouring villages are not to be trusted since the interests of these outsiders too often conflict with those of the villagers themselves. Even today in many small Italian towns the term *forestiero* – foreigner – is used to refer to a person who may come from no further than the next village.

Abroad

As we already know from Chapters 2 and 3, the notion of *campanilismo* is also applicable within migrant communities abroad where it constitutes an important social force. A minimum number of 50 *paesani* must be present before a real sense of *campanilismo* can become viable. Wherever a group of *paesani* is present abroad, they transfer with them their village-mindedness and *campanilismo* therefore becomes operational. For the Italians in the United States, the sociologist Suttles (1968) pointed out that *campanilismo* in all probability becomes more important abroad because in Italy a person's *paesani* would include practically everyone with whom he or she came into daily contact. Thus, *campanilismo* would be useless as a basis for selecting those one could trust or first approach for help. Abroad, however, a fellow *paesano* is certainly more trusted than a complete stranger. Because of *campanilismo*, after the family, *paesani* choose to interact firstly with their *paesani*.

However, in a large Italian Community, because of the proximity of many other Italians both from villages of similar geographical and cultural origin and also from other areas altogether, village loyalties are gradually broken down, firstly into provincial *campanilismo* and secondly into regional *campanilismo*. We have already seen in Chapter 3 how the *Lucchesi* of Glasgow naturally formed into such a provincial social set in the 1930s with the *Barghigiani* at their centre. After the *paese* and then the province, migrants of the same region of origin have more in common with each other than with migrants from different regions in Italy. The emergence of provincialism and regionalism depends on the overall composition of the particular Italian Community. The operation of *campanilismo*, its strength, influence and development depends on the local set of circumstances prevalent within each migrant setting. The most relevant factor is the origin composition of the entire Community.

With the development of regionalism in an Italian Community old loyalties are in an advanced state of breakdown. The way is then clear for an entirely new social development – a growing sense of identification with fellow migrants in the town of migration itself and the growth of a true 'Community'. There is often, however, a final stumbling block to this. If a Community is fundamentally split between a northern and a southern Italian population, it is unlikely, even after generations, that the two groups will fully merge into a corporate whole. Although this perpetuates factionalism and schism, it is often these very divisions which have kept the 'old' Italian Communities alive. It has been the very existence of two polarised sub-groups and the tensions between them which has often given a Community its definition.

We are now fully briefed to begin our origins analysis and to examine how these origins affect and influence the structure of the different Communities.

Scotland

As we have seen in Chapter 5, Scotland was least affected by 'new' immigration. The composition of the Communities has therefore remained similar to that of the 1920s and 1930s. The same two regional groups retain dominance, and fundamental differences in the pattern of origin are still apparent between the Glasgow and Edinburgh Italian populations.

The Glasgow Italian population remains split into two main regional origin groups; those from *Toscana* and those from *Lazio* which, when taken together, account for 54 per cent of the Italians.[6] In addition to the *Toscani* and the *Laziali*, three other smaller regional groupings can be identified: the *Molisani* who form 10 per cent of the total, the *Liguri* 9 per cent and the *Campani* 8 per cent. The relative contributions of the *Molisani*, who are almost exclusively from the province of *Isernia* (Is), and the *Liguri* who are *Spezzini* (Sp) have also remained very similar to the 1933 contingents as seen in Chapter 3. The presence of *Campani* who were not part of the 1933 make-up does, however, indicate that there was some 'new' immigration to Glasgow in the post-war period.

At the core of the Glasgow Community we still find the two main village groups from *Barga* (Lu) and *Picinisco* (Fr) who each have around 200 *paesani* present in the city, each accounting for 9 per cent of the overall total. The sense of identity of these two groups remains strong and many of the main families have become well-known businessmen. The Nardini family from *Barga* and the Crolla family from *Picinisco* are well-known examples.

The other main individual village sources of the Glasgow Italians are *Filignano* (Is) which has around 120 people in Glasgow, *Villa Latina* (Fr) and *Venafro* (Is) which each have representations of between 60 and 70 people. Although from different regions, people who originate in the provinces of *Frosinone* and *Isernia* are culturally similar, and over the decades in Glasgow have come to identify strongly with each other. Although Italians from *Lazio* and *Molise*, together with the 'new' *Campani* are in numerical dominance in Glasgow, it is the *Toscani* who maintain more influence and social dominance. They tend to retain their origin-based superiority, building, particularly in a business context, upon their strong links with a prosperous *Toscana* of the 1990s.

In summary, the Glasgow Italian Community has experienced the final stage development of *campanilismo*. Provincially and regionally based groups existed and still exist, but it is the north–south schism which is fundamental to attitudes and behaviour within the Community. The

179

continued distinction between the two main groups of Italians was reflected in the constitution of the *Casa d'Italia* which, until its closure in 1989, specified that the Board of Directors should be a balanced representation of both groupings.

In contrast to Glasgow, the Italians in Edinburgh continue, as they did in the 1930s, to form much more of an integrated Community. The main reason for this is that the less diverse origins have produced greater unity. Almost half, 46 per cent, originate in *Lazio*. *Picinisco* (Fr) people retain their dominance of the Community, numbering 270 persons, 20 per cent of the overall total, and form a solid social and economic base to the Community. The province of *Frosinone* in fact supplies all three of the major village groups in Edinburgh. Collectively the three sources of *Picinisco*, *Cassino* and *Atina*, account for 28 per cent of the total Edinburgh Italian population. The *Lazio* people have, however, lost some dominance to the 'new' migrants from *Campania*, who now account for 17 per cent of the total. A further 25 per cent of the total originate from central or southern regions, thus giving the Community its strong central–southern character.

The origins composition of the other smaller outlying Italian Communities in Scotland have also tended to retain their original structures, with no significant changes. With little 'new' immigration, the descendants of the original migrants, mostly now third and fourth generation, continue to characterise a particular source area. For example, the Italians of Aberdeen, third-generation people often in their 60s, talk mostly of *Val Dena* in the *comune* of *Borgo Taro* (Pr) when they talk of Italy.

The north of England

By choosing a sample of towns through north and central England, consistent with the overall pattern for England, we find that the majority host southern Italian Communities. Table 10 illustrates this fact.

Almost all these Italian Communities are strongly southern Italian in character, most outstandingly Burnley, at 91 per cent. Oldham, Bolton, Liverpool and Carlisle are good examples of towns which at one time hosted 'old' Communities whose origins were mainly in central and northern Italy, and which in the post war period were taken over by the 'new' immigrants from the 'deep' south. Although, some of these towns have a particularistic Italian Community, often outstanding in its degree of distinctiveness, this is not normally the case. More often the migrants come from a wide range of provinces and regions of the south of Italy with

Table Ten

Southern Italian Communities

Town	Identified Italians	Percentage Southern Italians
Burnley	222	91
Middlesbrough	233	88
Scunthorpe	400	88
Stoke on Trent	787	87
Nottingham	1,947	84
Oldham	339	81
Bolton	301	75
Liverpool	409	69
Carlisle	102	64
Huddersfield	372	50
Newcastle on Tyne	312	41

Source: *Anagrafe Consolare*, Manchester 1991.

no particular group – and certainly no particular village groups – gaining any significant dominance within the Community. Most tend to follow the national pattern with *Siciliani* and *Campani* being in predominance. There is however, one remarkable exception, the town of Nottingham.

The two largest regional groups which make up the Italian Community in Nottingham are from *Campania* (26 per cent) and *Basilicata* (25 per cent), with almost equal number of Italians from the two regions: 248 and 241 respectively. While the *Campani* are a mixture of the provinces which comprise that region, the people of *Basilicata* come almost exclusively from the province of *Matera*. There are a number of highly distinctive aspects to this group.

Firstly, they form the only large group of migrants from the region of *Basilicata* in Britain today. This fact alone makes them distinctive, but is highlighted by further features. Not only is the regional group almost totally dominated by people from the province of *Matera*, 80 per cent in fact come from just one village – *Accettura*. There are well over 200 *paesani* from *Accettura* living in Nottingham today. These *paesani* consequently have a very strong sense of identity and internal group cohesion as a result not only of their absolute numbers but also of the fact that they form 20 per cent of the overall Italian Community in Nottingham. Their presence is thus dominant in the city, giving a strong and individualistic character to this particular Italian Community. In

181

proportionate terms, amongst the 'new' Communities no other group of *paesani* in Britain make up 20 per cent of their Community; certainly not in an Italian Community as large as the one in Nottingham.

The third-largest regional group of migrants living in Nottingham comes from *Puglia* (125), making up 13 per cent of the whole Community. One province and one village again dominate the regional group. The *Foggiani* form 94 per cent of the *Puglia* regional total and then the people of *San Paolo Civitate* make up 59 per cent of the provincial total. This group are sufficiently numerous to operate on the basis of *campanilismo* and form a second smaller core group to the Community. All other regional and provincial groups in Nottingham are small. In the face of large group domination by the *Foggiani* provincial group on the one hand and the *Accettura paesani* on the other, they live rather on the fringes of the 'Community' being excluded from the larger *paesani*-based social, political and often economic networks.

The other towns given in Table 10 broadly follow the national pattern in that the two most dominant regional origin groups are *Sicilia* and *Campania*, although variations in the other regional contingents do inevitably occur. Three towns are strongly *Siciliano* in character. In Burnley, 71 per cent of the Community are *Siciliani*, with over half of these coming from the province of *Agrigento*, especially the village of *Racalmuto*. Stoke on Trent and Liverpool also have large *Siciliano* groups. Stoke on Trent in particular, although to a much lesser extent than Burnley, is a *Siciliano* Community with 60 per cent of the total coming from this region. Liverpool's *Siciliano* contingent is smaller, but still significant at 43 per cent. Like Burnley, both *Siciliano* Communities are mainly from *Agrigento*.

The other towns mentioned in Table 10 host small to medium-sized Italian Communities. Assimilation has often been hastened due partly to smaller numbers but also to the fact that no strong origin groups make up the Communities. The different origins of the migrants have worked to keep tham apart and no natural 'Community' sense has developed. Both *Sicilia* and *Campania* retain an equivalent predominance each making up 25 per cent of the Communities in Bolton and Oldham. In Scunthorpe there are few *Siciliani* but *Campani* account for 43 per cent of the total. The town of Middlesbrough is again dominated by *Campani* but here, most interestingly, and not found in any of the other towns, is a group of migrants, almost as numerous as the *Campani*, from *Sardegna*, and specifically from *Arbus* in the province of *Cagliari*.

Although Huddersfield and Newcastle upon Tyne do not have a

distinctly southern Italian character, both towns have sizeable groups of migrants from the region of *Lazio*, which in both cases make up 25 per cent of the total Italian Community. Closer to the south in a geographical and hence cultural sense, the addition of *Lazio* to the southern figures would move the composition of these towns too into the realms of the southern Italian Communities.

Wales

Only in the Welsh valleys of Mid Glamorgan do the 'old' migrants from *Parma* and particularly *Bardi* retain a dominance in the local Italian Community. It is from Porth and Merthyr Tydfil in Rhondda that the association of the *Amici Val Ceno Galles* is organised. The Italian presence in the other Welsh counties is now strongly southern in character. Dyfed, West Glamorgan and South Glamorgan, whose Italian Communities are centred on Milford Haven, Llanelli, Swansea and Cardiff, are now more than 80 per cent southern Italian. The county of Gwent retains more aspects of the 'old' migration with contingents from *Emilia* but is almost 50 per cent southern in nature, centred on the town of Newport. A further quarter of Italians in Gwent come from *Lazio* – Gwent being the only Welsh county to have formed this particular connection.

Particular province and village contingents within these small Italian Communities are never large. Sometimes, however, the provincial or regional make-up of a Community is distinctive. The northern county of Clwyd accommodates over 600 Italians, the majority in Wrexham, Mold and Buckley. Again these are 80 per cent southern Italian Communities. In the Community of Wrexham (175), the *Calabresi* comprise 26 per cent but are closely followed in numbers by the *Siciliani*. The only sizeable village contingent to have emerged in a specific location in Wales are people from *Montecorvino Rovella* (Sa) in Milford Haven of whom there are some 100 people.

London and the south

Southern Italians, particularly *Campani*, now also predominate in London. Indeed, the *Campani* outnumber the *Emiliani*, and the *Siciliani* also have a significant presence. Table 9 indicated a total of 8,500 *Emiliani* in Britain, the majority of whom are in London. The *Campani* in London now number around 10,000 and the *Siciliani* around 5,500.

Although the *Emiliani* retain their dominance in the catering industry, many of the southern Italians have also been able to infiltrate into this sector, so great is the range of opportunities at all levels of the trade. There are now several well-known *Siciliano* and *Sardo* restaurants in London who trade on their regional ethnicity, for example, 'La Famiglia' and 'I Sardi'. The majority of the *Siciliano* contingent are in unskilled jobs in other sectors. A significant number live in the Enfield area of north London and are connected with the market gardening and horticultural industries. Similarly, the *Campani* and other southern groups work as employees in light industry or the service sector. Many of these 'new' immigrants live to the south of the River Thames in the London boroughs of Southwark and Lambeth.

The two major counties of Italian residence in the south-east, Hertford-shire and Surrey, are home to large southern Italian Communities in which the *Siciliani* followed by the *Campani* predominate. Of 9,250 Italians in Surrey, 4,000 (43 per cent) are *Siciliani*. In Hertfordshire 40 per cent (3,000) are *Siciliani*. We saw in the previous section that several towns of the north of England hold *Siciliani* contingents and that these come mainly from *Agrigento*. In Hertfordshire and Surrey, by contrast, the major source of the *Siciliani* is the province of *Caltanissetta* with the villages of *Mussomeli* and *Acquaviva Platani* being dominant. In the small towns of Cheshunt and Waltham Abbey they form extremely tight-knit and close little Communities. Indeed in the 1980s when there was a series of *Siciliano* murders in the Lee Valley, dubbed by the *Harlow Gazette* as the 'Glass House Killings' since most took place in the green-houses where the Italians worked, so strong was the sense of 'Community' loyalty within the group that the local police were completely unable to penetrate the networks, gain information and thus solve the murders. The next largest *Siciliano* Community is in Bristol where almost half of the 1,500 strong Community come from *Agrigento*.

Like northern and central England, the pattern of *Sicilia* and *Campania* dominance prevails over most of the counties. In most Communities there is a balance between the two major groups and a slight variation in representation from the other southern regions. Generally, however, the *Campani* are from a wider range of sources and lack the coherence of the *Siciliani* who come from either *Caltanisetta* or *Agrigento* and from a much smaller range of specific villages.

Bedford

Southern Italy was the source area for over 90 per cent of the Italians resident in Bedford.[7] The region of *Campania* was the greatest source, supplying over 40 per cent – 1,500 Italians – of the Community. The three regions of *Molise*, *Puglia* and *Sicilia*, which fall into second, third and fourth positions, are also important source regions with over 400 migrants each in Bedford. *Lazio* is the only region of either central or northern Italy to have sent more than 100 migrants to Bedford. All the regions of northern Italy and the remaining regions of central Italy each contributed less than 49 migrants.

The migrants from the provinces of *Avellino* (668), *Campobasso* (618) and *Agrigento* (401), form the three main provincial cores of the Community. Each of these provincial totals are in turn composed of a number of *paesani* groupings. Only two villages – *Sant' Angelo Muxaro* (Ag) and *Busso* (Cb) – have more than 200 *paesani* present in Bedford. Even when the second-generation British-born Italians are also taken into consideration, no other villages rise above 200. There are, however, a further four villages which have around 100 migrants in the town. These are given in Table 11.

Taken collectively, these six main groups of villagers account for only 27 per cent of all Italians in Bedford. In such a large Community, built up mainly by impersonal recruitment migration, no particular village or even group of villages attained significant numerical superiority. The groups of *paesani* present in Bedford are greater in number and less numerous in membership that many people believe. Although there are six large *paesani* groups present, who operate with a degree of social exclusivity, many people (31 per cent) are not members of large groups.

Table Eleven

Villages with 100 *paesani* in Bedford

Villages	Italian-born	Non-Italian born	Total
S. Angelo Muxaro (Ag)	223	30	253
Busso (Cb)	206	46	252
Montefalcione (Av)	143	43	186
Buonvicino (Cs)	90	17	107
Castelluccio (Fg)	85	19	104
Petrella (Cb)	82	16	98
Total	829	171	1,000

Source: Current passports, Italian Vice Consulate, Bedford 1983.

It is in this context that the different provincial and regional totals and compositions become important.

Although not the largest regional group, the *Siciliani* are the most distinctive regional group in Bedford. As was the case in the other towns already surveyed, the *Campani* in Bedford are more wide-ranging in their provincial origins and are therefore less cohesive than are the *Siciliani*, 93 per cent of whom come from one province: *Agrigento*. This binds them and in addition their 'Sicilianness' serves to divide them further from the rest of the 'Italian' Community. The villagers from *Sant' Angelo*, who are probably the single largest group within the Community, are at their centre. They arrived later in Bedford, mainly in the 1960s and are generally younger then the rest of the Italians. Many second-generation members, not old enough for their own passports, are therefore missing from Table 11.

The most distinctive individual village group in Bedford are the *Bussesi*. Apart from their numerical dominance in overall Community terms, the *Bussesi* are also the best organised of all the *paesani* groups in Bedford and are the only village group to have a formal association, *'I Bussesi di Bedford'*, properly registered at the Italian Vice-Consulate, with a constitution and an elected committee. This organisational initiative has helped lead to the social and psychological dominance of the *Bussesi*, who are the most recognisable group and who are perceived to be the very heart of the Bedford Italian Community.

Indeed it is a *Busso* tradition, *La Pignata*, which has become one of the main social events of the Italian social calendar in Bedford. This annual event was originally attended only by *Bussesi* but now attracts over 500 migrants from all sources of origin. *Busso* has become the best-known village both inside the Community and also to the world at large. In an attempt perhaps at ethnic recognition, on first meeting, many *Campobassani* will tell you they come from *Busso*. The syndrome is somewhat self-perpetuating. Most people, from Community leaders and officials to the ordinary Italian migrant, think that the *Bussesi* form the single most numerous group in Bedford. As a consequence the Open University (1982) selected *Busso* to make a case study film on the Bedford Italian Community, which is shown periodically on television. In this way the general population now has the impression that most of the Italians in Bedford come from the village of *Busso*. *Busso* is certainly the only village that the ordinary Englishman in the street of Bedford can identify by name.

The villagers from *Petrella* (Cb) also form a large contingent in Bedford. *Campanilismo* keeps them apart from the *Bussesi* but other

186

Campobassani from less well represented villages with no *paesani* networks try to attach themselves to both the *Bussesi* and the *Petrellesi*. The large *Campobassani* contingent in Bedford is one of the distinctive features about the Community since, as we saw in Table 9, *Molise* was not a main source of migrants to Britain.

People from *Buonvicino* (Cs), the fourth-largest group in Bedford, are again identifiable – they are the only *Calabresi* in Bedford. They can be contrasted, however, with the more numerous migrants from *Montefalcione* who have merged naturally into their provincial group, the *Avellinesi*, who are the largest provincial set in the Community. The migrants from *Castelluccio* (Fg) form the fifth-largest group in the Community, sufficiently numerous to be organised along lines of *campanilismo*. Taken as a whole, the *Foggiani* are the last identifiable group. One reason for this is their distinct *Foggiano* dialect which is markedly different from the main *Molisano*, *Campano Irpino* and *Siciliano* dialects. Other migrants from under-represented villages have merged with their provincial and even regional groupings.

As the concluding section to this chapter and as a lead into Chapter 7, it is appropriate to look briefly at some everyday examples of *campanilismo* in operation.

Campanilismo in operation

Campanilismo was at its height in the early days of the 'new' immigrations. During this period, as we saw in Chapter 5, Communities were often in a state of internal turmoil and flux. Before the large *paesani* groups were gathered in Bedford, Peterborough and Nottingham, all the migrants, except single 'pioneer' male migrants from totally unrepresented villages, existed in small groups. Indeed Brown (1970), in his description of life in the brickyard hostels and lodging-houses in Bedford, tells how four Italian men lived together in the same room for a year, but in two separate pairs. Two were from *Busso* (Cb) and two from another village. They cooked and organised themselves in these two separate pairs with no interaction at all.

There is much discussion in the literature on ethnic minorities of the role of the immigrant community as a reception cushion for the newly arrived immigrant coming into an alien environment. In fact, this support mechanism is rarely provided by the 'community' – such a social entity is unlikely to exist in the early days of immigration. Rather, this service

187

is offered primarily by family. For the southern Italian migrants arriving in England the role of *paesani* was also very important, particularly where there was no family to aid its further arriving members. It was the groups of *paesani* who helped organise and provide basic collective needs and even services.

As a social process within southern Italian Communities *campanilismo* tends to be a rather divisive force. *Paesani* work together in networks of mutual aid and inevitably this puts them into conflict with similar groups of competitors over jobs, houses, prestige and honour. Each group of *paesani* normally has its leader or *padrone* who encourages this competition to maintain their own followings.

Campanilismo is primarily an informal social process. It is only rarely, for example at the time of the Italian Committee elections (discussed in Chapter 8), that a group will be mobilised to act as a political force by supporting certain candidates in preference to others. Where a large group of *paesani* are present in a town, even if their members are scattered, *paesani* know all other *paesani* and keep in touch. Often the *paesani* tie is interwoven with family ties which reinforces the connection. Obligation-visiting, particularly pertinent for *compari*, or honorary relatives, spills over into *paesani* contacts, albeit on a less regular basis. The *Bussesi* in Bedford, for example, are such a closed group that they behave almost as *compari* rather than just *paesani*. Of course, because of the numerous links through marriage and the *comparaggio* (discussed in Chapter 7) which have occurred over the years in the migrant situation many are now *compari*. With *paesani* being so central to life, much domestic discussion concerns them. People always mention the word *paesano*, even when it is superfluous both to clarity and meaning. Where an individual has not been raised to the status of being a *compare*, he will continue nevertheless to be given his due respect as a *paesano* by way of address. A *paesano* called Carmelo thus is addressed not just by his name but always as 'Paesano Carmelo'.

The main social events and collective efforts that the *paesani* groups are involved with are the organisation of, and attendance at, weddings of the second generation. People travel regularly to attend weddings of *paesani* living in other towns. It is not uncommon at a second-generation wedding, where both sets of parents are from the same *paese*, for an open invitation to be issued to all *paesani* in England. This way all the fellow villagers are automatically invited and no one is forgotten or offended by not receiving an invitation. The same occurs at inter-*paese* weddings when two sets of *paesani* are invited. It has been these inter-village as well as inter-province and regional weddings which, more than any other factor, have contributed to the breakdown of the old village loyalties and provided the basis for the development of a 'Community' in many towns.

Problems can occur, however, when people marry out of the Community. The southern Italian tradition of wedding administration is difficult for English parents to understand and is further complicated by the extreme generosity which accompanies it. In these cases considerable debate also surrounds the actual wedding celebrations – the Italian attitude is summarised in the view: 'If a *paesano* of mine wants another drink, how can I refuse him?' The resultant very grand scale of weddings is discussed in Chapter 7. Even though the cost of the wedding is normally shared by both sets of parents, the sheer numbers of people who 'have to be invited', just because they are *paesani*, can seem outrageous to the English unaccustomed to the concept of *campanilismo* and the village wedding. The wedding feast and celebration in fact offers the main social activity at which migrant *paesani*, as well as the extended family, can gather together. One saving on the costs at weddings is the fact that the wine on the table is normally made by the parents of either the bride or groom.

Wine-making is another important activity of the Italian Community in England. In Bedford, Peterborough and Nottingham as well as many smaller Communities, everyone is involved in the wine-making effort since production of sufficient wine to supply a family's consumption for a whole year is a major operation in which all must help. To be cost-effective in production, smaller families with modest needs must combine their operation with others: this most usually means with *paesani*.

The wine is made in exactly the same way as it was in Italy, except that the grapes have to be imported. All the simple machinery required for the natural fermentation process, and barrels used for decanting and storing also come from Italy. The pure grape juice is fermented and decanted in large demijohns and in the same sort of quantity as in Italy, between 400 and 1,000 litres per family. Nowadays, the Italian grocery shops are mainly responsible for chartering the lorries which travel to the south of Italy at the time of the grape harvest (October to November), and return with the grapes to sell. The subsequent bulk purchasing of the grapes from the shops is done mainly by groups of *paesani* working together to keep costs down. However, many small independent *paesani* co-operatives spring up at this time and organise their own consignment of grape imports from Italy.

After the acquisition of the grapes, further co-operative effort in the actual making of the wine is also the norm – not everyone has all the knowledge or equipment required. Within the *paesani* groups certain individuals will be known to possess more specialised or specific skills involved in the making of wine and these are generally at the disposal of the entire *paesani* group. Certain individuals are thus 'on call' to *paesani* during this period, which can last between two and three weeks. Because of the routine of the working week, wine is made at the weekend and in the evenings.

Very few members of the second generation who have married and set up household in their own right make their own wine. This is partly by conscious choice, but very few of the urbanised second generation possess the necessary skills to effect the operation without the expertise of the first generation. Their involvement is entirely passive: they help their parents but, since many do not even drink the fruity full-bodied red wine which is produced, it seems unlikely that this highly ethnic tradition will survive when the overall annual initiative rests in the hands of the second generation.

Finally, in Bedford the procession of village patron saints which takes place annually offers the large *paesani* groups of the Community the major event of the year at which to display their *campanilismo* and solidarity. Since only the main sending villages of the Community have their own patron saints' statues housed at the Italian Church, only they can participate in this event as an exclusive *paesani* group. The event has the specific function of redefining the old loyalties within the Community and at the same time clearly stating which are the dominant groups. Members of the Community from the smaller *paesani* groups, being unrepresented directly by their own saint at the *festa*, have the choice of joining in behind one of the non-village saints, or becoming supporters only in one of the large groups. The practical operation of the procession is decribed in Chapter 8.

Chapter Seven

Family and Community

Introduction

One of the crucial aspects of life in the large southern Italian Communities has already been introduced in the previous chapter, notably *campanilismo* and its operation. This chapter now zooms in to take a much closer look at how Italians lead their lives. The most important unit, basic to the way of life and the structure of the Community, is the family. Although individualism is the mark of Italianism, the family is at the very core of the Community. It is around the family that the main life-cycle events – births, deaths and marriages – are organised. While particularly important for the 'new' immigrants, the family ethic nevertheless still holds consider-able sway amongst the 'old' settlers and their descendants who are more family conscious than the population at large.

The families of the 'old' immigration are now all in the fourth or fifth, and some even in the sixth generation. By the 1980s the 'new' immigrant families had entered the third generation, and the young adult immigrants of the 1950s are now grandparents. The family passage of the 'old' and the 'new' to the present day has not been without challenge – but for different reasons.

The second main theme of this chapter, building on the family, is the other aspects of the way of life. Again, predictably, differences emerge between the 'old' and the 'new' immigrants. In the 'new' Communities there is a well-defined 'ethnic' way of life. Women of the first generation especially have been affected, socially and psychologically, by their emigration. In the 'old' Communities, apart from in London, assimilation is in an advanced state, but there is no doubt that an Italian factor con-tinues to be important in the lives of many people. Let us now begin to review life and family in the last four decades.

The old Communities

Family and life

The major challenge faced by the 'old' Italian families in the late 1940s was restructuring their lives after the War. For the large number of families who had lost men on the *Arandora Star* this was not always easy, but the Italians set about their task quietly and purposefully. Men had often been absent for five years – absent without leave in the internment camps. For example, Bruna Corsini, who was born in 1940 after her father was interned, saw him only three times in the first five years of her life. Her mother, Angela Corsini had both a brother and a brother-in-law on the *Arandora Star*. Fortunately both men were saved. The menfolk were delighted to be home but often took a while to adjust to normal family life, having spent so long in prison camps.

The older generation, men and women alike, who had experienced the war at first hand, tried in the post-war period to recreate their family lives and social patterns as they had been in the 'golden era'. In fact the old generation turned in on itself and people felt most secure within the ranks of the Community. As far as the family was concerned there was a restrengthening of old values, ties and bonds. Links with Italy were reopened. Naturally, during the war, people were unable to visit Italy or be visited in this country by their Italian relatives. Although splits had occurred within both family and Community because of different choices made during the war, this generation understood and valued the 'Community' and the importance of solidarity. The fact that members of the (often extended) family often worked with one another in small businesses meant that they spent much of their time together and kinship bonds were strengthened. In the expanding business environment of the 1950s, the new people employed were naturally family members 'brought over' from Italy, again strengthening the family network in this country. New arrivals varied from close relatives to 'distant cousins'. Those from small villages and hamlets such as *Bratto, Braia* (Ms) or *Fontitune* (Fr) were not only *paesani* but were often inter-related, strengthening enormously these village bonds.

People who had been children during the war often adopted a different approach in reorienting themselves in the post-war era. In Scotland, particularly, children who had grown up without their fathers and had to live with their 'tally bastard' status as the former enemy were often tainted for life by their experience. They internalised their Italianness and camouflaged their true identity. This was the generation who Anglicised their names and became Jimmy (Santoro), Edwin (Scappaticci), Tom (Conti), Archie (Tamburrini). They refused to speak or learn Italian, married Scottish girls and tried in every way possible for an alien ethnic minority to integrate and assimilate into Scottish society: in short, to become invisible. Through education, many Italo Scots and indeed Anglo Italians of the 1950s 'escaped' from the traditional occupations in which they were tied to their ethnicity. In the professions and in white collar positions it was much easier to hide their ethnicity. The 'shame' and confusion of this generation should not be underestimated.

In addition, the slightly older group, men now in their 70s, who served in the fiercely anti-Italian British Armed Forces during the War, perhaps more than any other sector of the Italian population, were forced to throw off their heritage, shake themselves adrift from their roots and pretend to be something they were not. There are some very sad cases of people today who are considered by the world at large to be 'Italian' because of their names, their looks, even their accents when speaking, who still try to deny who and what they are, so ingrained into them is their Italian denial experience.

In 'old' London Italian families the family ethos is still strong today. In the late 1940s in London there was a spate of weddings between second-generation members. Most young men who had been interned soon found Italian brides on their return to London. Double weddings were quite common and in fact fashionable. Out-marriage from the Community was not a feature. A major aspect of the infusion of new immigrants and blood in the 1950s was that it offered an increased pool of eligible spouses for sons, daughters and even grandchildren of 'old' families. Over the long decades of the Italian connection with London, individual families have absorbed immigrants from all the different periods of immigration, forming in fact the only Italian Community in the country to have received immigrants of all types during each of the phases of immigration. A boy who was 'brought over' after the First World War is now an old man in his late 70s. In the 1950s he may himself have 'sent for' nieces, nephews and 'boys' from his village to staff his then expanding catering business. Some of these newly arrived first-generation immigrants then married third-generation London Italians from other 'old' families. The offspring of such unions, people now in their 20s, are a complicated mixture of second and fourth generation. In London and the south east, we cannot talk simply of first, second, third-generation Italians; it is normally a more complex matter. Some of these young people have now married second-generation British-born southern Italians from the 'new' immigrations. The ongoing inter-marriage and intermingling of blood of different generations and often different regional origin is a striking feature of the London Italian Community.

Nowadays, in London and the south-east in general, there is an enormous choice of young Italians for spouses and much inter-marriage between the various Communities and generations takes place. The weddings themselves provide a major forum for family members to gather but also for young people to meet and enjoy each other's company in a family environment. We saw in Chapter 6 that the London Community is now evenly split between the 'old' *Emiliani* and the 'new' *Campani* groups. The result of this manifests itself in a continued desire and concern to find a partner from the 'north' if one's family are from the north and from the 'south' if the family originate in the south.

The weddings in the 'old' Communities have come to replicate those of British society at large, with emphasis placed on quality rather than quantity. Prestigious locations are chosen for the 'reception': a popular venue for wealthy families of the London Italian Community is the Hyde Park Hotel. There will, however, also be a distinctly Italian aspect at these events, through the food, wine, flowers and music, as the hotel is part of Lord Forte's organisation. The ultimate for a bride is the Valentino *bianco*, wedding dress.

Family networks are often extensive and there is still a strong obligation to keep in touch, visit and exchange information on the progress and well-being of the various family members. Socialisation within the family, even for the young today, is still common, with 'cousin friendship' being a particular feature in London. People are enormously proud of being part of a large family, and the prestige of a family is partly judged by the number of members as much as by their wealth. For example, one highly prominent member of the London Italian Community, Giuseppe Giacon, who had been a PoW, married into an 'old' London Italian family. Apart from relatives on his wife's side of the family, he was alone in this country. By fathering nine children, he personally is now at the head of a prestigious family of 34 people, at the last count, a fact which he himself enjoys pointing out. The network of relatives including the extended family on his wife's side runs to well over 100 people.

It was mentioned in Chapter 3, page 79, that London Italians felt there was a degree of discrimination against them, particularly in the employment sector. In the 1950s, much of the strong anti-Italianism expressed by the British population during the war continued. In an interesting study of Italian families in London, two anthropologists, Garigue and Firth (1956 p. 69), found that the majority of London Italians were:

> *convinced that having an Italian name may be basis enough for*
> *some discrimination to be directed against them, even if they are*
> *of British nationality and speak English as their mother tongue.*

The authors go on to say that there was no doubt about the presence of this discrimination and that most Italians sought out and preferred the company of other Italians. Integration, they said, was very slow.

It was mentioned in the Introduction to Chapter 4 that 'old' Italians have some difficulty in discussing the war. Apart from internalised pain, this is also partly due to Italy's defeat and the further shame and loss which that caused. Nowadays, it is difficult to find people in the old generation who are prepared to talk openly and sensibly about fascism.

Almost no one expresses a view either totally for or totally against the fascist period. On the one hand 'Mussolini did a lot of good for Italy', but on the other, 'I had nothing to do with fascism' or 'My father had nothing to do with fascism'. In many cases the people who express the latter view are the sons of *fasci* leaders, often men who were lost on the *Arandora Star*. When Italy was defeated many of the 'old' Italians felt they had lost all – a way of life and their ideal of Italy. They had, as we saw in Chapter 3, gained a considerable national pride in the 1930s because of fascism. It was not only the experience of the war which devastated the Italian Community. The loss of the way of life that they had had in the 1930s was a blow to the Community.

Men and women in the 1950s and 1960s were in the psychologically disturbing position of having to renounce not only their previous connection with fascism but also, by definition, with Italy. As one 'old' London Italian put it: 'We had our tails between our legs'. It would take the Community a long time to recover from this shame, confusion and also embarrassment at so whole-heartedly endorsing Mussolini. Many of the 'old' Italians, forced to renounce Italy in order to function in Britain, lost their heritage for ever. Their attitudes remained encapsulated in time and they never found the new Italy. This hastened the effect of assimilation tremendously in the 'old' Communities.

By the 1970s and 1980s life styles amongst the 'old' families had become less Italian as over many generations these Italians, long since integrated, became assimilated to a greater or lesser extent. With the exception of

195

London, where there is still a great deal of Italian Community activity and many people still lead their lives in an Italian way within the confines of the family and the Community, elsewhere in the country for most people their Italianness is secondary to them. Many people retain an Italian aspect to their life, particularly if they are in business and they trade on their ethnicity, but, for the majority their attitudes and behaviour are similar to the comparable British socio-economic group to which they belong. Similar to, but not entirely the same.

The process of assimilation has been hastened in the 'old' Italian Communities by inter-marriage to local people and the absence of the same level of 'new' immigration, particularly in Scotland. When the pool of eligible partners is reduced, out-marriage from the Community inevitably occurs with its consequent dilution of blood and loss of traditions. Outside London, third and fourth-generation Italians do not generally have Italian spouses. Where people have Italian spouses and are in traditional business activities many consider themselves to be 'Italian'. For example, Silvia Quarantelli, who was born in Aberdeen, holds a British passport and who has never lived in Italy, summed up a typical attitude when she said 'I don't feel as though I belong here. I was born here, I've lived all my life here but I feel different. I'm Italian.'[1]

Many people who are totally integrated choose to keep in touch with events in the Italian Community and their own networks of *paesani*. Nowadays, with increased mobility and communications, nationwide networks are easily maintained. This point is particularly pertinent within the business sphere. Where people are in catering or Italian service businesses they often maintain a countrywide Italian network of contacts. Activity in the business community is often connected both to developments in Italy but also more importantly, from the point of view of the British Italian Community, to the ethnic upsurge and interest of third and fourth-generation Italians. Unlike their fathers who sought to progress by leaving the business background behind, many third-generation people enter family businesses with university educations and often business qualifications. Sons of restaurateurs often train as chefs in Italy and induce a new level of standards and ethnicity to old businesses as a consequence.

The move into the professions, however, has not always resulted in a loss of ethnicity. In London, for example, the British Italian Law Association is composed mainly of third and fourth-generation London Italian lawyers who use their ethnic background at the highest level of bicultural occupational performance. Often those who are lawyers, doctors or accountants, although now professionals, take the family business approach to their independent operations. When a father has become a professional, his third-generation son often follows suit. Indeed one of the best legal firms in Glasgow, run by the well-known Glasgow Italian lawyer, *Comm.Avv.* Tino Moscardini, is actually called 'The Family in Law'.

In Scotland there have generally speaking been two main developments within the Italian Community as far as assimilation is concerned. Firstly, those families who have remained in business, ethnic or otherwise, have retained an Italian factor and indeed are normally extremely proud of it. Secondly, since one of the main avenues to progress in Scottish society involves entering the public sector and local government, many Italians have followed this path. This, however, has led in most cases to an 'institutionalised assimilation'. The capitalistic drive to progress has been lost amongst this group but, more importantly, so has their *Italianità*.

Today, people in business are in touch with Italy, feel Italian and see the very bright future of that country. They are part of the new and dynamic Europe. Unfortunately, it tends to be that the group who work in the public sector in Scotland remember the past, in their ethnic memory; the 'bad times' for the Italians in that Community, and the bitterness and shame, are still often visible. They have not been able to make either a cultural or economic leap forward into a new era. There are, however, some outstanding exceptions: people who have entered the public sector but, through force of personality, have been able, often in the face of strong pressures to the contrary, to maintain their Italianness. The most notable example is Frank Pignatelli, now Director of Education for Strathclyde Region.

Throughout Britain, Italians from the 'old' immigration are now present at all levels of society. In addition to this, within London, partly because of the diplomatic presence, the Italian Community itself has a pyramid-shaped structure, with the Ambassador at the apex. The status and position of an individual in this internal hierarchy is dependent upon occupation and wealth, and membership of the various non-official organisations such as the associations and clubs of the Community. It is through the institutions, associations and socio-political structure of the Community that status can be achieved, people recognised and evaluated. The conferment of *'Cavaliere'* is a key measure of status. We will pick up this interesting theme again in Chapter 8 when we look at the institutions of the Community. Let us now move to look at the 'new' immigrants.

197

The new Communities

The family

As we have seen in previous chapters, the vast majority of the 'new' immigrants came from the south of Italy; in fact almost exclusively from the *contadini* classes. Only a few people came from the cities and the provincial capitals, and therefore from less rigid and agriculturally dominated socio-economic backgrounds. At the time of the migration, levels of education within village society were low; illiteracy was still common. Many people did not have much experience outside restricted village life. In the normal course of their lives most villagers had little or no direct contact with the world beyond their own town. Many people never travelled beyond neighbouring towns and some women had never left their villages before coming to England.

The social traditions of village life were thus undiluted in form and almost unaffected by external influences or inputs. Remember this was the pre-television and pre-mass media era. Few people in the south even had radios before they left for England. Geographically the village was characterised by close residential clustering, and the members of the Community, at work and at play, were bound to each other by frequent social contact and unavoidable economic interdependence. Village society was determined by a way of life deeply embedded in tradition and controlled by a close-knit web of social relationships. The traditions and way of thinking – *la mentalità* – that the migrants brought with them were very rigid and strongly held. Inevitably, however, living in modern English towns, rather than Italian village communities, posed new challenges and necessitated some adaptations. Let us now see how these have occurred over the last 30 years.

Settling in

As we saw in Chapter 5, page 156, men nearly always arrived first with work contracts and, after a couple of years, wives and often children followed. The newly reunited family encountered an enormous range of difficulties, centred around adaptation to the new environment in both a physical and psychological sense.

All aspects of finding accommodation and suitable jobs for wives were extremely problematic and stressful. In the early phase of residency most families moved several times each year in the rented sector, desperately trying to improve their conditions. Needless to say, in Bedford and Peterborough, where the Italians were the first immigrant group to arrive in any noticeable numbers, finding rooms to let from increasingly reticent English landlords was no easy task. In Bedford particularly, there was such a massive build-up in numbers of Italians in the small town centre that, as we saw in Chapter 5, the Town Council refused to allow the brickyards to recruit any more Italians after 1959. Conditions became extremely crowded with whole families living in one room, often sharing kitchen and bathroom facilities with other families. As the numbers of Italians increased in many towns in the 1950s, landlords, particularly the less scrupulous ones, were quick to see the possibilities of subdivision and multi-occupation of large and already decaying Victorian properties, usually in central areas. The housing scandal of the mid 1950s was so acute in Bedford that the Town Council promoted a private Act of Parliament which required landlords to provide a rent book and make it available for inspection by the Council. During this phase there was a considerable degree of anti-Italian feeling, due mainly to multi-occupation and the inevitable problems this caused. According to the *Bedfordshire Times* (25 November 1960), the Italians were 'ear-shattering neighbours'. The main problem, apparently, was the 'din caused by these voluble and highly excitable people'.

Although in this early period of residence, life for the family was stressful, their traditions, way of life and sets of values could be maintained intact to a considerable extent. The children, only just settling into English schools, were not in a position to make any new demands on the traditional way of life. In general the overriding aim of the family was in any case to return to Italy. Although the women were for the first time going to work outside the home, in the domestic environment the traditional pattern continued with the division of the sexes in household chores and in family social patterns.

Throughout the 1950s and into the 1960s, as we have seen, chain migration increasingly came into play and it was of course due to strong family obligation that people found jobs for their relatives and assisted them in their emigration to England. Family here paid the fares and provided initial accommodation until the new arrivals established themselves. Newcomers were dependent for a while until they too began to learn their way around; the language, the housing market and so on. Increasingly, the family became a large extended network, often of up to 50 people when 'distant cousins' from the village were included.

While, as we have seen in Chapter 5, the availability of good, steady and well-paid employment worked against returning to Italy, it was the arrival of the second generation, born and bred in England, which perhaps more than any other factor led to very deep roots being put down in this country. It was, however, the social challenges and opportunities available to their children which more than any other factor led to conflict and changes in the traditional southern Italian family.

Conflict

The internal difficulty which emerged amongst the 'new' Italian families in the 1960s and 1970s was due to a struggle between parents and children and between the old values and ways and the new ones. The parents had the most to lose since acceptance of the full range of their children's demands would have meant an abandonment of everything they knew and understood, and an acceptance of a completely new way of family life. From opposite ends of the spectrum, these difficulties confronted first and second-generation members alike, with both sides anxious to resolve the conflict and maintain family unity.

Two major areas of conflict were the changing roles within the family and the acculturation into English norms of the second generation. The former unchallenged authority and high status position of the father was no longer taken for granted. In the new environment it could only be preserved superficially. The family no longer constituted a tightly-knit interdependent economic unit. In urban England, women and later children began to develop a degree of independence through the acquisition of employment, a situation unimaginable in the village. Also, in the first decade of residence, parents placed reliance on their children as interpreters of both language and social behaviour, as transmitters and disseminators of information. This gave the second generation an unprecedented position of influence in the family, again weakening the power of the father.

When the children went to school and later ventured out more and more from the home, the 'gap' between the generations widened. It was during the 1950s that the notion of the 'generation gap' was in fact first conceived. 'Teenagers' became a recognised group in their own right and parents and children became estranged and ideologically separated over a number of rapidly changing social issues. For the young Italian child growing up in England these difficulties inherent in the times were compounded by their ethnic and cultural heritage.

Attending school naturally encouraged Italian children to adopt English ways, of which their parents thoroughly disapproved, and they therefore had to cope with bridging the cultural and linguistic gap between home and school. In addition to this there was often further conflict within the family concerning education itself. Many parents did not value education and it is true to say that, unlike the Asian community in Britain which has encouraged education, at least for boys of the second generation, the southern Italian population has not generally seen education as a means of advancement. No motivation for learning was passed on to children and little encouragement was given for school work. Parents were shy and reticent to participate in 'parent–teacher' discussions since many of them could not speak English and had spent so few years at school themselves. This has meant that very few second-generation members have been able to take advantage of the education system and go on to tertiary education. This has been especially true of girls, because to go away to university or college would have been culturally inappropriate and indeed is still unusual in Italy today. Towns like Bedford and Peterborough with no university or polytechnic sent very few students into tertiary education in the 1960s and 1970s.

There are of course always exceptions. One example was Franca Torrano from Bradford who studied for a degree in geography at Oxford University in the early 1980s. Vincenzo Fattorusso was a pioneer of the second generation in Bedford, not only responsible for many initiatives affecting his own generation, but also the first Italian solicitor in the town. The Nottingham Community, with the nearby Loughborough University, has more recently had a better entry rate and according to Community leader, Fulvio Giretti, there are currently (1991) around ten Nottingham Italians studying there.

In general terms, however, since the first generation had migrated entirely for economic reasons, work and jobs rather than education were viewed as the best means of making progress, for child and family alike. Children were encouraged to leave school as soon as possible and in many cases it was the parents who found the school leaver his or her first job. Having worked for years as unskilled labourers the priority of the first generation was to see their children into 'skilled' jobs. They were keen to apprentice them to trades such as carpentry, plumbing, upholstery and most especially motor mechanics. For girls, jobs in shops or even offices, with the possibility of acquiring secretarial skills, were viewed as desirable. Hairdressing for both sexes became very popular.

In the larger Italian Communities particularly, very few of the first generation had much opportunity of learning to speak English with any degree of skill. Long hours in factory environments, often working with other Italians, and their firmly held hope of returning to Italy, were not conducive to learning English. Often the first generation had virtually no contact in an interactive way with English people. This aggravated the lack of communication between the generations especially when delicate inter-generational negotiation was necessary. Parents simply did not have the words to handle the new concepts introduced by the increasingly urbanised second generation: 'Youth Club? What is that exactly?' (see Plate 13).

As the children reached adolescence and relations with parents became strained over a number of issues, the worlds of the two generations moved further and further apart and the 'peer group' of second-generation Italians took on a special significance, particularly for boys. Parents were unaware that the culture they held out to their children did not supply the knowledge or practical guidelines for survival in urban Britain. The result was that the second generation began to build its own society relatively independent of the influence of its elders. Life was by no means straight-forward for the second generation, however, and despite peer group solidarity, many people lived with a sense of confusion and an identity crisis. Being socialised between these two incompatible cultures – traditional village society expectations and rapidly changing urban Britain of the 1960s – the second generation became muddled and acquired conflicting goals, habits and attitudes. On the one hand they strove to be independent and accepted by their English peers but, on the other, they had been moulded to accept the wishes of their parents and desired to maintain the good name of their family.

In a fascinating study of second-generation Italian Americans, three major types of reaction to, or ways of coping with, this difficult situation were identified by the American professor of psychology, Child, in 1943: the rebel, the in-grouper and the apathetic. The rebel is the person who throws off his ethnic heritage and tries to 'assimilate'. The in-grouper is one who identifies totally with his roots and the traditional way of life, feeling it to be superior and preferable. The apathetic individual tries to gain acceptance in both cultures by quietly refusing to identify completely with one or the other and is apathetic in the sense that he is not willing to take sides openly. This latter reaction is the most complex, but also the most common, since it involves an ability to perform correctly within either of the two different cultures.

In the 'new' Italian Communities of Bedford, Peterborough, Nottingham, and the Surrey and Hertfordshire agglomerated Communities of the south east, including the 'new' families in London too, very few true rebels emerged in the 1960s and 1970s. The second generation did not reject its Italian heritage and the vast majority adhered to it in varying degrees. Today people who were born in Italy and brought to this country as children in the late 1950s and early 1960s, admit to very little Anglicisation. They consider themselves to be 'Italian'. Young women especially, even when born in England, because they were kept closer to home and the traditional codes of social behaviour were more strictly applied to them, in general consider themselves more Italian than English. Where people were born in this country and are entitled to British nationality few take this up and the majority 'opt' for their Italian (by parentage) nationality.

The reality of this dual ethnicity is, however, complicated. The second generation may claim to be and indeed be considered 'Italian' when amongst their friends in this country, both Italian and English, but when in Italy they are considered *Inglesi*. Neither society is yet ready to cope with the notion of the bicultural, bilingual person. This is a social phenomenon which can really only exist at the highest levels of society with high levels of education, status and wealth.

In general terms, the second generation in England has been between the 'apathetic' and the 'in-group' reaction in their behaviour and attitude. Most were 'apathetic' until the time of marriage and were able to operate in both worlds by keeping them separate and by behaving appropriately within each. The majority of the second generation married within the Italian Community and became strongly in-groupish as they followed the Italian family way of life. Rebels wishing to become English and disown their Italian origins could not, and still cannot, do this within the larger Italian Communities, particularly the large Community in the small town. To pursue this course of action it became necessary to move away completely. There are two main reasons for this.

Firstly, the family did not and does not tolerate rebels. In the 1960s and 1970s particularly it was virtually impossible for girls to become rebels, so strict were the social controls. Although there is a certain double standard in the codes applied to boys, with far greater freedom allowed, some restrictions also apply to them. The most notable is that boys are required to live with their parents until they marry. In the Italian family this is linked to the very strong bond between the Italian mother and her son.

One vivid example will amplify this point. It relates to the Bedford Italian Community in 1980 and demonstrates the continued power of the family. Franco (pseudonym), a 27-year-old unmarried, Italian-born

203

member of the second generation, decided to leave home and move into an all-male shared flat in the town centre with a few friends, one of whom was Italian and two of whom were not. *Signora* Balduccio (pseudonym), Franco's mother, was so upset, and more importantly so 'ashamed' since such an act brought shame on the entire family causing a collective loss of honour, that she decided drastic steps would have to be taken in order to get her son home. Accordingly, *Signora* Balduccio decided to go on a hunger strike and announced to the Italian Community in general that no food would pass her lips until Franco returned home. As the weeks passed, the level of tension and outrage grew. During this critical period, the incident became widely if not totally known throughout the Italian Community in Bedford and was a subject of constant conversation and debate. The barometer of opinion never changed: few voices were raised except in support, from first and second-generation members alike, of the righteousness of the mother's act and despair at the despicable behaviour of her son.

As *Signora* Balduccio became increasingly weaker, the pressure upon Franco to abide by the most sacred rule and code of the Community – honouring the family – mounted. Finally, after pleas and persuasion from several 'important' and 'successful' people, *Signora* Balduccio won her battle for the supremacy of the family and errant Franco returned home, where he remains to this day, still unmarried at 38. (The other Italian boy very quickly returned home, long before Franco, when the Community pressure began to bear.) A major and full-scale public battle of this type between the generations served as a warning and at the same time as a lesson. The power of the family and of the first generation are still intact and are forces to be reckoned with. Second-generation members with rebel tendencies have to think carefully before they act, knowing that the consequences could well be drastic.

The second aspect of the difficulty of being a rebel within the larger Italian Communities has also been touched upon in the above example; the 'Community' has a certain power, and its pressure can be brought to bear on the individual. But even if the rebel escapes the pressure of both his own family and the Italian Community, the second-generation Italian person will always be recognised for what he is by the indigenous population, 'an Italian'. Hence the view that if a member of the second generation truly wishes to abandon his Italian heritage it is necessary to leave his home town altogether and to break away from the Italian Community and the mould that this sets.

Members of the second generation do have English acquaintances but socialise mainly within their Italian Community. As we will see below there are many family occasions and social events which in the extended family, now with three generations, can offer more rewarding socialisation than English-style adolescent 'party-going' and 'pub-crawling'. Many boys have English girlfriends but most feel it is important to try to find an Italian wife since they very much wish to continue life in the type of household that they know. This is especially relevant where food is concerned.

The selection of marriage partners has been one of the greatest areas of conflict between the generations. The second generation have been influenced by the ideals of marriage in Britain and indeed modern-day Italy, with its emphasis on individual choice, romance and love. The old generation could not understand these values, particularly if such a 'choice' involved marrying out of the Italian fold. In the village a 'good marriage' was tantamount to survival and the choice of partners became a family rather than an individual matter. ('Arranged' or contracted marriages did not exist in the south of Italy, although a good deal of discussion and negotiation between families did occur.) Attempts to impose the old system of courtship on the second generation were in the main rejected and although the second generation sought parental approval it insisted on free choice and to an extent free 'dating'.

The adolescent years and the passage towards marriage were particularly difficult for second-generation girls. In the south of Italy a girl beyond childhood was closely supervised and when the time came for marriage the family networks helped her find a partner. In England, from the point of view of the parents, it has been less easy to supervise the activities and movements of girls, who after leaving school usually work some distance from home. This sometimes led to complications like getting to know and 'falling in love' with the wrong sort of person. But because family networks are reduced in size and range, it has not been possible for parents to rely on the old spouse-finding system. Nevertheless, independent efforts by daughters to seek and select their own spouse have not been encouraged. Girls had to live within a 'catch 22' situation. On the one hand, they were under pressure to marry and have a family, but on the other their opportunity for identifying partners was limited.

The informal social institutions of southern Italian life, such as the village *feste* in the summer months and the pre-Lenten *carnevale*, which allow young people to associate casually although under the watchful eye of village elders, are not available to the girls 'cooped-up' in urban

England. Only in the large Italian Communities where *scampagnate* or picnics are organised in the summer do girls acquire a certain freedom.

A complicated courtship system consequently developed in England which made it practically impossible for young people to meet 'casually'. Meeting surreptitiously and briefly on the way home from work and at lunchtime was often the only means of passing time with male friends. Girls were not generally allowed out in the evenings on 'dates'. Italian boys were expected to 'visit' the girl at home, effectively under the supervision of the parents. This level of relationship, however, sealed a firm commitment which was extremely difficult to break. Once a boy stepped over the threshold of a girl's house a certain unspoken agreement had been struck. There is no word for boyfriend or girlfriend in Italian – from friend (*amico, amica*) one is immediately elevated to the status of *fidanzato, fidanzata (fiancé)* – which, of course, implies a much less casual relationship. Bad behaviour by young men who tried to rescind on this could damage not only the future marriageability of the girl in question, but also the chances of his sisters, whose honour could be tainted by association. Since young men were freer to date and wished to avoid the complications of becoming too involved too soon with an Italian girl, they socialised with English girls on a casual basis, which did sometimes, despite initial intentions, lead to marriage. Out-marriage from the Italian Community among the second generation was, as a result, greater for boys than it was for girls. Consequently, there are many more spinsters than bachelors in the Community today.

Harmony

Through the marriages of the second generation, the second-generation family was formed. By the mid-1980s, this was the phase of development that the 'new' Italian families had reached, with the first generation becoming grandparents. Although the life-style of the second-generation family leans towards English ways, many of the traditional patterns and attitudes are maintained, even amongst the more upwardly mobile. The separation of roles between husband and wife is still common and relationships with same sex kin are often still very strong, particularly in the big family where the second-generation women, now in their 20s and 30s, rely on their sisters, cousins and *comare* for a support network. Even when a residential move from the traditional area of Italian settlement in a town to better housing and more prestigious addresses has occurred, face-to-face contact is maintained on a daily basis with first-generation parents.

People rely on the many services that the family network can offer. These include a considerable amount of financial help from both sets of parents in the early days of marriage, practical as well as economic help when the third generation emerges, and provision of certain ethnic items such as home-made wine, where the relevant manufacturing skills have not generally been acquired by the second generation. It is not uncommon for the second-generation family to eat their evening meal at the home of either set of first-generation parents for several years after marriage. This not only saves money but allows the family to continue to 'live together' in the Italian way rather than become isolated in nuclear units in separate suburban houses. Unlike the 'old' Italian families, where people often work together on a daily basis in their family-run businesses, the 'new' families have been separated at least between 9 a.m. and 5 p.m. because of employment constraints. When the third generation appears, grandmothers (now retired) are often crucial in their care, especially when the second-generation mother goes out to work, as is most often the case.

Not until the third generation reaches school age and then adolescence will aspects of assimilation, as opposed to integration, begin to appear. It is they who may well begin to discard the traditional life-style in a way that their parents, the second generation, have not. Girls may wish to leave home to gain a tertiary education. It will be the third generation too who will struggle for a place in British society in a way that their parents have not. Recognition at a local level, now so prominent in the 'old' Communities, in local government and public sector, lies ahead of this group.

The second-generation family must also deal with a further problem: that of the aging first-generation parents and whether their dream of returning to Italy will become a reality or remain a myth. Many of the now married and British-born second generation themselves harbour a nostalgic dream of returning to Italy although most qualify this by saying 'not to the village though'. Contacts with Italy are often still strong and the building of holiday villas by the second generation indicates their commitment to their origins.

One of the most important family traditions to have been transplanted by Italians to this country is the *comparaggio*, applicable mainly in the southern Communities. However, in the 'old' Communities of Edinburgh and Manchester which were based on migrants from *Lazio* and *Frosinone*, people placed an enormous importance on this tradition. In these cities the network and importance of these *compari*, or honorary relatives, has

207

declined although the term *compare* is still understood and used. The important role of the Italian Catholic Church in keeping the family traditions alive within the Community is discussed in Chapter 8.

Comparaggio

The *comparaggio* which provides the family with a network of adopted relatives is extremely important in the south of Italy and is, if anything, more important for the Italian immigrants in England. The privileges and obligations of *compari* approach those of kin with blood ties. Since to be invited to become an intimate and trusted member of the family is one of the great honours of the Community and to refuse the invitation a great insult, the selection procedure is done with great care. The acquisition of *compari* revolves around the life-cycle ritual, the *rites de passage*, of the Community and is church-dependent, based on the life-cycle sacraments: christenings, confirmations and marriages.

The role of *compari* takes several forms. At marriage the *compare* and *comare* act as best-man and best-woman; at confirmation the male or female sponsor; and at christenings as godmother and godfather.

Christening

The first life-cycle event is birth and the baptism of the child. For a christening, two *compari*, usually a married couple, are chosen, although two or more sets of *compari* can be selected. The most normal procedure for the first-born child is to ask the couple who were *compari* at the wedding. For any subsequent children new *compari* are chosen for each child. The godparents are expected to provide for the godchild in any family emergency, remember the godchild at Christmas, on the feast of the child's patron saint, and at any other special family occasions.

Tradition requires that the first-born male child be named after the paternal grandfather and the first female child after the maternal grandmother. First-born male cousins whose fathers are brothers therefore always have the same names (christian and surname). To avoid confusion the use of *soprannome* is thus common. Other family first names are also used for subsequent children. More and more this tradition is losing its hold on the second-generation parents who prefer to name children according to their own choice. The trend is still to give saints' names, but many shortened forms have become common, not just in usage but on the birth certificate and in the actual christening ceremony, for example,

Leonardo becomes 'Dino' and Pasqualina 'Lina'. Baptism takes place at the weekend, normally Sunday, since in the church calendar Saturdays are reserved for marriages.

The ceremony involves the *compari* as much as the parents; it is the *comare* who is expected to hold the baby throughout the ceremony. A baby who cries is thought to have been badly prepared by the mother and badly handled by the *comare*. Nowadays more than one christening usually occurs at the same time and, because of this, the ceremonies often take place in main churches rather than, as was traditional, in the baptistry. As we will see in Chapter 8, the Italian missionary priests who conduct the ceremonies are dependent on agreeing dates with and having the co-operation of the local priests in order to be able to use their churches.

Many superstitions which derive from a bygone era in the south of Italy still surround the birth and the christening of children today. It is felt, for example, that if a baby is taken out of the house before it is christened it will be vulnerable to evil influences (the 'evil-eye') since it has not yet been purified by the sacrament of baptism. For this reason the christening normally takes place shortly after the birth of the child, at a time when the mother has perhaps not fully recovered physically or psychologically from the birth. Hence the importance of the *comare*. Also it is thought unwise to cut a baby's hair until after it has been christened, again for fear of evil influences.

The christenings which occur today in the 'new' Italian Communities are of the third generation. The second generation, as we have seen, were born either in Italy or in England at a period when the first generation of migrants had not become economically established or socially organised. The christenings in the 1950s and 1960s were very different events from the grand celebrations which became the norm for the third generation born in the early 1980s. These christenings, particularly if for a first born, offer an opportunity for displaying economic well-being as well as for reinforcing family ties. The underlying philosophy of the event is that the family should organise a gathering, the size of which is determined by their economic situation. It is normally the two sets of grandparents who cover the costs of the christening.

The typical christening party involves 30 to 50 people, although nowadays wealthy families can have up to 100 people at a christening 'reception'. After the baptism itself, the party move, in the early afternoon, either to the couple's home, an Italian restaurant or, in the case of the very large groups, a hired hall. If outside the home, the christening reception is organised on similar lines to a wedding reception, with a lavish but traditional Italian meal provided for the guests. After eating, some form of musical entertainment is provided, with guests having the opportunity to dance, the *tarantella* being a favourite. The event can continue into the late evening. The child who has been christened is naturally the centre of attention and will be kept 'on show' until the departure of all the guests. In this way the skill of the mother and the *comare* in their ability to handle the baby can be directly assessed by all the women present.

Confirmation

After the christening of a child the next event which requires adoption of *compari* into the family is confirmation. The sacrament 'confirms' the child in the Catholic faith and membership of both church and Community. For confirmation, one further person will be asked to join the family. If the child is male, a *compare* will be selected, and if female, a *comare*.

In England today, since the age of confirmation is increasingly postponed, the trend is for the confirmee to select a *compare*, often therefore choosing a 'peer group' member, a personal friend. This particular development of the *comparaggio* can cause some friction between the generations, but because of the ethnic and religious nature of the procedure an Italian friend is, however, nearly always chosen. A period of instruction of the confirmee, which at a later stage also involves the *compare*, takes place during which time the priest decides when the applicant is ready for confirmation.

Confirmation was until recently an area of difference in practice between the Italian ethnic church and the local Catholic church since the latter organises the ceremony through the local Catholic schools. Although in the local Catholic church a 'guardian' is now chosen for every child to be confirmed, this is a fairly recent innovation since it was normal for confirmation to be done in large groups, organised through the Catholic schools and in particular age groupings or school classes, with one guardian or sponsor for the entire group. The individual guardian for each child is thus more similar to the individual *compare/comare* system, although the strength of the bond between the child and the guardian is extremely weak compared with the *comparaggio*. Where Italian children are present at the Catholic schools they do not participate in the local 'batch schemes' and continue to choose their own *compari* and are thus confirmed in their own time and in their own way by the Italian missionaries. The sacrament of confirmation is, however, a diocesan function and it is the local Bishop who conducts the confirmations.

Marriage

Marriage forms the most important life-cycle event for the 'new' Italian families. It is true to say that marriage and weddings form the core of the culture and the ethnic identity of the Italian Communities in England today. The continuation of the family is ensured by marriage and its centrality to the culture has been maintained.

For the wedding, a couple, who are normally married, will be chosen as *compari*. While the translation of *compare* in this context would be best-man, the translation of *comare* is not bridesmaid (a concept which does not exist at the southern Italian wedding) and would be closer to 'best-woman'. While it is usual to select a married couple, sometimes a sister and brother will be chosen, or an engaged couple, or more rarely an unmarried relative from one side of the family, who will be paired with an unmarried member from the other side of the family. These are the *compari d'anello* – the *compari* of the ring.

Something of the form and scale of the Italian wedding celebrations has already been mentioned in Chapter 6, on *paesani* and weddings. Not only do weddings ensure the continued future of the family but they offer the main opportunity for extended family and *paesani* reunion. However, according to the socio-linguist Arturo Tosi (1984), because of the 'supreme officiality' of marriage, 'enemies' have to be invited as well as family, and tradition dictates that these attend in person – rather than sending representatives – to be eye-witnesses of the standard that the family has achieved in respectability, power and wealth.

Many writers have described Italian weddings in North America, which offer a picture very similar to the typical southern Italian wedding in England today. For example, the anthropologist, Boissevain (1970, p.12), says of the Italian wedding in Montreal:

> *As the success of these functions is usually measured by the lavishness of the arrangements as well as by the number of persons attending, a good deal of informal pressure is placed on relatives to attend and help make a good showing. In order to accommodate the many guests invited (at times as many as 200 people), such receptions are often held in specially hired halls.*

At the weddings in England, between 200 and 300 guests would be normal and many celebrations in fact exceed 500. For example, the largest hall in Bedford, the only place in the town which can accommodate over 500 people, the Bunyan Centre, is regularly hired during the summer months for Italian weddings, although most receptions take place in the town's smaller school halls. Receptions are indeed lavish, with abundant food served and eaten over several hours, against a background of continuous entertainment. Many family-run catering firms have been established to service the considerable Italian wedding industry in the south-east. Any families seen not to be 'doing their best' would be considered to show a great lack of respect to *compari*, *paesani* and especially to the bride and groom. Such efforts indicate the level of adherence to, and recognition of, the importance of maintaining the old value system. The considerable sums of money spent on these weddings reflect the economic well-being of the Community. Nevertheless, the cost of each wedding can only be covered by several years of hard work and saving.

This cost tends to be shared between the parents of the bride and groom. A tradition has emerged where it is normal for the groom's parents to pay for the honeymoon. One father in Bedford spent £7,000 (in 1982) to send his son and his bride for a honeymoon in Hawaii. He did, however, recognise his good fortune in only having one son, but gained tremendous prestige in the Community by such action. A good big wedding and a proper honeymoon indicate the economic status of the two families and signal the future economic well-being of the young couple, who will, for some time and in a number of ways, continue to be dependent on their parents.

It is normal for the guests to bring their gifts to the wedding reception and, with a flourish, present these to the couple at the 'top table' which consists of the immediate family and the *compari*. The gifts usually consist of money in envelopes and are given to the bride. Guests are expected to give an amount which would represent the cost of their food plus their personal contribution on top. There is, however, a certain reciprocity in the giving of gifts, since all the guests, on leaving the reception, are presented with a *bomboniera* as a keepsake of the event. The expenditure on *bomboniere* varies considerably and the general impression of the event will be judged as much on the *bomboniere* as on the food, wine and entertainment.

Plate 14 illustrates three *bomboniere*, from a simple bunch of sugared almonds attached to a trinket, through an intermediate example, to a solid silver bell. The bell was presented to around 500 guests at the wedding of the daughter of one of the *padroni* of the Bedford Community in 1985.

Death and the family

After weddings, the main family occasion at which all members, including the extended branches, gather are funerals. Attendance at a funeral involves the same level of obligation, although since these are often held on weekdays, it is more acceptable to send representatives, one from each nuclear family. In the 'old' Italian families, particularly in London, there is a tradition of sending cards to inform members of death in their ranks. Attendance at funerals at the Italian Church in London often reaches capacity levels, especially for well-known members of the Community who have given years of service.

In all Italian Communities, 'new' and 'old', it is the cemeteries, perhaps more than anywhere else, where memories of the past are preserved. Cremation is not acceptable to Italian Catholicism, and burial in the local cemeteries has always been customary, although this too is not entirely coincident with southern Italian ritual. In larger towns and cities the specifically Catholic cemeteries are used where available. Italian sections of graveyards are always distinctive. Most of the gravestones bear enamelled portraits of the person and the inscriptions often give an impression of the person's life. The gravestones are often large and elaborate, made of the best marble, and the graves themselves are meticulously attended even years after the death.

At various periods there have been difficulties between Italian Communities and local authorities over cemetery policy. In the early 1980s, a considerable controversy developed between the Italians in Bedford and the Town Council. According to the Council, the Italians were turning the graves of their relatives into 'gardens' which is against cemetery policy. The tradition of the Italians in Britain is to delimit the grave, perhaps with a little fence, and to 'grow' rather than 'place' flowers. In 1982 the *Bedfordshire Times* (7 October 1982) carried a front-page article with the title 'Relatives Fight to Honour Dead'. Since many of the Italians in question were indeed prepared to 'fight' and go to prison over the issue, the local council did not pursue its demands and the Italians have been allowed to maintain their graves in the traditional way. There is now a growing lobby for a separate section in the cemetery to entomb bodies rather than bury them in the ground, which is not a custom in southern Italy.

A similar row erupted in Edinburgh in 1990 where the Italians have for several generations kept these sorts of graves. As burial space became short in the Mount Vernon Cemetery in Edinburgh, digging began for fresh graves between the lines of burial plots. Some of the Italian graves were damaged by tractors. The cemetery claimed that these Italian family lairs exceeded the permitted size for burial plots, and said they should be scaled down. One prominent Edinburgh Italian waged a battle against this 'desecration' of the Italian graves.

In London's Highbury Cemetery where there are restrictions not only on the size of plots but also the height of the monuments erected, there are numerous rather dumpy looking statues, especially of the *Madonna*, as the Italians try to conform to the regulations, but at the same time maintain their own traditions.

A death in an Italian family will be formally mourned for a considerably longer time than is the tradition in Britain. In the southern Italian family, a little shrine is often set up in the house in honour of the memory of the dead person. This 'grotto' consists of a photograph of the person, a constant flame – either a candle or more usually now a little electric light – and some flowers in a small vase. Shortly after the death, all the family, *campari* and *paesani* will visit the house to pay their last respects to the dead person, whose body is usually kept at home until the funeral. After a death in the family, it is not decorous to attend any celebrations such as weddings or christenings – only in these circumstances is it acceptable to decline an invitation.

The women of a southern Italian family at the time of a death and for a considerable length of time afterwards are required by tradition to assume black clothes as a mark of respect. If a husband dies, the widow is traditionally expected to wear black for the rest of her life. A daughter is expected to wear black clothes for between three and five years after the death of a parent. If a woman is of a large family beyond a certain age, she will be dressed in black for the rest of her life because deaths in the extended family become frequent. Because of this tradition, it is not difficult to identify Italian women of the first generation on the streets of English towns, since many of them are now permanently dressed entirely in black.

A final aspect of the ritual of death in the Italian Communities is that bodies of the dead are often sent back to the native village in Italy to be placed in the family tomb. Often, monetary collections are made by *paesani* if a family wishes to send a body back to be buried in the village of origin. The bureaucratic procedure is co-ordinated through the Italian Consulates and the coffins must be sealed by the official Italian Republic wax seal. It was mentioned in Chapter 5 that since the 1970s many Italians have been successful in their initial aim of returning to Italy with their families. One aspect of this has been a dramatic increase in the number of exhumations from cemeteries in this country. The southern Italians are anxious to reunite 'all' family members. Returning migrants do not wish to leave their dead behind with no one to tend their graves, so their bodies are exhumed and they too return to their native *paesi*. In Bedford, for example, an exhumation register was opened in 1977 and since then 90 per cent of the exhumations have been Italians. This tradition is strongest of all amongst the *Siciliani*.

Way of life

The 'new' immigrants from the south of Italy lead their lives almost totally through family, *compari* and *paesani*. The social 'clique' is fairly static and unchanging. Notions of assimilation or social mobility are inappropriate in the first generation. People without a large *paesani* network and extended family lead more isolated lives than those who are fortunate to be members of large groups. Outside the family circle, the other groups which emerge are usually single sex. In fact, as was the case in the villages in the south of Italy, the men and women of southern Italian families in England tend to lead rather separate lives. Men depend largely on other men for their social activities and women rely on female relatives, *comare* and perhaps neighbours to make up their social or support groups.

First-generation women

Southern Italian women of the first generation have made more sacrifices and suffered most in the adaptation to living in England. They tend to be rather isolated, spending much of their free time within their own homes; the range of their socialisation is more restricted than it was in their villages of origin.

In England, there are no small-scale informal social organisations equivalent to the street sewing groups or communal wash-houses of the village. Apart from casual visiting of neighbours in the evenings during the week, and paying social calls on geographically accessible relatives at the weekends, women do not go out of their houses in a leisure context. Few first-generation southern Italian women have found the motivation or nerve to learn to drive in urban Britain. Nor do they have the confidence or 'knowledge' to take a trip unaccompanied on public transport. Remember, acquisition of English in the larger Italian Communities has been limited. The range of their independent socialising is therefore

215

restricted mainly to points within walking distance from their own homes. It would not, in any case, be culturally appropriate for a woman to travel or 'do' something alone, especially in the evening.

The female is the guardian of the family nucleus and the concept of mother is the symbol of what is most sacred within a family. Any questionable behaviour on the part of the mother not only damages her personal reputation but that of the whole family. The codes which surround the expected behaviour of the mother are therefore extremely strict, arguably even more strict than those which are applied to the unmarried girl, and they must be rigidly upheld.

First-generation women take an enormous pride in their homes and in 'looking after' their families. The immaculate condition, inside and out, of Italian houses is a noticeable aspect of many areas of English towns. The traditional areas of Italian residence in Bedford (Queen's Park and Castle Road), Peterborough (Stanground) and Nottingham (Lenton) all retain many members of the first generation. Often the distinctive condition of their homes as well as one or two tell-tale ethnic signs make them instantly recognisable. Sheds and garages are used for making and storing wine, gardens are used for growing vegetables rather than flowers, colourful but well maintained paintwork on window and door frames is preferred, exterior string curtains are hung on front doors, wrought iron work is often extensively used, and finally in the larger Italian Communities where there are Italian bakeries a shopping bag can often be seen hanging from a side or back door. Delivery of the large loaf of Italian bread is made early in the morning by way of the shopping bag. Fresh milk is not delivered to Italians. The best way to make *caffelatte* in the morning is with long-life milk.

In addition to full-time jobs, often with much overtime in factories, first-generation women have run their homes to these exceptionally high standards and looked after their children at the same time, completely single-handedly. In the first generation, because of the traditional value system, there was absolutely no question of first-generation males helping with the household chores or the raising of the children. In the cuisine of the migrants everything is prepared from fresh ingredients and therefore involves a certain amount of time and work. People simply would not dream of buying 'fast foods' and are very concerned about the quality and the naturalness of the food they consume. For the women though, in order to be ready with an evening meal, this often involves getting up early in the morning to make some preparation before going to work.

Tradition requires a large family lunch on Sunday. Three or four main courses are typical, often with extra appetisers such as olives, and digestives such as nuts and fruit, *torrone* and coffee. If fresh *pasta* is to be made, perhaps for up to ten people, which is not uncommon, the woman must rise at 6 a.m. in order to have time for all the necessary preparation. The reward of having the family happily gathered together makes the effort worth while. In general, however, the lives of these women have, in the past, consisted of a great deal more work, of one kind or another, than leisure or play of any kind. Leisure activity, however, is not an accepted concept in southern Italian society for women. The social groups which emerged there were based around 'doing something', for example sewing groups. Idle hands were not approved of for women.

The lives of the first-generation women became organised around work. However, the workplace often offered an opportunity for a new kind of socialisation. This was certainly true in Bedford, for example, where until the mid 1980s hundreds of first-generation Italian women were employed at the Meltis factory, and to a lesser extent at Texas Instruments. Production line work allowed chatting and acquisition of new 'friends'. In the 'mixed' Italian Communities of England and Wales, where there are few large *paesani* groups and people were forced to get to know 'outsiders', it has been through work contacts that *compari* have been found.

At the Community level, there are no places for women to gather and socialise. The wash-house of the village, the major social centre exclusively for women, has no equivalent in urban England. The main opportunity for socialisation has undoubtedly become the weddings and dinner dances. Italians, particularly women, attend church on a Sunday partly for social reasons and to keep in touch. Women do go shopping and they use their local Italian shop to meet and chat, albeit briefly.

In most Italian Communities there is little residential clustering; after the early days of immigration, families have tended to spread out from the initial areas of settlement. Even in the largest Italian Communities no particular streets can be identified which are exclusively, or almost exclusively, Italian. But even in areas where there are several Italian families, *campanilismo* may come into play and prohibit women from talking to their neighbours.

In sum, we can appreciate the longing to return to Italy; women particularly have had hard lives because of their emigration. They remember Italy as the land of their childhood, their parents, sun and happiness. Of course they see it with rose-tinted glasses and forget the reasons that forced them to leave. But Italy has changed and, as we know, has outstripped Britain in economic growth (*il sorpasso*). First-generation Italians with a *nostalgia* for Italy see a way of life there today very much preferable to the one they

217

lead in England when they make their return visits in the summer. First-generation women of the southern Italian communities are the least contented perhaps of all the Italians in Britain today. They are the living embodiment of the difficulty and sadness of emigration.

First-generation men

Compared with women, men of the first generation have more life and more group activities available to them. Men are considerably more mobile than women: most of them can drive and have a car, have more places to go and are less psychologically imprisoned in social terms. They too work hard, but the demands on their free time have been considerably less.

Men, unlike women, are permitted to indulge in leisure time. Women as women do not meet as pre-organised groups in each other's homes. Men on the other hand do; they gather in the houses of *paesani* and other social contacts to play cards, watch something of interest on television such as a football match, or simply to chat, for example about the forthcoming wine-making season. Men as well as women make use of their local Italian shop as a social centre, as well as to buy ethnic products. Men, however, are allowed the luxury of loitering in groups, and 'going to the shop' on no other mission than to meet up with other men is permissible. The social function of the shop is thus in many ways greater for the men than it is for the women, even although it is women who buy the food.

At the Community level, if there is no equivalent of the wash-house for the women, there is no institution similar to the *piazza* or the *cantina* as meeting-places for the numerous male groups. There are, however, more places for men to gather outside the home, such as the Italian clubs, English working men's clubs and inevitably that unique British institution, the pub. The annual wine-making is a major recreational activity for men requiring much debate and co-operation. In addition to this mainly agricultural activity preserved by the southern Italians in the towns of England, many men have allotments on the outskirts of towns where they grow vegetables for the family's consumption. This too is now as much recreational as functional, particularly for the first-generation men who are often retired.

Given the segregation of the sexes, social visiting by married couples in other people's homes is somewhat rare. Small gatherings of couples of *paesani* and *compari* do occur, however, at home in the evenings. But, once under way, these gatherings follow the pattern of segregation with the men in one room playing cards, and wives in another chatting and watching television (which is always 'on' in the evenings in the Italian households) and waiting to serve food, wine and coffee to the men when they request it. Even at home, women never seem to relax; they are always busy and, in the presence of guests, will sit on the arm of a chair ready to prepare food or drinks.

Second-generation boys

Some of the family aspects of life for the second generation were discussed earlier. The 'peer group' or clique of friends was mentioned. Let us now see how these operate. The 'peer group' is important for the second generation, especially for males. The second generation tended to create their own life with their own values, codes and morality. Soon after going to school, cliques, gangs and male-only social groups formed.

The freedom accorded to boys compared with girls has already been mentioned. It is through friendship with their peers that this freedom finds expression. Young men have numerous places to gather, including the Italian 'pool-clubs', and the Italian youth clubs. The Italian five-a-side football teams of the popular Anglo Italian Football League has spawned a national network involving over 600 people. Most boys 'do' something, and hobbies and interests are considerable, although there is an almost universal obsession with cars. Conspicuous consumption related to cars and clothes is widespread and the 'image' of these young men, based often on their ethnicity, including driving red Italian cars, is often a priority. The conspicuous red Alfa Romeo cars with Italian emblems and flags indicating their ethnicity are very popular. Few achieve the required level of economic success to acquire the Ferrari *Testarossa* to which many aspire.

At weddings and dinners and dances within the Community, the young males are a prominent feature, physically and psychologically attached to their peer group rather than their family. They arrive late and remain together clustered at certain strategic points within the hall, usually the bar.

Second-generation girls

In total contrast to the male peer groups which are independent and can be relatively large, the position of girls within the Community structure is relatively weak and invisible. Friendship cliques do form during school days and may be maintained into late adolescence and after marriage, but in comparison with those of the boys they are small in membership and

219

restricted in social remit. The movement of girls is more controlled by their parents, and in any case, perhaps because of this, girls have nowhere to gather, nowhere to go as girls. They are not as a consequence members of large peer groups; at most, outside the family circle, each girl has two or three close female friends upon whom she relies for her socialisation. Often, as we have seen, friends are cousins or *comare*. The social life of the young Italian girl is based around the family, visiting her friends and by being visited by them, at home and under the supervision of parents. Because of this limited social environment and controls built into it, young girls of the second generation have very few interests and 'do' very little.

The great difficulties faced by girls in meeting members of the opposite sex were discussed earlier. The main complication derives from the fact that girls are not 'allowed out' and if a boy enters the house his involvement is irreversible. Active males of the second generation established youth clubs in the 1960s and 1970s in many Italian Communities in England. (See Plate 13.) Even where these came under the auspices of the Italian mission, as was often the case, they were not considered suitable for girls since parents, who were not usually invited to attend, did not in any case understand the concept. Only parents who were more far-seeing and perhaps more urban in their origin tended to allow daughters to attend. Permission to attend the classes of the *doposcuola* was, however, more readily given. As parents saw Italian slip out of use by their children most were strongly in favour of these after-school classes which taught Italian language to their children. For girls these classes were enormously popular in the 1970s since they were a social escape hatch which had parental approval. Fathers were extremely protective, however, and would ferry girls to and from these classes by car, allowing no opportunity for any deviation.

Like their male counterparts, Italian girls are attracted by consumerism and the popular cultures of the day and they display an inordinate interest in popular fashions and clothes. One of their main opportunities to 'dress up' is for Sunday mass. They, however, unlike their male counterparts who loiter outside waiting to attract the attention of the girls, actually attend the service. Friendships can tentatively be formed and conversations struck up in the crowd which develops outside after the mass, particularly at the Italian churches of St Peter's, London, Santa Francesca, Bedford and San Giuseppe, Peterborough.

With a clear picture now in mind of the occupational structure of the Community, the geographical origins in Italy, the family and the way of life in the 'old' and 'new' Communities, we are now ready to contemplate the institutions and overall organisational structure of the Italians in Britain.

Chapter Eight

Institutions of the Community

Introduction

The overall level of institutional development within the British Italian Community is varied and striking. The structure of these institutions and organisations represent two types of development: those which have grown organically from within the Communities and those which have been implanted by external bodies. With over 150 years of Italian presence there are several very old institutions such as St Peter's Italian Church in Clerkenwell, the *Mazzini Garibaldi Club* in Bloomsbury and the Italian Catholic Society in Manchester. In addition, there is the Italian diplomatic and consular presence which has a remarkable geographic spread across the country and which sustains hundreds of diplomats and bureaucrats in its employ.

Then there is a nationwide network of clubs, circles and associations, many of which are extremely active and which form the main internal structure to the Community. The Italian Welfare Agencies, which have grown up since 1965 and are attached to the various political parties in Italy, work mainly within the 'new' Communities where the industrial work-forces grew up. These, together with the Italian missionary priests and new churches, provide a remarkable degree of institutional completeness for the Italians. There is no doubt that because of this highly developed and ever evolving structure the Italian Community has been able to maintain its identity and to retain contact with Italy. A review of these Community institutions, both old and new, completes our study.

Italian authorities

The Italian diplomatic and consular presence in Britain is considerable. It ranges from the Embassy in Grosvenor Square, Mayfair; the Institute of

Culture in Belgrave Square; the Military Attaché in Ebury Street; the two Consulate Generals in London and Edinburgh, through a well-organised hierarchical structure of Consulates, Vice-Consulates, consular Agencies down to a plethora of consular Correspondents nationwide. The Embassy itself has little to do with the Italian Community although the Ambassador attends many Community events as a guest of honour. The rank of the Consul General is normally equivalent to that of the First Councillors at the Embassy, responsible for the various briefs and departments of which consular affairs is one.

Let us now look at the consular structure and the other departments of the diplomatic presence which impact on the Italian Community.

Consular organisation

It is with the consular structure that Italians have most frequent contact. Its importance to the Italian Community is considerable because of the complex nature of Italian bureaucracy. The consular authority takes care of the administrative and bureaucratic needs involved in regularising the legal and civil positions of Community members under British and Italian law. The paperwork involved, even in simple procedures, is onerous and can often take a long time to complete. Residency, property, land owner-ship and transferrals within the family, registration of births, deaths and marriages in Italy, military service exemption papers, return migration are all dealt with by the various consular offices. There is also a welfare department which handles social problems and most importantly procur-ing pensions, old age and other types, from Italy.

In addition to the administrative services there are also education departments. These organise, fund and supply teachers for Italian lan-guage and culture tuition to Italian children. This continued contact with, and commitment to, the children and the grandchildren of the migrants is, for the Community, perhaps the most important area of consular activity since this teaching helps ensure continuity of contact with the mother tongue and culture through the generations. Tuition occurs both within and outside the main curriculum at local schools up and down the country. There are education offices in London, Birmingham, Bedford, Manchester, Nottingham and Edinburgh. Hundreds of teachers are employed, each of whom cover several schools or areas, travelling between them to conduct the Italian lessons two or three times a week.

In conjunction with the consular education structure, a number of semi-voluntary bodies and parents' committees have grown up. The consulative committees are registered charities and work closely with the consular authorities. They are organised by the *Co.As.It.* In the London consular jurisdiction there are 43 schools committees, made up of parents and teachers, indicating the high level of Community support for, and involvement in, the Italian language tuition. These are organised by FASFA.

The organisation and distribution of consular offices across the country reflects the location and concentration of Italians and also the changing character of the Community with closures and openings of consular offices. For example, as we know from Chapter 2 and the Italian Diplomatic Year Book of 1887, Liverpool was the main Consulate General outside London. During the 1970s the Consulates in Liverpool, Glasgow and Cardiff closed, with a centralisation at this level of bureaucratic presence in Edinburgh and Manchester. Further down the hierarchy, the number of consular Agents and Correspondents has increased, reflecting the wide geographic distribution of the 'new' Communities.

Map Five illustrates the structure and organisation of the Italian consular presence in Britain today. There are the two Consulate Generals, one in London and one in Edinburgh; one Consulate in Manchester; one diplomatic Vice-Consulate in Bedford; four honorary Vice Consulates in Aberdeen, Glasgow, Nottingham and Birmingham; 14 Agencies and 42 Correspondents. At the Correspondent level, the people who carry out these services are volunteers, often Community leaders, and in one case an Italian missionary priest (*Padre* Silvano Bertapelle of Woking). They do an enormous amount of work within the Italian Community for their fellow compatriots and although they have no signatory powers in terms of issuing or renewing documents, they act as brokers between the Italians and the Consulate authorities. These individuals are generally very highly regarded in their own Communities.

Such praise is not achieved by the Italian Consulates themselves. In the mind of the ordinary Italian resident in Britain, the Italian Consulates are synonymous with the Italian government. While the physical presence of the Consulates is valued, very few people among the rank and file of the Italian Community have any real understanding of the actual operation of the consular service and how it is constrained by London, by both the Consulate General and the Embassy, and how these in turn are constrained by *Roma*. Severe criticism of the Consulates, and of the individuals who work within the system, is widespread. The anthropologist and Italian missionary, *Padre* Bruno Bottignolo, in his book on the Italian Community in the Bristol area, reported in 1985 that the Italian

MAP FIVE: ITALIAN CONSULAR ORGANISATION IN GREAT BRITAIN

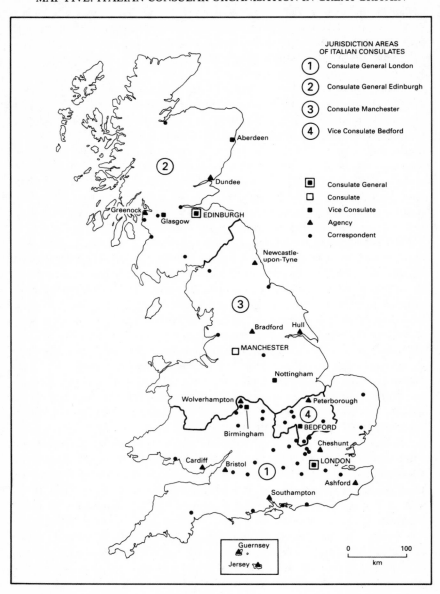

immigrants were critical of the various Italian institutions but especially of the Consulate, towards which no criticism was spared.

In Bedford the attitude to the Vice-Consulate is similar. When over 100 Italian people were asked if they thought the Vice-Consulate did a good or a bad job for the Community, not a single person, either of the first or the second generation, responded in a positive manner and some were highly critical.[1] The main complaint centred around the complicated procedures and the long delays in resolution of various bureaucratic matters. Most people, however, answered passively, saying that the Vice-Consulate 'did nothing' but at the same time implying that they did not expect it to 'do anything' for the Italian Community. The migrants fail to understand, of course, that the Vice-Consulate in Bedford is essentially a bureaucratic presence and that it has no decision-making powers of its own. It can take no real independent initiatives which might help or benefit its particular local Italian population with its own particular set of circumstances and needs. Nor does the Vice-Consulate have a budget independent from the Consulate General in London; all policy decisions must first be approved higher up the administrative ladder, and possibly by the Ministry of Foreign Affairs in *Roma*. The migrants thus, rightly from their point of view, see the Vice-Consulate as a rather ineffectual, even uninterested, administrative presence.

From the point of view of the Italian authorities, on the other hand, the problems are often intractable. Shortages of quality personnel, cramped premises, particularly in London, and control from *Roma* mean that even a very active and dedicated Consul General has very little room for manoeuvre. Policy and procedure are enmeshed in a grand bureaucratic web which requires conformity and standardisation.

Particularly enthusiastic Consuls can, however, take initiatives, some of which have produced extremely successful results. Two examples of this type of activity were, firstly, a conference organised in 1985 by *Console Generale* Marsili of Edinburgh, in conjunction with the local education authorities, to discuss the 'Scottish Italian Community: its Language and its Culture'. This two-day symposium brought together experts from various fields, not only from Scotland but from all over Britain and also Italy: sociologists, historians, educationalists, linguists and Italophiles. The publication of the conference proceedings was highly acclaimed and the general feeling was that, after over 100 years of settlement by Italians in Scotland, such a meeting to assess the current situation was very worthwhile. In the absence of such a gathering, no documented assessment of the Italian Community in Scotland would exist. Secondly, an exhibition of photographs and its accompanying booklet, organised by *Console* Mercuri and the Committee of Italian Emigration *Co.Em.It.* of Manchester in 1990, was enormously successful not only within the Italian Community but within the city as a whole. By visual presentation, the history of the Manchester Community was articulated and recorded and its contribution to local history and development underlined.

One major initiative, currently under way and determined from *Roma*, is a census of all Italians resident abroad, an exercise not undertaken since 1933. In conjunction with this, and as an integral part of the work, the further computerisation of the Consulates is under way. Because of different sets of local problems, this operation is still in a piecemeal state and, as we have seen in Chapter 6, the Consulates are at varying levels of achievement and implementation within Britain.

European elections

The first European parliamentary elections were held in 1979 when Italian expatriate citizens, resident in EEC countries, were given the opportunity of voting for the Italian delegates to Brussels. The Italian consular authorities in Britain were responsible for the organisation of electoral constituencies and establishment of polling stations across the country in localities with concentrations of Italians. It was a colossal operation, the first of its kind, and in the pre-computerised era involved the Consulates of London, Edinburgh, Manchester and Bedford in lengthy preparation.

The 1984 and 1989 European elections were again major bureaucratic operations for the Consulates, involving the hiring of locally recruited personnel and the despatch of temporary help from the Ministry of Foreign Affairs in *Roma*. The organisation of these elections was chaotic; beyond a point, local Consuls had little control. Virtually all of the practical aspects of organisation were dictated from *Roma*, which attempted to standardise procedures throughout Europe. Three different government ministries were involved and instructions were often contradictory, resulting in muddle and confusion. The worst problem was the dependence on every town hall in Italy sending polling cards to the electorate in this country. Addresses were often incomplete, out of date, misspelt and incorrect, and thus never reached their destination. Although the Consulates themselves often had up-to-date details on the Italians under their jurisdiction, even by 1989 these had not been fully computerised into a workable system where they could be transmitted to the town halls. British Italians resigned themselves to the mistakes and inefficiency of *la burocrazia italiana* and the turn-out on both occasions was predictably low.

In addition to these operational problems, many of the issues seemed remote and inconsequential for the expatriate Italians, and although representatives from the various political parties did make campaign visits to the main Italian Communities in England, notably in London, Bedford and Peterborough, little enthusiasm could be engendered. This was particularly true where, as was often the case, no polling station had been established. The majority of people in small Italian Communities did not consider it worth the effort to travel to their nearest polling station, often some distance away.

It was, however, due to this involvement of the expatriate Communities in Italian national politics that a new attitude began to take root in political circles in Italy concerning the emigrants. Their potential as a political force in the national political arena was realised and a movement developed which sought to re-envelop the expatriate Communities, in a way which had not occurred since the 1930s.

The Italian committees

Since the time of Mussolini, there had been little serious attempt on the part of various Italian governments to involve the Italian Communities abroad in Italian affairs. After the Second World War, Communities once again became *abbandonate*. From 1979 and the first European elections, however, there began a fundamental change in attitude towards the emigrants partly because they were seen to be able to exert some influence on politics at home. The ideological movement which ensued was reflected in developments such as a new law which provided for the election of the Italian Committees in 1986 – a major initiative by the Italian government to recognise the expatriate Italian Communities.

In a unique experiment in international democracy, in November 1986 elections were held in 86 Italian Communities of the world (23 countries) for each to elect Committees of Italian Emigration (*Co.Em.It.*). The elections were organised by the Italian consular authorities and the Committees elected from the ranks of the Communities' populations. For the first time 'leaders' were officially recognised and their position given credence by formal election; they were given a mandate and the means to 'do something' for their Communities. The Committees were financed by the Ministry of Foreign Affairs and were to collaborate with the consular authorities and the Italian Communities in the organisation of new initiatives for the good of the Community as a whole.

As part of this reinvolvement in the Italian political arena and wish on the part of the Italian government to organise the Communities abroad, a major international conference was held in *Roma* in 1988 with the title *Italiani nel Mondo* – 'Italians of the World'. The conceptualisation was thus 'still Italian, but resident abroad'. Again the word 'emigrant', which implies a loss of current dialogue with the mother country, was abolished. The 1988 conference in bringing together leaders of Italian Communities from throughout the world, strengthened not only links between these individuals but also their confidence in the sense of belonging to the Italian Republic. One of the consequences of the conference was a decision to rename the *Co.Em.It.*, or emigration committees as Committees of Italians Abroad (*Com.It.Es.*).

In May 1991 the Committees were re-elected and are now known as *Com.It.Es.* There are four Committees in Britain – London, Bedford, Manchester and Scotland – one for each consular area (see Map 5). Each Committee has twelve members who represent various factions and sub-groups within the Communities. The candidates organised themselves along political, interest group, geographical and associational lines. For the London consular area there were 40 candidates in total, arranged in four 'lists'. The major list, which won over 50 per cent of the committee places, was the *Unione Associazioni Italiane* (Union of Italian Associations).

The consular area of Bedford presented 42 candidates, the Peterborough Community fielding its own list of 12 candidates. Manchester presented a total of 26 candidates in three lists, and Scotland 36. Interestingly, the main list of the Manchester area was called 'Italians of Europe'. The overall turn-out in 1986 had been 41 per cent of the electorate. In 1991 this had declined to 21 per cent. Over the five-year period of the *Co.Em.It.*, enthusiasm had waned a little in the Community, and the Committees increasingly became seen as ineffectual. The budget, scope and potential of the *Com.It.Es.* has, however, been widened and the leaders are hopeful of being more effective and thus inspiring more Community participation in the next five-year term.

A milestone for the Italian Community in Britain was the visit of President Cossiga of Italy in November 1990. After a state visit, lasting three days, President Cossiga met with the Italian Communities in London at the Grosvenor House Hotel, as guest of Lord Forte and then at the City Chambers in Glasgow. On both occasions many coach loads of Italians assembled from outlying and smaller Italian Communities. The London event was especially successful with more than 1,500 Italians present.

President Cossiga gave a long and often rousing speech in which he spoke knowledgeably on the history of the Italian connection in Britain but in which he also debated the continuing ties and contacts that the migrants had with Italy. He was keen to impart the 'We are all Italians' ideology, now prevalent in Italian government circles. The president of the *Com.It.Es.* (then *Co.Em.It.*), Lorenzo Losi, made an impassioned and highly political speech, demonstrating the fact that there are a number of 'live issues' with which Italians in England are concerned. For example, the necessity to return personally to Italy for participation in local and national government elections and also the fact that Italians in this country have no political voice even at local government level.

In Glasgow, although there was an equally warm and enthusiastic response from the Scottish Italians to President Cossiga, the speeches focused on the historic, nostalgic and integration aspects of the Community. There was no indication from either President Cossiga or the gathered Italians that the relationship with Italy was current, political or symbiotic.

The Italian Institute of Culture

The Italian Institute of Culture has two autonomous offices in Britain: one in London, the other in Edinburgh. The London Institute was opened in 1950, the purchase of the building in Belgrave Square made possible by the sale of the Charing Cross Road *fascio* after the War. The Edinburgh Institute was an off-shoot of the London operation until 1988 when it gained its autonomy.

The remit of the Cultural Attaché is to bring Italian art, literature and culture to Britain and the British people. There has not tradionally been much interface or interaction between the Institute and the Italian Community. This has changed in recent years, but actual policy depends very much on the Italian Ambassador of the day. Both Institutes run extremely interesting and varied programmes of events throughout the year including exhibitions, talks, book launches, small round-table talks and discussions, concerts and other arts-related entertainments. The general change in attitude towards the Italian Community can be witnessed by the encouragement given to young Anglo and Scottish Italian artists such as the 'light sculptor' Umberto Di Zenzo in London and the painter Claudia Petretti in Edinburgh, both of whom were given exhibitions in 1990. Similarly, many initiatives have been taken in London between the Institute and the associations of the Italian Community. In this way many ordinary Italians of the London Community entered the rather grand building at 39 Belgrave Square.

The only other time Italians in London gather at the Institute is for the annual *Festa della Repubblica*. This event has become the most important social and patriotic venue for the Community when its leaders and prominent members gather to celebrate Italy's National Day. The *festa* at the Institute is different from the parallel events which take place elsewhere. In London, the Embassy fulfils the diplomatic function and at the event guests are in the majority non-Italian, representing other Embassies and many British institutions. At the Consulates in Edinburgh, Manchester and Bedford, invited guests to the *Festa della Repubblica* are again mainly local dignitaries, personalities and representatives with only a smaller number of Community representatives present. These are, in effect, local versions of the national event at the Italian Embassy in Grosvenor Square. The *festa* at the Institute in London, organised by the Consul General, is therefore unique as the guests are exclusively Italian. Many people travel from the outlying areas of the London Consulate's geographical jurisdiction, such as Swansea, Wolverhampton, Jersey and Guernsey. It is seen as an important date in the calendar and a good opportunity to maintain and renew contacts.

The Italian ethnic church

This section discusses the Italian churches and missionary presences in Britain and assesses their role within the Italian Community. It is the ethnic church which more than any other institution preserves the culture of the Italians. It is the custodian of the language, and the religious artefacts symbolise a certain culture, tradition and way of life. In order to understand fully why this is so, let us begin with a little history on the Catholic Church in general which will help to explain how and where the Italians fit into this structure.

Given that it was only in 1829 that the Catholic population of Britain was re-embraced into mainstream society with the passing of a law which allowed Catholics their civil rights – to vote, to enter parliament and to occupy almost all public offices – it is not surprising that until then Catholicism had retained a persecution complex and a secretive air. From 1829 onwards, the religion was able to develop religious orders and diffuse with a new missionary spirit throughout the country, restoring its hierarchy and following.

The Italian presence and connection was to prove instrumental in this movement to normalise Catholicism in Britain. The importance of the procession of the *Madonna del Carmine* was mentioned at the end of Chapter 1. The most noted Italian religious men who helped work towards the rebirth of British Catholicism were Luigi Gentile (1801–48) who arrived in England with his colleague *Padre* Pagani in 1835, Blessed Domenico Barberi (1792–1849) and Fathers Raffaele Melia and Giuseppe Faà who founded St Peter's Italian Church. These men, together with Cardinal Newman and the Oxford Movement, helped to open up the Church again and draw it nearer to the Anglican Church. From the 1840s, however, the Irish influence became increasingly dominant on the indigenous Catholic Church. This, as well as other local factors, had a significant effect on how the Italian ethnic church developed in Britain.

It is an interesting question why Catholic immigrants to countries with established Catholic minorities, such as the United States, Australia and Great Britain have, with differing degrees of success, felt the need to form their own separate national or ethnic parishes. The fact is that social community and religion are closely related to, and reflected in, each other. Religion becomes a restatement on a mystical plane, where the most basic traits of social organisation are made sacred and put beyond question. Religious expression is then a projection of the social structure of a community which provides at the same time a context of meaning for man's actions, experiences, frustrations and anxieties. It therefore follows that, since religion and social community are inter-linked, as long as any given community, such as an immigrant group, remains a distinct social entity, it will tolerate only its own kind of religion. The church of an ethnic group, threatened with the loss of its identity, serves more than any other institution to organise and maintain the group as a functioning community.

As a result of the mass immigrations to the United States during the second half of the nineteenth century, even a Church which is as international as the Catholic Church had, in that period, to weather severe conflicts between the various Catholic sub-groups, who displayed religious antagonism due to their ethnic differences. The establishment of an ethnic church is not only dependent on a large and cohesive ethnic community, which feels the need for the establishment of its own church, but also on the attitude of the indigenous Catholic hierarchy. Both Italian and Polish Catholics applied pressure to the existing American Catholic hierarchy, which was Irish-based and dominated, for the establishment of dioceses based not on territorial but on national lines.

The Italian immigrants and their priests, although not going as far as the Poles who severed from the main Catholic hierarchy, were from the 1880s onwards successful in establishing a number of Italian ethnic parishes in the United States. When the process of ethnic parish building was concluded, New York City, for example, had 74 Italian churches and the Catholic Directory for 1918 reported 580 Italian churches and chapels in the United States.

There were several reasons why the early attempts to incorporate the Italian Catholics into the existing Irish-based Catholic hierarchy failed. They were essentially two differing socio-religious systems which came into conflict. The cultural expressions of the faith common to Italians and Irish people were at opposing ends of the Catholic spectrum and therefore did not merge readily. Russo (1970), in his study of the religious acculturation of New York's Italians over three generations, listed the following characteristics of the dominant Irish-American Catholic establishment within which the Italian immigrants found themselves: it was English-speaking, Jansenistic, excessively reverential and loyal to the clergy, activist, conservative, very concerned with fund raising and pervaded with a super-nationalistic spirit identified with all things Irish.

By contrast, Italian Catholicism, particularly southern Italian Catholicism, was extremely casual and informal, personal and parochial. It was characterised by an intense devotional attitude to the *Madonna*, and to the saints. Excessive deference paid to statues and image worship was seen as idolatry and superstitious by the Irish, but this helped make Catholicism more comprehensible to the unlettered mind. These differences were sufficient to generate a resentment which often precluded co-operation between the two groups.

There are a number of similar traits in the development of, and the relationship between, the Italian ethnic church and the native Catholic hierarchy in Britain and those experienced in the United States. Although the Catholic Church in Britain is indigenous and was not founded and developed by Irish Catholics as it was in the United States, there is nevertheless a strong Irish influence, particularly in areas of high Irish immigration such as Liverpool and Glasgow. The main contention in Britain is not between Irish Catholicism and Italian Catholicism directly, but rather between the existing hierarchical structure which is Irish influenced, and the imported Italian Catholicism. Problems of cultural and social differences in worship and organisation are, however, apparent in this country. Italian Catholicism is considerably more relaxed than the indigenous British Catholic Church, while at the same time being more colourful and more ritualised.

In Britain, the local Catholic hierarchy has consistently tried to integrate the Italian immigrants into its structure and is traditionally and fundamentally opposed to the establishment of ethnic parishes and attempts at independence by the Italian missionary priests. *Padre*

Umberto Marin pointed out in his book *Italiani in Gran Bretagna* in 1975 that the statement of Vatican policy on the ethnic church published in *Exsul Familia* (from the Apostolic Constitution given by Pope Pius XII in 1952) has been largely ignored by the indigenous British Catholic hierarchy. This document, based on 80 years of involvement in, and study of, the religious consequences of migration, supported ethnic parish establishment in countries with immigrant Catholic populations. *Padre* Bruno Bottignolo (1985, p. 119) supported this view and summarised the stance of the Catholic hierarchy in the following way:

> *English religious officials show an attitude of benign tolerance in relation to the Italian missions. In any case they do not consider them necessary. For the English religious authorities, the Italian immigrants 'are like everybody else' and consequently there is no need to do anything special for them. They have at their disposal the same Catholic organisation, the same apostolate movement that the indigenous people have.*

The indigenous Catholic hierarchy is uncomfortable with Italian Catholicism and holds a rather critical view of the Italians' religious convictions and practices. As *Padre* Bottignolo (1985, p. 57) explained, according to English Catholics:

> *Italians did not go to mass every Sunday (which for the English Catholic is central to his faith), during the ritual they used to talk and laugh and in any case participated with little attention and devotion and finally used to give little money for the collection . . . the Catholicism of the Italians was rather superficial, vague, and perhaps even superstitious.*

The extreme devotion paid to the saints and some of the ritual and tradition that surround worship, particularly in the southern Italian Catholic tradition with exaggerated devotion to the dead, are examples of incompatible aspects of Italian Catholicism in the minds of the local hierarchy. In fact, these practices are discouraged by the Italian missionary priests, and the role of these traditions, which are central to the socio-religious aspect of the southern Italian culture, are often misunderstood. From the point of view of the Italian migrant in this country the English Catholic Church is not an institution with which he or she readily identifies. Added to this are the language difficulties inherent in participation since the Catholic

233

Church began to worship in the vernacular in 1964 in this country (Vatican Council Document on the Liturgy, promulgated 4 December 1963).

The less numerous and less geographically concentrated population of more heterogeneous Italian Catholics in this country compared with the United States has, in the light of the above, not made the desire for independence and autonomy any less important from the point of view of the Italian missionaries and migrants here.

As we saw in Chapter 1, the Italian Church of St Peter's was established in 1864 and owed its existence to the high absolute number of Italians who were at that time clustered in Clerkenwell. This church is entirely independent of the local Catholic hierarchy and is the only Italian church to have a national parish status. As indicated in Chapters 1 and 3, the presence of the Italian Church and priests formed not only a spiritual service to the Italian Community but also took care of a vast range of social and welfare activities. For the immigrant arriving into the alien environment, the presence of Italian priests, who were usually better educated than the immigrants and who were prepared to act as social workers and mediators, was a very comforting phenomenon. This was just as true for the post-Second World War Italian immigrants as it was for the immigrants of the nineteenth century.

The first Italian missionary priests who came to minister to the 'new' immigrants began to arrive in the 1950s. They were crucial in setting up the institutional and organised life and they initiated the procedures to establish bureaucratic links between the Community and the encapsulating society, as well as links with the Italian authorities. In short, they acted as social workers. With the build-up of the 'new' Communities, three new Italian churches were established in the 1960s. These were:

(1) San Giuseppe, Peterborough 1962;
(2) Santa Francesca Cabrini, Bedford 1965;
(3) Chiesa del Redentore, Brixton, London 1969.

All three new churches were founded by the *Scalabrini* missionary fathers who minister to Italian emigrants throughout the world. The churches have their own premises in the form of a parish church, parish rooms or hall, day nursery and social club, but are only semi-autonomous since they remain under the jurisdiction of their respective diocese. The parishes have some degree of jural autonomy and are ethnically rather than territorially based. Appointments of the *Scalabrini*, although sanctioned in *Roma*, have to be approved by the respective bishops in these areas. The Italian priests at these churches also have responsibility for the surrounding areas and they therefore cover wide-ranging geographical territories in order to minister to the Italian Communities. Co-operation from the existing hierarchy is therefore essential since the Italian priests must negotiate to use their churches and facilities.

All of the major life-cycle events, most of which are ritualised through church ceremony – formal engagements to be married being the only exception – provide the main opportunity for the extended family, often separated geographically by migration, to reunite. All of these events are steeped in ritual and tradition and it is mainly in this area that differences between British and Italian Catholicism are highly visible. Each ceremony provides the occasion for the meeting of a large body of persons who are either blood relatives or relatives by marriage. Such occasions very often offer the means for more distant relatives to remain in contact with each other, as well as for younger members of the family to learn the names of, and to meet personally, those who make up the kinship network into which they were born and which will become increasingly important to them in their own social life.

San Giuseppe, Peterborough

Italian priests first arrived in Peterborough in 1956 and said mass for the Italians in hired halls and private rooms. At this time the Community was clustered in the town centre around Gladstone Street. In 1962, the Scalabrini fathers purchased an old school and converted it into a church. It was named after the patron saint of workers, San Giuseppe. By 1991 over 3,000 christenings of second-generation Community members had been carried out there. As we shall see below, from this church an annual procession of saints occurs. Now the Scalabrini fathers also say mass at St Anthony's Church in the Fletton area of Peterborough where many Italians are resident.

Santa Francesca, Bedford

On 28 March 1965 the Italian church in Bedford, Santa Francesca, was officially consecrated. Appropriately, the church was dedicated to Santa Francesca Cabrini, who is the patron saint, or 'mother', of Italian emigrants. Canonised in 1948, this remarkable woman devoted her life (1850–1917) to helping Italian immigrants in America until her death in Chicago. Although most of the money raised to build the church was collected from within the local Bedford Italian Community, money devoted to the shrine of Santa Francesca in Rhode Island in the United States was

235

sent to Bedford to help with the building costs. The location of Santa Francesca near the town centre reflects the initial area of residence of the town's Italian population.

That the Italian Community in Bedford was able to fund the creation of its own parish church, a church which has become the showpiece of the British post-war Italian Community, was a remarkable achievement. This accomplishment proved both the growing economic stability of the group and its commitment to the migrant situation as well as the centrality of this socio-religious institution in southern Italian culture. The church is the rock upon which the Community is founded. It is around the key aspects of the life-cycle ritual – birth, first communion, confirmation, marriage and death – that the social traditions of the Community find expression and are formally institutionalised. (The actual operation of these events and the *comparaggio* have already been described in Chapter 7.)

In 1990 Santa Francesca celebrated its 25th anniversary and held a weekend of celebrations within the Community attended by the Italian and local Bedford authorities alike.

Chiesa del Redentore, London

South of the River Thames this church, together with the *Centro Scalabrini* from where the British Italian fortnightly newspaper, *La Voce degli Italiani*, is published, provides a focus for the Italians resident in this area of London.

First opened in 1969, the church and centre underwent a complete renovation in 1978 and was officially reopened by the Archbishop of Southwark. The church serves mainly the 'new' immigrants of London who are not necessarily resident in the area but feel it is more 'their church' than the Italian Church in Clerkenwell which is steeped in the historical tradition of the 'old' Community. No procession, however, has been inaugurated at the Redentore Church and for this annual event all Italians must look to the *Madonna del Carmine* and St Peter's.

The missionary priests

The other 14 missionaries and chaplains stationed across the country are without their own churches and must negotiate with the local hierarchy for the use of premises to say mass and hold other meetings. Most have wide geographical territories to cover and only periodically visit some towns in order to say a mass for Italians who are more scattered and seldom come together. The priests are based within the larger Italian

Communities and from this central point they conduct their mission. Of the 14 missionary presences eight are in London, their location reflecting the current geographical distribution of the capital's Italian population. The exception is Mons. Giuseppe Blanda who is based at St Patrick's in Soho Square where, as we saw in Chapter 3, there has been an Italian chaplain since the early part of this century. His work is now mainly with young Italians arriving in London at his *Centro Giovanile Italiano* rather than any locally resident Italian population.

The other six missionaries are in Birmingham, Bradford, Glasgow, Manchester, Nottingham and Woking. All cover large territories, particularly *Padre* Zorza in Glasgow whose parish is the whole of Scotland and who therefore spends a good deal of time travelling to visit Italian families as far north as Inverness and Dingwall. *Padre* Morone in Nottingham does not have such a large territorial area to cover, but he is solely responsible for large Italian Communities in Nottingham, Derby, Chesterfield, Scunthorpe, Leicester, Loughborough and Burton on Trent. Similarly, *Padre* Gonella in Bradford ministers to Italians in several towns of the north of England including Bradford, Halifax, Huddersfield, Keighley, Leeds, Sheffield and Shipley.

The saints, Madonnas and processions

The procession of the *Madonna del Carmine* and that of the *Madonna del Rosario*, mentioned in Chapters 1 and 2, continue today and are the major annual events for the Italian Communities in both London and Manchester. Both events continue to attract large numbers of people and the London procession has in fact grown in recent years. This growth in London has been due to the popularity of constructing 'floats' depicting various biblical or religious scenes and themes in general. Also many of the associations now participate. There has in fact been an increase in the number of statues and portraits of saints of particular village, province and regional groups which join the procession. Also, the *festa* of the *Madonna del Carmine* follows the traditional Italian pattern in that the religious pageantry is followed by a range of social activities – the *festa*.

Over the years, this day of festivities has been held in many locations around Back Hill; in parks, vacant lots and open ground where buildings had been demolished. In 1990 the *festa* returned to its traditional location in Warren Road, behind the church and under Rosebery Avenue. Here, up to 50 stalls and thousands of people congregated on a hot summer's day. Again at the *festa* many of the associations are responsible for putting

237

up stalls and particular areas of expertise have developed. For example, the *Alpini* always run a coconut shy and the *Veneti* are known for their wonderful *salsicci*. Other stalls are put up by well-known Italian businesses who offer bargains and a range of competitions and prizes. The general atmosphere is highly ethnic and closely reproduces the general ambience of the Italian village *festa*.

The Manchester procession is part of the Whit Walk in which many other Catholics of the city participate. The procession is not followed by a *festa*. The number of people involved is fewer and a more religious atmosphere has been maintained – there are no floats. The women and young girls who follow the statue, which is magnificently decorated with arum lilies, continue to dress in the traditional *Ciociaria* costume. In the 1950s a small statue of Sant' Antonio was added to the procession to encourage the participation of children. This statue is borne by young boys who thus become involved with the tradition, the hope being that they will remain involved through adulthood.

The routes followed by the processions in London and Manchester trace out the old Italian quarters: Clerkenwell and Ancoats. Few Italians live in these areas today and the territorial delineation no longer has any meaning. This is particularly true in Manchester where not only is there no longer any residential concentration of Italians in the area, but St Michael's is no longer the Catholic church used by the Italians of the city. Thus the statue of the *Madonna del Rosario* is kept in storage and only brought out on the occasion of the procession. The Italian Church in London, on the other hand, still very much forms the emotional and ritualistic centre of the Italian Community in London, with several thousands of Italians visiting on a weekly basis.

The building of Santa Francesca in Bedford was not considered complete by the town's Italian population until statues of the village patron saints had been housed. The village saints form an integral part of the traditional form of worship. There are seven statues of saints in the Italian church in Bedford. Four of these represent the patron saints of four of the major sending villages: San Lorenzo of *Busso* (Cb); Sant'Antonio of *Montefalcione* (Av); Sant'Angelo of *Sant'Angelo Muxaro* (Ag) and San Ciriaco of *Buonvicino* (Cs). A fifth statue also depicts a *paese* patron saint, Santa Lucia of *Cava dei Tirreni* (Sa), but its presence is idiosyncratic since it was paid for by a single *padrone* rather than by a group of villagers. The other two statues are San Giuseppe, which was added in 1983, and Santa Francesca Cabrini, the patron saint of emigrants, after whom the church is named. The presence of the first four of these statues in the church can be attributed to the organisational and co-operational abilities, based on the sense of *campanilismo*, of the *paesani* from these villages. (It was estimated by the priest that each statue cost, in the 1970s, between £1,000 and £1,500.) The patron saint of *Castelluccio* (Fg), San Giovanni Battista, is represented in a painting in the baptistry of Santa Francesca.

A *festa*, following the tradition of the southern Italian village, which combines religious celebration with general festivities, takes place annually in Bedford on the last Sunday of August, which is a bank holiday weekend. In the early history of the church many inter-*paese* disputes focused on arranging a date for the *festa*. Rather than attempt to organise several individual events, agreement was reached to hold a joint *festa* for the saints represented in Bedford; the event is in fact called '*Festa* of the Patron Saints'. It is, however, not entirely coincidental that the end of August is the *festa* time of Sant' Antonio of *Montefalcione*, given that the *Montefalcionesi* have always been active on the *festa* committee in Bedford and this saint is becoming the patron saint of the Community as a whole.

The *festa* in Bedford comprises two major parts: the procession of saints and church ceremony (or *sagra*), and a dance and other social activities which take place in the evening. The statues are mounted on purpose-built carriers for the procession and are borne out of the church in a set order at around 5 p.m. on Sunday. The priests of Santa Francesca and perhaps from some other Italian churches are usually supported by the presence of an eminent member of the local English Catholic hierarchy, such as the Canon of the diocese, but not usually the Bishop of Northampton. These men head the procession and are robed in full ecclesiastical dress for the occasion. The pilgrims have been declining in numbers throughout the 1980s and very few young people were participating by the early 1990s. Nevertheless a turn-out of 500 or so is still usual.

In Peterborough a procession of saints is held on the feast day of Sant' Antonio, 13 June. Four statues are involved: Sant' Antonio, San Giuseppe, San Gerrardo and a *Madonna*. The pilgrims normally number around 500 evenly distributed behind the statues with a slight preference for Sant' Antonio. Again a *festa* is held in the early evening.

The southern Italian practice of segregation of the sexes amongst the pilgrims is seen in both Bedford and Peterborough. The women, who are often dressed in black, bear colourful *paese* banners depicting their saint or some aspect of local tradition, and follow behind the statue and the men. The men congregate around the statues, awaiting the honour of shouldering the weight of the statue. It is the custom in the south of Italy

239

for money to be pinned to the statue as it passes along the route. This practice has been discouraged by the Scalabrini fathers who feel that the gesture would be misunderstood by observers and even the local Catholic hierarchy. The offering of gold jewellery still occurs, however, and, in both towns, many items of gold are normally visible on a satin cushion placed on the statue of Sant' Antonio.

Scotland

The Italians in Scotland although significant in numbers, especially in the early part of this century, never succeeded in setting up their own church or even chapel. As we saw in Chapters 2 and 3, in Glasgow the Italians were clustered in the Garnethill area of the city. The existence of the Italianate Jesuit church, St Aloysius, obviated the need to set up a meeting place in culturally sympathetic surroundings. The nature of the occupational structure of the Italians led to the dispersal of them not only to small towns, but also throughout Glasgow and Edinburgh. Because of the long hours involved in these small businesses, there was not a great deal of free time for social activities, or the social aspect of religion. In any event we have seen that by the 1930s the *fasci* had monopolised the social activities of the Italian Communities, gathering everything under the same umbrella, both ideologically and physically.

There is, however, in the Scottish context a further factor which needs to be mentioned, that of Scots Presbyterianism. The general effect of this extreme version of Protestantism on the indigenous Catholic Church, which had become almost exclusively Irish dominated, especially in the west of Scotland, was to push Catholicism to an extreme position also. In Glasgow in particular there exists considerable tension between Protestants and Catholics. In a country which in any case has not experienced large-scale immigration of the coloured ethnic minorities, the main tension within society continues to be of a religious rather than a racial nature. The Irish Catholic population, in the minority, lives with a high level of institutionalised religious racism.

Irish Catholicism, as noted earlier, in its Hibernian tradition is very different from the more relaxed Italian Catholicism. Resentment to Italian missionary priests from the local ecclesiastical structure has been particularly pronounced in Scotland where the local Catholic hierarchy, in the face of Presbyterianism, has been at pains to calvinise Catholicism. The cult of the saints was destroyed during the Reformation. For example, the procession of St Giles in Edinburgh, down the High Street every

1 September, was one of the most famous in Europe. During the Reformation, the statue of St Giles was thrown into a sewer, never to be resurrected. Unlike in America, Australia, England and most of Europe, the Italians in Scotland have been incorporated into the existing hierarchy, or, as in the case of many, have lost touch with their religion altogether. They have certainly lost all touch with the cultural aspect of Italian Catholicism, and as a consequence have lost contact with much of Italian culture and language.

Associations and clubs

The third most important layer in the structure of the Italian Community is formed by the associations, clubs, circles and societies. Indeed, one of the most significant developments within the Community over the last 15 years has been the development of associative life. This has been particularly significant in London where there is now an intense political and social activity centred around the associations and circles, many of which have substantial membership.

Unlike the consular and ethnic church structure these associations are formed mostly, but as we shall see not exclusively, from within and by the Community itself. There are several hundred clubs and associations of Italians, formed for different reasons and with different areas of activity, in Britain today. These associations fall into one of five categories based on:

(1) the club houses – old and new;
(2) occupational groups;
(3) geographical origins in Italy;
(4) location of members in this country;
(5) other interest groups.

The club houses – old and new

There are two types of club houses within the Italian Community: those which have been formed naturally from within the Communities and those which have been developed for the Italians, normally by the missionary priests.

Within the first category, one of the oldest Community associations still surviving in London today is the *Mazzini Garibaldi Club*. At its Red Lion Street premises the club continues to form a centre where many older

241

Italians gather, and is still responsible for a number of prestigious annual events within the Community. The annual *scampagnata* at Woodford Green remains extremely popular with the London Italian Community. In June 1991 over 1,000 people attended and the committee of the Club pride themselves on the organisation of this 'old-fashioned family picnic'. The main change in the *scampagnate* is that nowadays everyone arrives and departs independently with their own transport. In years gone by the Community would set out together in coaches from central London and, while the picnic was under way, there was no threat of numbers dwindling in the afternoon, since everyone had to wait for the collective departure of the coaches.

The dinner dance of the *Mazzini Garibaldi Club*, held annually for around 400 people at Café Royal, is one of the most 'classy' of these events in the Community. As we shall see below, almost all associations now hold dinner dances at London hotels, and at similar venues nationwide. These have become popular, often large-scale, events for up to 700 people.

The membership of the *Mazzini Garibaldi* is effectively all male. Wives are automatically members but there are no women members in their own right. It is the equivalent of a gentleman's club for the Italian Community. The current membership stands at around 150 and is mostly middle-aged. The committee is anxious to renovate the premises and encourage more young members in whose hands the future of the club lies. It is hoped that some of the money gained through the sale of the Italian Hospital will be used to help renovate the facilities of this oldest and most venerable club of the Italian Community.

The *Casa d'Italia*, of Glasgow, which was the grandest Italian Club to survive into the post-war era, closed in a bankrupt and shabby state in 1989, having long ceased to attract the new generations of the city's Italians. One of the first and longest serving presidents of the *Casa, Comm. Avv.* Tino Moscardini in Glasgow, summed up the general attitude of Italians in Glasgow to this closure.[2] 'If you go into Glasgow and ask a thousand Italians, they'll say it's disgraceful that the *Casa* has folded. But if you asked those thousand people, "Why didn't you support it?", at least 995 of them would say it was a terrible place, a terrible place. So we couldn't win.' The Italians in Glasgow today are thus without a centre at which to meet. The need for such a 'club house', however, has passed and as we shall see below some new associations which formed in the 1980s have become extremely popular, reflecting as they do the changing social structure of the Community. This is also true for the London Community.

Elsewhere in Scotland, however, two old clubs do still survive: the *Club*

Romano in Dundee and the *Circolo Italiano* in Greenock. Both Italian Communities are small and fairly tight-knit, and have a large proportion of the Italians coming from similar origins. As we saw in Chapters 3 and 6 similar origin produces more cohesion within the Community. This has been the case with the club in Greenock where most Italians are *Spezzini*, and in Dundee where a large proportion of members originate in *Frosinone*, particularly *Belmonte Castello*.

In the 'new' Communities only in Peterborough have the Italians become sufficiently united and organised to open their own club. The ICA – Italian Community Association – at the Fleet Centre in the Fletton area of the town, under the active presidency of *Cav.* Marco Cereste is sponsored by the local authority in Peterborough.

The second type of Italian club, attached to the various Italian missions, exists in proliferation across the country. These groups are therefore not entirely independent or spontaneous in their development. The Italian missions and churches themselves exist where there are concentrations of Italians, and the missions have normally organised a church hall for club and social activities. The most notable of these clubs are attached to the two Italian churches in London: the *Club Italia* at the Scalabrini Centre in Brixton and the *Casa Pallotti* at the Italian Church in Clerkenwell. Both of these clubs are gathering and meeting points especially on Sunday after the various masses, and both have spacious premises and a bar for both coffee and drinks. In addition several associations and circles meet at and use the facilities of *Club Italia* and the *Casa Pallotti*. At Brixton a youth club is held, the highly successful *Club delle Donne* meet and also the *Alpini Monte Rosa* choir rehearses. The *Casa Pallotti* similarly has a social club and a youth club. The committee of the adult club is particularly active and organises the procession of the *Madonna del Carmine*, and also the youth Olympics for Italians (*Olimpiadi della Gioventù Italiana*), an event which involves over 1,000 young Italians who gather from all over Britain. The Scalabrini also organise a *scampagnata* which rivals in size the *Mazzini Garibaldi* event.

Similar smaller clubs are attached to the Italian missions in Nottingham, Bradford, Bedford and Peterborough and form important social centres to these Communities.

In London the FILEF Italian Community Centre, funded mostly by the London borough of Islington, has a large membership, its own premises, offers a wide-ranging and active programme of events and serves both the 'old' and 'new' Communities of north London. Like the clubs set up by the priests, this is not an internal Community development.

243

Occupational groups

The oldest occupational association is that of the *arrotini* and indeed, apart from this, all other old occupational group associations have folded. There is an Ice Cream Alliance, which is composed primarily of Italian ice-cream makers and others related to the industry, but there are many non-Italian members also. As we have seen in Chapter 3 there were many associations in the 1920s and 1930s related to the catering trade. Recently, there has been a revival of these types of bodies with the establishment in London in 1985 of AMIRA (*Associazione Maîtres Italiani Ristoratori ed Alberghi*) and *Ciaò Italia*, a rival association for all people who have an interest in the catering trade. Both run courses and competitions for their members and are generally committed to improvement in the industry and seeking standards of excellence.

In the 1980s, and reflecting trends towards Europeanisation of commerce and business as well as the increasing numbers of professionals within the Italian Community, a few professional associations have been founded. The most notable of these is the British Italian Law Association which has 150 members and is dedicated to promoting understanding and links between the British and Italian legal systems.

Geographical origins in Italy

The theme of Italian geographical origin runs through this book. Always important to the informal social organisation of the expatriate Italian Community, since the mid to late 1970s this importance has been enhanced by the formation of associations based on Italian provincial and regional loyalties. Associations based on village, province and region of origin in Italy have sprung into life. One of the main reasons has been the interest shown by the Italian regions in the emigrant Communities and the mobilisation of these groups can accordingly become politically based. Generally, however, the initiative to form an association comes from within the Community and it is only later that links with the relevant region are formed. The regionally based associations, predominantly in London, have been operational for some time and are formed around the 'old' origin groups.

The oldest of these is the *Associazione Italiana della Val D'Arda*, founded in 1968, which combines people from villages in the *Val D'Arda*, in the province of *Piacenza*, and has over 400 members today. There are four other associations of *Piacentini* in London: the *Associazione Pedina*

Val D'Arda founded in 1979 with 150 members; the *Associazione Amici di Santa Franca* also founded in 1979 with 300 members; the *Associazione Valchero* founded in 1982 with 185 members and the new (1989) provincially based, rather than valley based, *Associazione Piacentini* which combines the membership of the other associations. These associations are all very active within the London Community and are paralleled by the various *Parmensi* or *Parmigiani* associations which also total five.

The oldest association of *Parmigiani* is the village-based *Amici di Casanova Valceno* founded in 1972 with 200 members. Shortly after, in 1975, the *Associazione Parmigiani Valtaro* began and now has 750 members. (See Plate 15.) The first *Amici Valceno* association was founded in Wales in 1976. It was followed in 1983 by the village-based *Amici Bardigiani* in London. By 1985 the growth of these *Val Ceno* associations culminated in the founding of the *Parmigiani Val Ceno* which claims a membership of 1,500 – effectively a total of the other associations excluding the *Valtaro*.

Both sets of *Piacentini* and *Parmigiani* associations are highly active and indicate the 'old' dominance over the London Community. These two groups form the two main power bases of the Community. The range of annual events organised by them is impressive, particularly the Park Lane dinner dances, normally attended by a host of celebrities and *prominenti* both from Italy and England. These events reflect the high level of economic and social progress of the group.

As we know from Chapter 6, however, the London Italian Community is now fairly evenly split between the 'old' and the 'new' immigrants. Accordingly, also in the 1970s, two main associations of *Campani* were founded – the *Campani nel Mondo* and the *Associazione Regionale Campania Emigrati*. Both associations have around 200 members, but are not so well organised as the *Parmigiani* and *Piacentini* contingents. During the 1970s associations of *Campani* formed elsewhere in England, notably in Bedford, and by 1985 a *Federazione* of all *Campani* associations had been formed with 600 members. Also, in 1987 a breakaway association called *Campania Felix* formed in north London, which now has 250 members. Unlike the *Parmigiani* who are a provincially based group but who also, as we have seen above, have village-based associations, the *Campani*, as a regionally based group, are much less tightly knit. The breakaway faction was based not on geographical origins but rather on political lines.

The second-oldest regional association is the *Lucchesi nel Mondo* founded in 1970 in both London and Glasgow with 230 and 100 members respectively. A *Toscani* association was set up to encompass the wider regional group in London in 1980, but most of its 80 members are, however, also members of the *Lucchesi* provincial group. The most recent development within the *Toscani* was the formation of the *Associazione Lunigianesi* in London in 1988. Heavily backed by the region of *Toscana* and the Italian Socialist Party, and with a dynamic president, this new association was able to launch itself with a considerable splash on to the associational scene. A superb photographic exhibition of emigration from the *Lunigiana* was staged at the Italian Institute of Culture and the new association quickly gathered over 150 members, most of whom were already members of either the *Lucchesi, Piacentini* and even *Parmigiani* associations. The *Lunigiana* cuts across the boundaries of the three regions of *Toscana, Emilia* and to a lesser extent *Liguria*.

Other southern Italian associations sprang up, mainly in the 1980s. These are: the *Associazione Calabresi* with 485 members; *Associazione Abruzzo e Molise* with 275 members; *Associazione Trinacria (Siciliani)* with 200 members; *Associazione Sarda Ichnusa* with 120 members. With the exception of the *Calabresi* which is based mainly in Swindon the others are London based.

Most of the associational life based on regional and provincial origins does in fact occur in London. In addition to all the associations mentioned above there are several others, the *Circolo Trentini, Associazioni Piemontesi, Laziali, Veneti* and the *Fogolar di Gran Bretagna* whose members are all *Friulani*.

In Scotland too in recent years new regionally based associations have been formed. These, however, have centred around an upsurge of interest amongst the 'old' groups and their descendants. For example, in 1989 an *Associazione Parmigiani della Scozia* was formed which now has over 100 members. Most of these are located in Aberdeen, Dundee, Perth and Stirling. Similarly an association of *Laziali*, based on the 'old' *Frosinone* group in Scotland was founded in the 1980s. The most active association in Scotland, however, is the Scottish Italian Graduates Society under the presidency of Dr Eileen Millar of the Department of Italian at Glasgow University. Founded in 1975, since the close of the *Casa d'Italia* in 1989 it has become extremely popular and organises a varied and interesting programme of events.

Although the development of regionally based associations outside London has not been a feature because, as we saw in Chapter 6, most Communities are now 'mixed' in their origins, there has been considerable activity in the development of other forms of associative life.

By geographical locations

A fourth type of association, normally called *circoli*, or circles, have been a feature of the 'new' Communities for some time. Their function and orientation is normally social and they gather together the Italians of their town on a regular basis for dinner dances at specific times of the year, for example, *Carnevale* or Christmas. These *circoli* do not have their own premises. Such circles exist in Worcester, Coventry, Basingstoke, High Wycombe, Croydon, Slough, Leamington Spa, Bristol, Horsham, Sutton, Watford, Oxford, Aylesbury, St Albans, Swindon, Scunthorpe, Stoke on Trent, Blackburn, Chorley, Leicester, Derby and Rochdale. The Committee of the circle will normally organise representations to any major events in the Italian Community which often take place in London, such as President Cossiga's visit to Grosvenor House when he met with Italians from all over England.

In many 'old' Communities too, where no regionally based associations have formed, *circoli* have also grown up, for example, Inverness, Ayr, Edinburgh, Carlisle and Sheffield.

Other interest groups

A number of specific interest associations have always been popular amongst the Italians, most notably the *Alpini* and the *Cacciatori*. The *Associazione Cacciatori* was founded in 1977 and has 250 members who are very active in shooting over the winter season in and around the Home Counties. Members are almost all *Piacentini* and *Parmigiani* from the mountain valley areas who enjoyed these activities in their home environments. The choir of the *Alpini*, which is well known for its mountain songs and had the honour of singing for President Cossiga when he visited Britain in 1990, has already been mentioned. Like all associations the *Alpini* and the *Cacciatori* now both host dinner dances in London's West End hotels. The *Alpini*, founded in 1967 and the oldest association to be registered with the Italian Consulate in London, now has over 150 members and a branch association in Wales with a further 25 members.

The two other main interest groups are the political parties and the cultural associations. Cultural associations such as Dante Alighieri and Antonio Gramsci have spawned a nationwide network, some of which are extremely active and many of which involve non-Italian members.

All of this association building led in 1975 to the foundation of a governing body, FAIE (the *Federazione Associazioni Italiane England*), which tries to regulate matters and affairs between the associations. The majority, though not all, of the associations are members of FAIE.

Welfare Agencies

It was due to the growth of the southern Italian industrial workforce in provincial England that the welfare agencies grew up in the 1960s and 1970s. All now have offices in London as well as a network of provincial agents. The largest of these is the ACLI (*Associazioni Cristiane Lavoratori Italiani*) with ten regional offices including London, and a total of 16 representatives nationwide. Similarly the *patronato* INAS (*Istituto Nazionale di Assistenza Sociale*) now has headquarters in London, and a network of 17 representatives. The three smaller *patronati* are INCA (*Istituto Nazionale Confederale di Assistenza*), ITALUIL (*Istituto di Tutela ed Assistenza ai Lavoratori della Unione Italiana del Lavoro*) and IPAS (*Istituto Patronato Assistenza Sociale*), the latter located only in Birmingham.

These *patronati*, which are affiliated to the Italian political parties, offer a wide range of welfare agency services mainly to first-generation Italians. Much of the welfare work in fact duplicates that of the welfare officers at the Consulates, but the brokerage or go-between function of the *patronati* is important given the complicated nature of Italian bureaucracy. For example, people seeking to initiate the proceedings for the application of an Italian pension would rarely do so without the help of one of the *patronati* who liaise professionally and persistently between the British and the Italian authorities. Contact with the English authorities in fields such as health and social security is equally daunting for first-generation Italians because of language difficulties.

Other institutions

The Italian Hospital

After over 100 years of service to the Italian Community, the Italian Hospital at Queen Square, London, finally closed in 1989. For the previous decade or so the hospital had had falling patient numbers and had been plagued by management and financial problems. In the end, however, its closure was sudden, following a decision by its trustees Lord

Thorneycroft and Lord Forte, and there was a great sense of loss within the Community. Relatives of the founders were rather upset by the action and a spate of articles appeared in the Community press decrying the decision and the perceived lack of 'consultation' about it.

Apart from its medical care, for which patients even came from Italy, the hospital was renowned for its kitchen. An Egon Ronay survey of hospital cooking in the 1980s found the Italian Hospital to have the best food in London. Its closure signified two facts: the demise of the need for a specifically Italian Hospital within the Community, as most people felt entirely comfortable in the local hospital system, either public or private; and, secondly, the ongoing difficulty of the management committee in identifying a course of strategic development for the hospital.

Villa Scalabrini

Founded in 1986 under the directorship of *Padre* Alberto Vico, *Villa Scalabrini* in Shenley, Hertfordshire, is the first old people's home for the Italian Community in Britain. It is a registered charity and is funded mainly by contributions from the wealthy business Community as well as a considerable amount of fund-raising activity.

Despite the family-oriented nature of the Italian Community, there are now old people without family support and such a home was considered necessary. Places are restricted to around 40 people. *Padre* Vico also acts as a missionary to the Italians in Watford and St Albans.

Ethnic press

The main publication is the British Italian fortnightly newspaper, *La Voce degli Italiani in Gran Bretagna*, produced by the Scalabrini fathers in London; *Padre* Gaetano Parolin is the director. With a subscription of over 5,000 and a readership close on 25,000, *La Voce*, founded in 1948, is not only the longest running Community newspaper but has the widest coverage of Community events.

During the late 1940s and 1950s the news and Community events content of the newspaper reflected the distribution of the 'old' Communities and Scotland, particularly Glasgow, were regularly featured in the pages of *La Voce*. With the build-up of the 'new' Communities in the mid 1950s the balance of the editorial coverage shifted to reflect this. Throughout the 1970s and 1980s very little news was reported from any of the 'old' Communities, with Scotland and Manchester being particularly absent.

249

Subscription also reflected this and by the late 1980s and early 1990s *La Voce* had come to represent mainly the London and Home Counties Italian Communities. A new initiative was taken in 1990 to recruit Scottish subscribers and a 'Scottish page' was reintroduced. With the death of *Avv.* Osvaldo Franchi, who not only co-ordinated and organised the events of the Scottish Italian Community but reported them to *La Voce*, it may be that interest will not be maintained in reporting the issues and events of the Scottish Italian Community at a national level.

The Scottish Italian Community has its own newspaper – *Italiani in Scozia* –edited by the missionary priest *Padre* Pietro Zorza. It appears roughly four times a year and although also heavily religious in content (unlike *La Voce*) reports on the main events of the Scottish Italians.

A recent attempt to publish a Community newspaper in the north of England – *il Corriere del Nord* – lasted only a year or so after the election of the first *Co.Em.It.* Committee in 1986.

There are two other smaller publications in London. Firstly, the rather individualistic *Londra Sera* which covers mainly 'glitterati' events in the London Italian Community and rarely concerns itself with lower level or small-scale events. Its editor, Tomasso Bruccoleri, is also a photographer and is often to be seen in person covering the Community events at which the *prominenti* gather, especially in the banking sector. Secondly, *Back-hill*, a news magazine, is published monthly by St Peter's Italian Church under the editorship of *Avv.* Francesco Giacon. This has no subscription and is mainly a free news sheet picked up by people who attend the Italian Church.

In addition to these regular Community-wide publications there are a number of smaller more specialist publications such as *Nuova Presenza* published by the ACLI, *Pino L'Alpino* of the *Alpini* association, *La Gazzetta* published by the *Amici Val Ceno Galles*, and *Rivista* published by the British Italian Society. There are also some small Community news sheets at the individual town level such as *Il Tricolore* in Peterborough, *L'Informatore* in Aylesbury and *Bollettino* in Bedford.

There is now in addition to this impressive list of Community publications, the radio station, *Radio Londra*, which broadcasts for two hours a day in Italian and is popular with the Community. Finally it should also be noted that many Italians now have satellite dishes which allow them to receive Italian television, RAI UNO and DUE, a phenomenon which helps enormously in keeping in touch with Italy.

Most of the people who are presidents of the associations and involved in the running of the institutions are personalities and *prominenti* within the Community. Let us now as a final section to this chapter consider the leaders of the Italian Community.

Leaders within the Community

Broadly the leaders of the Italian Community fall into two categories: 'successful' and 'important' people. Some people, although not many, fit both categories. A combination often leads to unacceptable levels of conflicting interests.

Important people

The 'important' people within the Community are firstly individuals appointed to official positions in the general bureaucratic framework. They represent the establishment of the Community. The most 'important' person, by definition, is His Excellency the Italian Ambassador, at present the popular Boris Biancheri. The Ambassador is closely followed in level of perceived importance (although not linked to actual diplomatic rank) by the Consul Generals and Consuls. The priests, the various welfare agents, the members of the *Com.It.Es.* and the consular Agents and Correspondents all have high public profiles within their individual Communities and are thus 'important'. A number of these individuals also have a significant level of exposure and prominence within the national structure of the Community particularly if they have dedicated many years of service to it. Often when this is the case, the Italian Government recognises the contribution of these people to the Community and confers upon them various titles of civil merit. Reflecting life in Italy today, Italians are very status conscious, and titles such as *Dottore, Avvocato, Ingegnere* are always used when referring to people, particularly superiors. Within the Italian Community the 'important' people nearly all have the titles *Cavaliere* or *Commendatore* reflecting their status.

A second group, more from the ranks of the Community, are also 'important'. Almost all of the people are men. The prevalence of the single sex groups described in Chapter 7 for the southern Italian Communities in general, applies at almost all social and economic levels within the Community. With only a few exceptions (notably *Cav.* Roberta Mutti and *Dott.essa* Maria Pompei in London, *Dott.essa* Nadia Dalziel in Edinburgh and *Cav.* Maria Schiavo in Cardiff), the 'important' people are men.

251

These 'important' men and women are often linked to the associations and/or Italian political groups. Most are political animals and considerable manoeuvring within the Community occurs as they build up and maintain their support networks. A number of individuals have considerable personal followings, and command high levels of patronage.

Each of the smaller Italian Communities tends to have at least one 'important' person. Because of the nature of the Italian personality, however, as well as political considerations, even small Italian Communities often have two 'important' leaders who are prominent at the national level within the Community. The most notable example of this is in the town of Watford which has two Italian consular Correspondents, and loyalties appear to be quite clearly divided between them. Most of the 'important' people, however, not only at the individual Community level but also the national level, are concentrated in London. The degree of internal organisation within the Community and the array of factions, each with its own leader, is an important feature of the London Italian Community. It is to these leaders that the Italian government turns when any major Community event is to be organised, such as the State Visit of President Cossiga. Each leader mobilises and organises his own faction. In general the competition between groups for status and prominence can be intense. In overall terms, however, the number of 'important' people is dwarfed by the numbers of 'successful' people.

Successful people

Those in the 'successful' category are the businessmen of the Community who have generated considerable personal wealth through entrepreneurship in satisfying either some of the consumer demands of the Community itself or the population at large. These men are not leaders in the sense that they take any active decisions or initiatives within the Community, although some do, but each has a high profile and prestigious position and each has his own group of loyal followers. Aspects of the classic notion of the *padrone* within the Italian migrant situation are well applied to these men, particularly when they are employers of large numbers of Italians. These 'successful' men support the Community. They give to its charities, such as the recently closed Italian Hospital, or the old people's home at *Villa Scalabrini*, and they donate gifts for the lotteries and raffles at the dinner dances. The annual ball at the London Hilton of the British Italian fortnightly newspaper, *La Voce degli Italiani*, receives each year a Fiat Uno car to raffle from *Cav.* Carmine Leo, the most 'successful' Fiat dealer in the country. Many other businesses give generously and, in the traditional Italian way, a list of who has given what is published, in order that all may assess the generosity and commitment to the Community of the various 'successful' leaders.

When the roles of 'successful' and 'important' are combined in the same person, conflicts can occur which often lead to difficulty and allegations of corruption within the Community. When an honorary Consul tries to combine his bureaucratic functions with his private legal practice, Community members can suspect that proceedings may not be conducted entirely in the individual's own interests. Men in traditional restaurant or provisions shop businesses have often, however, been able to combine the roles of 'successful' and 'important' very efficiently.

To summarise, the Italian Communities in Britain are often characterised by the outstanding level of leadership which has developed both from within the Community and by being imposed as an external structure. Many individuals abound and many small Italian Communities have a larger-than-life place in the British Italian Community mental map because of the character, dedication and flair of the individuals in their midst. It is these individuals who have built and created the diverse range of institutions of the Italian Community.

Having surveyed the Italian presence in Britain, past and present, let us now conclude by drawing some of the main threads of the book together and by looking to the future.

Chapter Nine

Conclusion

In the preceding eight chapters of *The Italian Factor*, the depth of history, spanning more than 150 years, the diversity of geographical and social origin in Italy and the fascinating range of occupations of the Italians in Britain have been discussed. In the early 1990s, as we move towards the twenty-first century, the Italians constitute a multi-faceted Community with a high level of internal organisation and a strong sense of 'people-hood'. Almost every decade has witnessed a new development: indeed the longevity of the Italian factor in British life has been due to constant adaptation and evolution. This inherent versatility has resulted both from an on-going and dynamic relationship with Italy and from a natural organic growth within the Community itself.

There have been periods of strife, especially for the 'old' Italian Community. The prejudice and discrimination which many old Italians remember from the first half of this century, when the Italians were the most 'visible' immigrant group in Britain, and the trauma and difficulties of the Second World War and its aftermath, are now well in the past. The 'new' Communities of the post-war era have become well established, integrated not only into the existing framework of the Italian Community itself, but also into the fabric of British society. The British Italians are again proud of their heritage, not just their Italian roots, but also their own history in this country, and the members of the Community have increasingly grown prosperous and again outward-looking.

It has not, however, been the passage of time alone which has produced these conditions for a new 'golden era'. In the last decade or so, there have been three main inter-related elements which have had a cumulative impact on the lives and self-confidence of the Italians in Britain. These are: firstly, Italy's increasing economic prosperity; secondly, the Italian

255

government's renewed and growing interest in her emigrant Communities; and, thirdly, the influence of the European Community.

The rapid economic growth of Italy in the 1980s led not only to substantial structural change within Italy, including we should note, the first waves of overseas, particularly Senegalese, immigrants to a country which previously had been characterised by a long tradition of economically motivated emigration, but also to a marked increase in the European and international orientation of the many successful Italian firms and businesses. Italy as a whole began to look outwards, to become a major international player, a fully fledged member of the 'group of seven'. Benetton and Olivetti have now colonised the world and Fiat, Gucci, Fendi, Pirelli, Zanussi and many others are household names across Europe. Linked to this economic expansion has been a small but important migration from Italy of high-level managerial and professional people.

From the early 1980s therefore, as Italian business became more international and the movement of capital and people within Europe intensified, yet another new wave of Italian immigrants arrived in Britain, in fact almost exclusively in London. It is interesting to recall the discussion of the early Italian immigrants at the beginning of our study. In many ways this new movement represents Italian immigration coming full-circle to this country – it is again an élite immigration. The new migrants are highly educated, highly mobile professionals posted here on a temporary basis as diplomats, bankers, technocrats, businesspeople and Eurocrats. They generally already speak good English, are often associated with the Arts and Italian culture; in short they are sophisticated emissaries and ambassadors of Italy today. While in the past, and indeed over most of our period of study, the Italians who have arrived in Britain have been from the poorer sections of Italian society, this latest group have come from the upper echelons. Socially and economically rather than numerically significant, they too have come to work, but have added a new and interesting layer to the Italian presence in Britain.

All of the major Italian companies such as those mentioned above as well as the official state entities such as Agip UK, Alitalia and Snia UK, maintain offices and substantial personnel in Britain. Although not often directly involved in the social activity of the Italian Community, there are many business links between these people and the permanent Community. As we have seen, British Italian entrepreneurs have often concentrated on selling some aspect of their Italianness. Today Italian companies are keen to use British Italians to promote their products not only in catering and the motor car industry, but also in fashion, design and many other areas.

256

The Italian Chamber of Commerce and the Italian Trade Centre are active in promoting Italian products and concepts in Britain and provide a range of information services for businesspeople wishing to trade with Italy. Naturally, many of these are British Italians. In addition, the growth of banking and the financial markets in both London and Italy has been responsible for bringing many Italian bankers to London. There are now 23 Italian banks in the capital which employ hundreds of Italians.

A final aspect of this new wave of Italian immigration has been the growth of the Italian government presence in Britain. This is closely linked to the second major element currently shaping the Italian Community. We saw in Chapter 8 that there has been a renewed interest and involvement in the global expatriate Italian Communities by the Italian government. The introductory pages of *The Italian Factor* pointed out that Italy is unparalleled internationally in terms of emigration history. Italians throughout the world, in the United States, in Latin America, in Australia, as well as in Europe including Britain, are currently making their presence felt not only in their adopted homelands, but have successfully demanded the right to remain involved with and be recognised by their mother country. Italy has again begun to re-envelop her global compatriots. The result of the world-wide census of all Italians living abroad will shortly be available. Not only does such activity in conjunction with a host of other political and cultural initiatives encourage Italians – second, third and fourth-generation Italians – to remain within the ethnic fold, but it requires the maintenance of a colossal governmental and semi-governmental structure and presence throughout the world. The 1980s also saw the arrival and recruitment of unprecedented levels of diplomats, bureaucrats and clerical staff within the Italian consular structure in Britain. Unlike the other professional migrants, these people often have a high level of involvement with and commitment to the Italian Community.

The 1990 visit of President Cossiga to the British Italian Communities, the first official visit since 1969, was important. The frequent visits by various Italian government ministers indicate commitment at the highest level to the Italians and to some of the initiatives being taken by them in Britain today. Of outstanding note is the recently opened *Accademia Italiana* in London. Now not only a major Arts venue in the capital, it is also beginning to emerge as the first truly 'European' independent institution in Britain today with its wide-ranging cultural and political programme. Also of significance is the recent acquisition by the Italian Ministry of Foreign Affairs of the Richard De Marco Gallery in Edinburgh for a major new Italian cultural institute. Such an initiative indicates an awareness of the unique contribution of this Italian Scot to the cultural map of Scotland and a continued desire to bring Italian art, culture and literature to the people of this country.

The third major element affecting the position of the Italians in Britain has been the increasing influence of the European Community. Moves towards the free circulation of capital and labour within the member countries has spurred efforts to develop links between countries. Italy is a leading force within the European Community; the Italian people are frequently shown to be more in favour of further integration than other members states. They can cope with the linguistic, cultural and bureaucratic challenges of Europe and are thriving on them. Britain, sadly, is not.

Most of the 250,000 Italians resident in Britain already feel themselves to be not only partly British and partly Italian, but also European – a concept which few other British people are ready to endorse whole heartedly. The British Italian Community is well-placed to think positively about Europe and about retaining its own identity within that structure, to look to 1992 and beyond and to help Europeanise Britain.

Life in the early 1990s in Britain for the Italians has many, many positive aspects. Indeed, it would be difficult to identify negatives. The Italian Community, especially in London, is alive with activity: events, issues, developments. This vibrancy can be appreciated at such events as the procession of the *Madonna del Carmine*, the annual national 'Olympics' organised for the young Italians of Britain and the many and varied country-wide arts, cultural, sports and social activities. To have all one's senses fully switched on to Italy and Europe one only has to step inside the many Italian provisions stores nationwide. (See Plate 16.) Such premises are the 'Little Italies' of the 1990s, but today their economic success is as much dependent on the local population who now buy *prosciutto, provolone, porcini,* etc. as it is to the Italians.

The British Italian Community is today in a strong position, perhaps stronger than at any time in its history. Britain has become more tolerant as she has absorbed waves of coloured immigrants from her former empire and the Italians have become ever more acceptable. For almost two centuries Italians have brought new ideas, products and concepts to Britain; they will no doubt continue to do so. Their level of creativity linked to a capacity for hard work and an appreciation of quality are invaluable assets. This Italian factor in the fabric of life in Great Britain is now being fully recognised, appreciated and indeed valued. Long may it continue to be so.

Notes

CHAPTER TWO

1. A census of all Italians resident in Scotland was carried out by the Italian Consular authorities in 1933. One of the questions asked the migrants when they had arrived in Britain.

CHAPTER THREE

1. This is my deduction since no similar documentation exists in either the Italian Consulate General in London or the Consulate in Manchester. These papers most probably would be found in the archives of the Ministry of Foreign Affairs in *Roma*.
2. Author Interview, Elpidio Rossi, *Chiavari* (Ge), 28.8.1990.
3. Author Interview, Pietro Beschizza, Middlesex, 17.10.1990.
4. Author Interview, Kathleen Fusco, Edinburgh, 13.7.1989.

CHAPTER FOUR

1. Foreign Office File FO 371 25193, folio 87.
2. The *Guardian*, 2.7.1990. Churchill's 'Collar the lot' referred to 60,000 Category 'C' Jews as well as all Italians.
3. Author Interview, Joan Ottolini, Glasgow, 21.3.1991.
4. Author Interview, Vivian Santoro, Milngavie, 7.2.1991.
5. Foreign Office File FO 371 25192, folio 131.
6. Transcription of author interview, Rando Bertoia, Glasgow, 2.3.1990.
7. Transcription of author interview, Nicola Cua, London, 23.4.1990.
8. Transcription of author interview, Romolo Chiocconi, Glasgow, 16.3.1990.
9. Transcription of author interview, Gino Guarnieri, London, 21.5.1990.
10. Transcription of author interview, Enrico Casci, Falkirk, 12.3.1990.

11. Foreign Office File FO 371 25210 includes a printed but undated 'Embarkation List' which gives a total of 712 Italians on board the *Arandora Star* – 486 lost and 226 saved. Home Office File HO 215 429 1942 'List of Missing' lists 446 lost. In his report on the *Arandora Star* to the Cabinet in October 1940, Lord Snell said there were 717 Italians on board and sidestepped the more difficult question of how many died. The War Office gives 734 Italians on board and 486 lost (FO 916 2581 folio 499). The *St Laurent* claimed to have picked up 264 Italian survivors.
12. Home Office File HO 215 429 1942.
13. Foreign Office File FO 916 2581 folio 548.
14. Foreign Office File FO 371 25210.
15. Transcription of author interview, Amilcare Cima, Padivarma (Sp), 29.8.90.
16. Author Interview, Luigi Beschizza, London, 8.4.1991.
17. Home Office File HO 200 117 163.
18. Foreign Office File FO 916 2581 folio 548.

CHAPTER FIVE

1. The data for these figures was based upon a full survey of records held on Italian immigrants to Bedford at the Aliens Office, Bedfordshire Divisional Police Headquarters. See Colpi (1987).
2. Author Interview, Antony Rea, Manchester, 15.2.1991.

CHAPTER SIX

1. The Vice-Consulate in Bedford is dependent on the Consulate General in London and only semi-autonomous. From 1987 the jurisdiction of the Vice-Consulate in Bedford was expanded to include Suffolk, Norfolk, the northern half of Buckinghamshire and the north-west corner of Hertfordshire, areas previously directly under the jurisdiction of the Consulate General in London.
2. The 1981 British census collective counties total for each of the consular jurisdictions was: Edinburgh 4,789; Manchester 18,708; Bedford 9,008 and London 65,343.
3. This work has been possible by extensive statistical gathering carried out at the Italian Consulates in London, Edinburgh and Bedford in the 1980s and in Manchester in 1991. Further up-to-date statistics were supplied in 1991 by *Consoli Generali* Buonavita in Edinburgh

and De Ceglie in London. There is some variation in the underlying parameters used to compile the figures, so they should not be interpreted as more than a guide, although they are the most accurate and up-to-date guide currently available.

4. A further 73 people were enumerated in Belfast in Northern Ireland which comes under the jurisdiction of the Edinburgh Consulate. The size of the Belfast Italian Community has declined greatly during the last two decades because of the 'troubles'. Many Italians moved to Eire, swelling the ranks of the Dublin Italian Community, almost all of whom originate in *Frosinone*.

5. These figures are drawn from a full survey of consular records held in Bedford in 1983. See Colpi (1987).

6. These figures are drawn from a full survey of consular records held in Edinburgh in 1983. See Colpi (1986).

7. See note 5.

CHAPTER SEVEN

1. Author Interview, Silvia Quarantelli, Aberdeen, 16.2.1991.

CHAPTER EIGHT

1. Questionnaire survey conducted in Bedford 1985. See Colpi (1987).

2. Author Interview, *Comm.Avv.* Tino Moscardini, Glasgow, 30.10.1990.

MAP OF ITALY: AREAS AND REGIONS

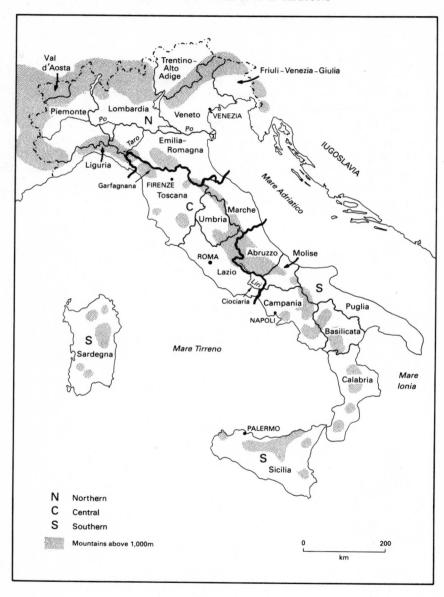

Val d'Aosta
Trentino-Alto Adige
Friuli-Venezia-Giulia
Piemonte
Lombardia
Veneto
VENEZIA
Po
N
Po
Taro
Emilia-Romagna
IUGOSLAVIA
Liguria
Garfagnana
FIRENZE
Toscana
Mare Adriatico
C
Marche
Umbria
ROMA
Abruzzo
Molise
Lazio
Liri
S
Ciociaria
Campania
Puglia
NAPOLI
Basilicata
S
Sardegna
Mare Tirreno
Calabria
Mare Ionia
PALERMO
S
Sicilia

N   Northern
C   Central
S   Southern

▨   Mountains above 1,000m

0   200
km

Appendix One

Glossary of Italian words and terms

Abbandonato	Abandoned
Albergo	Hotel
Alpini	Mountain soldiers of the Italian army
Ambasciatore (Amb.)	Ambassador
Amico/Amica	Friend
Arrotino/Arrotini	Knife-grinder/s. These emigrants came from the *Val Rendena* now in the province of *Trento*
Associazione	Association
Avellinesi	People from the province of *Avellino*
Avvocato (Avv.)	Lawyer
Balilla	Part of the fascist youth movement
Bardigiani	People from the small town of *Bardi* (Pr)
Barghigiani	People from the small town of *Barga* (Lu)
Befana	Epiphany. Good witch
Bomboniera/e	Keepsakes. For both christenings and weddings, *bomboniere* are distributed to all the guests as a keepsake of the event. Some sugared almonds are the basis of the gift (different numbers and different colours representing different celebrations) but these are attached to gifts of varying value from small trinkets to solid silver bells
Briscola	Italian card game
Burocrazia	Bureaucracy
Bussesi	People from the village of *Busso* (Cb)
Cacciatori	Hunters
Caffélatte	Milky coffee
Calabresi	People from the region of *Calabria*
Campani	People from the region of *Campania*

Campanile	Bell tower. The church and its bell tower are normally dominant both physically and psychologically in the villages of Italy. From *campanile* comes *campanilismo*
Campanilismo	Can be translated as 'localism' or spirit of the bell tower. *Campanilismo* involves an emotional loyalty to the place of one's birth and to one's *paesani*. *Campanilismo* is evident both in Italy and abroad in the emigrant communities, where it takes on new forms. It should be understood that *campanilismo* is usually a group feature and not normally an expression one would attach to an individual in isolation, i.e. it is shared experience
Campobassani	People from the province of *Campobasso*
Cantina	Cellar
Casa	House. *Casa d'Italia*: House of Italy
Casa del Littorio	House of the Emblem. (*Casa d'Italia*)
Cavaliere (Cav.)	Title of civil merit. Knight
Chiesetta	Little church. *La nostra chiesetta*: our little church
Ciociaria	Geographical area name relating roughly to the province of *Frosinone*, but in the past also including sections of *Isernia* and *Caserta*. People from this area were often, mistakenly, called *Napoletani*
Ciociari	People from the *Ciociaria*
Co.As.It.	*Comitato di Assistenza Scuole Italiane*
Co.Em.It.	*Comitati Emigrazione Italiana* (1986) Italian Emigration Committees
Commendatore (Comm.)	Title of civil merit – superior to *Cavaliere*
Compari	Pseudo or fictive kin. The assignment and acquisition of *compari* occurs around the life-cycle ceremonies, the *rites de passage* of the south of Italy. These are coincident with ecclesiastical function – i.e. births, confirmations and marriages. The closest translation for *compari* at a christening would be godparents, for a wedding, best-man and best-woman, and for a confirmation, guardian

Compare	Masculine form
Comare	Feminine form
Comare D'Anello	Literally *comare* of the ring, i.e. at a wedding. Best-woman
Com.It.Es.	*Comitati Italiani all'Estero* (1991) Italian Committees Abroad
Comparaggio	The institution of acquiring *compari*
Comune/Comuni	Smallest administrative area. The *comune* comes after the region and the province in Italy's three-tier administrative system. The *comune* can be either the small *paese* or the city
Console	Consul
Console Generale	Consul General
Contadino/Contadini	Peasant, farmer. People who live and work on the land. Nowadays in Italy *contadino* is applied to all rustics who live on and from the land, mostly the southern Italian small farmers
Contadina/Contadine	Feminine form
Conte	Count
Credere, Obbedire, Combattere	Believe, Obey, Fight
Croce Di Guerra	War Cross. Decoration
Direzione Didattica	Education office of the Italian consular authority
Don	Priest
Dopolavoro	After work
Doposcuola	After school
Dottore (Dott.)	Title given to a person with a university degree
Emigrante	Emigrant
Emigrazione	Emigration. *Vecchia emigrazione*: old emigration
Emiliani	People from the region of *Emilia*
Ex Combattenti	Veteran soldiers
Fascio/Fasci	Fascist club/s
FAIE	*Federazione Associazioni Italiane England*
FASFA	*Federazione delle Associazioni e Comitati Scuola Famiglia*

265

Festa/Feste	Holiday, saint's day, festival, party. Sometimes called *sagra*
Fidanzato/Fidanzata	Fiancé/fiancée
Figurinaio/Figurinai	Makers and travelling sellers of statuettes and figurines
FILEF	*Federazione Italiana Lavoratori Emigrati e Famiglie*
Foggiani	People from the province of *Foggia*
Forestiero	Foreigner, stranger. Used to refer to people outside the group of intimates. See *straniero*
Friulani	People from the region of *Friuli*
Garibaldini	Followers of Garibaldi
Garzone/Garzoni	Boy apprentice/s
Genovese	Person from *Genova*, in the region of *Liguria*
Ghetto	Ethnic quarter of a town. Originally Jews in *Venezia*
Giornata Delle Fedi	Day of the wedding rings
Guida Generale Della Comunità Italiana in Gran Bretagna	General Guide of the Italian Community in Great Britain
Inghilterra	England
Inglesi	English
Italiantà	Italianness
Lago	Lake
Lavoratore Italiano All'Estero	Italian worker abroad
Laziali	People from the region of *Lazio*
Liguri	People from the region of *Liguria*
Lire	Italian currency
Londra	London
Lucchesi	People from the province of *Lucca*
Madonna	Mother of God, Our Lady, The Virgin Mary
Madonna del Carmine	Our Lady of Mount Carmel
Madonna del Rosario	Our Lady of the Rosary
Marchese	Marquis
Mentalità	Mentality. Way of thinking
Meridionali	People from the south of Italy
Mezzogiorno	Geographical name given to the south of Italy

266

Ministero del Lavoro	Ministry of Labour
Moleta	Wheelbarrow equipment of the *arrotini*
Molisani	People from the region of *Molise*
Mondo	World
Napoletani	People from *Napoli*
Nonni	Grandparents
Nostalgia	Nostalgia and home sickness
Onore, Famiglia e Patria	Honour, family and country
Padrone/Padroni	Master or boss. (Root word is *padre*: father.) In the context of emigration/immigration the *padrone* is a person who either looks after and helps his fellow countrymen in the immigrant situation, or one who exploits them
Padronismo	Power/patronage system of the *padroni*. Master/servant relation
Paese/Paesi	Village, place/s
Paesano/Paesani	A person from the same village of birth as oneself
Paesana/Paesane	Feminine form
Parmigiani	People from the province of *Parma*
Patronato	Agency, institution
Pensione	Guest house
Petrellesi	People from the village of *Petrella*
Piacentini	People from the province of *Piacenza*
Piemontesi	People from the region of *Piemonte*
Pignata	*Busso* pre-Lenten *carnevale* tradition
Porcini	Edible wild mushrooms
Prosciutto	Ham
Provolone	Kind of cheese
Quartiere	Quarter, area
Raccomandazione	Literally recommendation. Much more than that in fact. The entire socio-economic system in the south of Italy favours only those who have been 'recommended' by sufficiently influential people. Without a *raccomandazione* it is impossible to obtain work etc.
Regno di Piemonte	Kingdom of *Piemonte (Sardegna)*

267

Ristorante	Restaurant
Sacrifici	Sacrifices. *'Ho fatto tanti sacrifici all' estero'* – I have made so many sacrifices abroad – is a key phrase used by the migrants in England. It is employed often and sums up their attitude, both to emigration and to their experiences (i.e. being abroad is conceptually inseparable from hardship, both material and psychological)
Sagra	Feast. See *festa*. Religious part of the celebrations
Salsicci	Spicy home-made sausages
Sardo	Sardinian
Scampagnata	Picnic. Countryside excursion
Scopa	Italian card game
Scuola Popolare	Public school
Siciliano	Sicilian
Siciliani	People from the region of *Sicilia*
Soprannome	Nickname
Sorpasso	Overtake. Economic overtaking of Britain by Italy
Spezzini	People from the province of *La Spezia*
Straniero	Stranger, foreigner
Tarantella	Folk dance
Terrazzo	Specialist floor-work
Tesserati	Membership card holders, subscribers, ticket holders or full members
Torrone	Italian nougat delicacy
Toscani	People from the region of *Toscana*
Trattoria/Trattorie	Informal restaurant/s
Vecchia Emigrazione	Old emigration
Veneziano	Venetian
Via Vittime Arandora Star	Road of the *Arandora Star* victims
Voce	Voice. *La Voce degli Italiani in Gran Bretagna*: the voice of Italians in Great Britain
Zampogne	Bagpipes from the *Ciociaria*

Appendix Two

List of Italian provincial abbreviations

(Ag)	Agrigento	Sicilia		(Lt)	Latina	Lazio
(Al)	Alessandria	Piemonte		(Le)	Lecce	Puglia
(An)	Ancona	Marche		(Li)	Livorno	Toscana
(Ao)	Aosta	Valle d'Aosta		(Lu)	Lucca	Toscana
(Ar)	Arezzo	Toscana		(Mc)	Macerata	Marche
(Ap)	Ascoli Piceno	Marche		(Mn)	Mantova	Lombardia
(At)	Asti	Piemonte		(Ms)	Massa-Carrara	Toscana
(Av)	Avellino	Campania		(Mt)	Matera	Basilicata
(Ba)	Bari	Puglia		(Me)	Messina	Sicilia
(Bl)	Belluno	Veneto		(Mi)	Milano	Lombardia
(Bn)	Benevento	Campania		(Mo)	Modena	Emilia Romagna
(Bg)	Bergamo	Lombardia		(Na)	Napoli	Campania
(Bo)	Bologna	Emilia Romagna		(No)	Novara	Piemonte
(Bz)	Bolzano	Trentino Alto Adige		(Nu)	Nuoro	Sardegna
(Bg)	Brescia	Lombardia		(Or)	Oristano	Sardegna
(Br)	Brindisi	Puglia		(Pd)	Padova	Veneto
(Ca)	Cagliari	Sardegna		(Pa)	Palermo	Sicilia
(Cl)	Caltanissetta	Sicilia		(Pr)	Parma	Emilia Romagna
(Cb)	Campobasso	Molise		(Pv)	Pavia	Lombardia
(Ce)	Caserta	Campania		(Pg)	Perugia	Umbria
(Ct)	Catania	Sicilia		(Ps)	Pesaro	Marche
(Cz)	Catanzaro	Calabria		(Pe)	Pescara	Abruzzo
(Ch)	Chieti	Abruzzo		(Pc)	Piacenza	Emilia Romagna
(Co)	Como	Lombardia		(Pi)	Pisa	Toscana
(Cs)	Cosenza	Calabria		(Pt)	Pistoia	Toscana
(Cr)	Cremona	Lombardia		(Pn)	Pordenone	Friuli Venezia Giulia
(Cn)	Cuneo	Piemonte		(Pz)	Potenza	Basilicata
(En)	Enna	Sicilia		(Rg)	Ragusa	Sicilia
(Fe)	Ferrara	Emilia Romagna		(Ra)	Ravenna	Emilia Romagna
(Fi)	Firenze	Toscana		(Rc)	Reggio Calabria	Calabria
(Fg)	Foggia	Puglia		(Re)	Reggio Emilia	Emilia Romagna
(Fo)	Forlì	Emilia Romagna		(Ri)	Rieti	Lazio
(Fr)	Frosinone	Lazio		(Roma)	Roma	Lazio
(Ge)	Genova	Liguria		(Ro)	Rovigo	Veneto
(Go)	Gorizia	Friuli Venezia Giulia		(Sa)	Salerno	Campania
(Gr)	Grosseto	Toscana		(Ss)	Sassari	Sardegna
(Im)	Imperia	Liguria		(Sv)	Savona	Liguria
(Is)	Isernia	Molise		(Si)	Siena	Toscana
(Aq)	L'Aquila	Abruzzo		(Sr)	Siracusa	Sicilia
(Sp)	La Spezia	Liguria		(So)	Sondrio	Lombardia

269

(Ta)	Taranto	Puglia	(Ud)	Udine	Friuli Venezia Giulia
(Te)	Teramo	Abruzzo	(Va)	Varese	Lombardia
(Tr)	Terni	Umbria	(Ve)	Venezia	Veneto
(To)	Torino	Piemonte	(Vc)	Vercelli	Piemonte
(Tp)	Trapani	Sicilia	(Vr)	Verona	Veneto
(Tn)	Trento	Trentino Alto Adige	(Vi)	Vicenza	Veneto
(Tv)	Treviso	Veneto	(Vt)	Viterbo	Lazio
(Ts)	Trieste	Friuli Venezia Giulia			

Appendix Three

Arandora Star: Missing persons list

Surname and Christian Name	Date of birth	Place of Birth		Last place of residence	
1. Abrardo, Eraldo Giuseppe	15.04.1892	Fubine	(AL)	London	E
2. Abruzzese, Giocondino	26.08.1875	Filignano	(IS)	Glasgow	S
3. Adami, Paolo	29.05.1909	Trieste	(TS)	London	E
4. Affaticati, Riccardo	02.08.1893	Caorso	(PC)	London	E
5. Aglieri, Mario	21.05.1887	Milano	(MI)	London	E
6. Agostini, Oliviero	29.04.1904	Barga	(LU)	Glasgow	S
7. Albertella, Giovanni	13.01.1893	Cannero	(NO)	Lancaster	E
8. Albertelli, Carlo	30.05.1899	Morfasso	(PC)	Pontypridd	W
9. Alberti, Humbert	28.10.1881	Barga	(LU)	Manchester	E
10. Albertini, Constante	08.04.1885	Milano	(MI)	London	E
11. Allera, Lorenzo	17.09.1900	Ivrea	(TO)	London	E
12. Alliata, Publio	19.08.1884	Roma	ROMA	London	E
13. Amodeo, Tullio Edouard	29.07.1882	Roma	ROMA	London	E
14. Andreassi, Giuseppe	19.03.1880	San Demetrignei	(CS)	London	E
15. Angella, Emilio	02.07.1896	Pontremoli	(MS)	Bolton	E
16. Angiolini, Domenico Giuseppe	15.03.1900	Genova	(GE)	Glasgow	S
17. Aniballi, Giuseppe	06.09.1896	Amatrice	(RI)	London	E
18. Antoniazzi, Bartolomeo	20.01.1908	Bardi	(PR)	Newtown	W
19. Anzani, Decio	10.07.1882	Forlì	(FO)	London	E
20. Arnoldi, Ercole	03.09.1910	Taleggio	(BG)	London	E
21. Avella, Alfonso	04.07.1889	Tirreni	(PI)	Glasgow	S
22. Avignone, Giovanni	02.05.1887	Port St Martin	—	London	E
23. Avignone-Rossa, Italo	12.10.1907	Bollengo	(TO)	London	E
24. Avondoglio, Fortunato	03.07.1888	Chiaversano	(TO)	London	E
25. Azario, Efisio Remo Vitale	18.06.1885	Mosso, Santa Maria	(VC)	London	E
26. Babini, Lorenzo	16.11.1885	Lugo	?	London	E
27. Baccanello, Marco	03.04.1898	Venezia	(VE)	Harpenden	E
28. Bagatta, Angelo	26.03.1883	S.Columbano Al Lambro	(MI)	London	E
29. Baldieri, Armando	26.06.1912	Roma	ROMA	London	E
30. Ballerini, Roberto	02.05.1895	Galluzzo	?	London	E
31. Banino, Luigi	21.08.1904	Cerione	(VC)	London	E
32. Barone, Francesco	13.09.1889	San Paolo	—	London	E
33. Baroni, Alessandro	11.08.1880	Milano	(MI)	London	E
34. Basilico, Cesare	15.06.1885	Cavonno Milanese	(MI)	London	E
35. Basini, Bartolomeo	12.10.1908	Bardi	(PR)	Tre Herbert	W
36. Battistini, Umberto	23.05.1899	Stazzema	(LU)	Ayr	S
37. Bava, Claudio	20.03.1887	Montechiaro D'Asti	(AT)	Gateshead	E
38. Belli, Antonio	08.11.1885	Bardi	(PR)	Maestag	W
39. Bellini, Pietro	08.07.1878	Morfasso	(PC)	London	E
40. Belmonte, Gaetano	16.09.1876	Cassino	(FR)	Edinburgh	S
41. Belotti, Leone	17.02.1904	Bergamo	(BG)	West Wickham	E
42. Beltrami, Alessandro	20.12.1874	Egypt	—	Glasgow	S
43. Beltrami, Leandro	11.08.1890	Massemino	(SV)	Middlesbrough	E

271

Surname and Christian Name	Date of birth	Place of Birth		Last place of residence	
44. Benigna, Pietro	01.11.1904	Chiuduno	(BG)	Leicester	E
45. Benini, Giuseppe	14.03.1881	Bologna	(BO)	London	E
46. Berigliano, Antonio	17.01.1899	Dorzano	(VC)	London	E
47. Berni, Attilio	10.05.1899	Bardi	(PR)	Weston-Sp-Mare	E
48. Berra, Claudio Giacomo	16.07.1890	S.Quirico	(VI)	London	E
49. Bersani, Carlo	07.06.1889	Sarmato	(PC)	London	E
50. Bertin, Antonio	11.10.1901	Sequals	(PN)	London	E
51. Bertoia, Luigi	04.06.1921	Montereale	(PN)	Middlesbrough	E
52. Bertolini, Vincenzo Silvio	14.06.1876	Barga	(LU)	Glasgow	S
53. Bertoncini, Pietro	24.11.1887	Camporgiano	(LU)	London	E
54. Bertucci, Siro Celestino	01.02.1885	Vercelli	(VC)	London	E
55. Beschizza, Anselmo	29.04.1878	Bratto	(MS)	London	E
56. Beschizza, Raffaele	12.11.1910	Pontremoli	(MS)	London	E
57. Biagi, Luigi	16.04.1898	Gallicano	(LU)	Ayr	S
58. Biagioni, Ferdinando	06.07.1895	Barga	(LU)	Glasgow	S
59. Biagioni, Francesco	06.03.1897	Castelnuovo G.	(LU)	Rothesay	S
60. Biagioni, Umberto	23.04.1878	Castelnuovo G.	(LU)	Glasgow	S
61. Biagiotti, Carlo	04.06.1877	Pistoia	(PT)	Glasgow	S
62. Biagiotti, Nello	25.02.1893	Pistoia	(PT)	Glasgow	S
63. Bich, Clement Daniele	21.12.1887	Valtournenche	(AO)	Thames Ditton	E
64. Bigi, Mansneto	08.08.1885	Gualteri	(RE)	Highcliffe on Sea	E
65. Bigogna, Giuseppe	10.11.1900	Acqui	?	London	E
66. Bissolotti, Carlo	24.11.1900	Soresina	(CR)	London	E
67. Boccassini, Attilio	10.10.1890	Barletta	(BA)	London	E
68. Bombelli, Mario	18.09.1885	Roma	ROMA	Cardiff	W
69. Bonaldi, Andrea Luigi	18.06.1898	Songavazzo	(BG)	London	E
70. Bonati, Alfonso	02.07.1893	Riccò Del Golfo	(SP)	Glasgow	S
71. Bonetti, Giovanni	23.02.1881	Lograto	(BS)	Southampton	E
72. Bongiovanni, Pietro	20.04.1891	Savona	(SV)	London	E
73. Bono, Luigi	24.01.1890	Arona	(NO)	London	E
74. Borgo, Carlo	03.04.1897	Casatisma	(PV)	London	E
75. Borrelli, Federico	12.12.1887	Schiava	?	London	E
76. Borsumato, Alessandro	02.11.1896	Cassino	(FR)	Middlesbrough	E
77. Boscasso, Magno	02.06.1881	Montechiaro D'Asti	(AT)	London	E
78. Bragoli, Pietro	23.05.1880	Morfasso	(PC)	London	E
79. Bragoni, Ilario	14.01.1897	Villa Franca	(FO)	London	E
80. Bravo, Francesco	30.03.1892	Bollengo	(TO)	London	E
81. Breglia, Salvatore Gaetano	13.07.1895	Napoli	(NA)	Cambridge	E
82. Broggi, Vittorio	08.07.1902	Gavirate	(VA)	London	E
83. Brugnoni, Mario Maximilian	25.08.1904	Paris	—	London	E
84. Bucchioni, Lorenzo	23.03.1899	Pontremoli	(MS)	London	E
85. Caldera, Carlo	21.01.1896	Alice Castello	(VC)	London	E
86. Calderan, Emilio	06.09.1900	Torino	(TO)	London	E
87. Callegari, Luigi	27.03.1899	Torino	(TO)	London	E
88. Camillo, Giuseppe	04.10.1882	S.Cosmo	(LT)	Glasgow	S
89. Camozzi, Cesare	02.11.1891	Iseo	(BR)	Manchester	E
90. Capella, Giuseppe	13.04.1885	Borgotaro	(PR)	London	E
91. Capitelli, Carlo	28.04.1899	Borgotaro	(PR)	London	E
92. Capitelli, Eduardo	18.07.1882	Albareto	(PR)	London	E
93. Cardani, Carlo	28.04.1886	Sesto Calende	(VA)	London	E
94. Cardarelli, Quirino	17.05.1889	Roma	ROMA	London	E
95. Cardellino, Giovanni	18.12.1886	San Damiano	(LT)	London	E
96. Cardosi, Nello	17.02.1902	Brunswick	—	London	E
97. Cardosi, Valesco	24.12.1910	Camporgiano	(LU)	London	E
98. Carini, Francesco	15.07.1893	Bardi	(PR)	Pontypridd	W
99. Carini, Giuseppe	21.05.1898	Bardi	(PR)	Ebbw Vale	W
100. Carpanini, Giovanni	05.01.1919	Bardi	(PR)	Britton Ferry	W
101. Carpanini, Giuseppe	17.07.1892	Bardi	(PR)	Cwmcarn	W

Surname and Christian Name	Date of birth	Place of Birth		Last place of residence	
102. Casali, Giuseppe	03.08.1909	Morfasso	(PC)	London	E
103. Castelli, Antonio	18.10.1894	Bettola	(PC)	Aberdare	W
104. Castellotti, Giovanni	15.06.1899	Pontremoli	(MS)	London	E
105. Cattini, Giacobbe Pietro	01.06.1918	Bratto	(MS)	London	E
106. Cattini, Pietro	02.11.1881	Bratto	(MS)	London	E
107. Cattolico, Mario Fedrico	16.04.1891	Napoli	(NA)	Stanmore	E
108. Cavaciutti, Pietro	06.06.1893	Morfasso	(PC)	London	E
109. Cavadini, Achille	26.03.1891	Como	(CO)	London	E
110. Cavalli, Giovanni	04.02.1889	Bardi	(PR)	Neath	W
111. Cavalli, Nicolas	06.05.1892	Felizzano	(AL)	London	E
112. Ceresa, Antonio	20.06.1889	Bollengo	(TO)	London	E
113. Ceresa, Eduardo	29.05.1890	Bollengo	(TO)	Chorlton Medlock	E
114. Ceresa, Stefano	22.05.1900	Bollengo	(TO)	London	E
115. Chiappa, Emilio Domenico	16.09.1900	Bedonia	(PR)	Bridgend	W
116. Chiappelli, Oraldo	14.05.1920	Pistoia	(PT)	Glasgow	S
117. Chiarcossi, Giovanni	09.01.1875	Gradisca di Sedegliano	(UD)	London	E
118. Chietti, Emilio Ottavio	03.09.1886	Monte Folonico	(SI)	London	E
119. Chiodi, Domenico	29.10.1912	Braia	(MS)	London	E
120. Ciampa, Salvatore	07.02.1884	Messina	(ME)	London	E
121. Ciarli, Vittorio	31.07.1897	Quagneto	(NA)	Edinburgh	S
122. Ciotti, Pasquale	09.11.1890	Coseiago	?	London	E
123. Cimorelli, Giovanni	23.06.1875	Montaquila	(IS)	Edinburgh	S
124. Cini, Armando	09.06.1886	Cairo	—	London	E
125. Colella, Vincenzo	25.04.1895	Viticuso	(FR)	London	E
126. Coniola, Celeste	06.04.1883	Pontari Genova	(GE)	Bradford	E
127. Conti, Abramo	04.09.1894	Venezia	(VE)	London	E
128. Conti, Guido	26.12.1908	Bardi	(PR)	Newport	W
129. Conti, Giuseppe	19.03.1898	Bardi	(PR)	Treharris	W
130. Copolla, Philip	07.01.1895	Picinisco	(FR)	Edinburgh	S
131. Coppola, Paolo	05.09.1878	Picinisco	(FR)	Edinburgh	S
132. Corrieri, Leonello Giuseppe	16.10.1888	?	?	Wallasey	E
133. Cortesio, Giuseppe	13.01.1899	Savigliano	(CN)	London	E
134. Cosomini, Giovanni	03.05.1880	Barga	(LU)	Bellshill	S
135. Costa, Diamante	28.10.1882	Parma	(PR)	London	E
136. Cristofoli, Domenico	14.04.1905	Sequals	(PN)	Birmingham	E
137. Cristofoli, Ettore	12.09.1896	Sequals	(PN)	London	E
138. Cristofoli, Renato	10.02.1908	Autun	(PN)	London	E
139. Crolla, Alfonso	24.05.1888	Picinisco	(FR)	Edinburgh	S
140. Crolla, Donato	07.09.1880	Paris	—	Edinburgh	S
141. D'Ambrosio, Francesco	02.12.1879	Picinisco	(FR)	Swansea	W
142. D'Ambrosio, Silvestro	30.12.1872	Picinisco	(FR)	Hamilton	S
143. D'Annunzio, Antonio	22.09.1905	Villa Latina	(FR)	Glasgow	S
144. D'Inverno, Francesco	17.04.1901	Villa Latina	(FR)	Ayr	S
145. Da Prato, Silvio	27.02.1878	Barga	(LU)	Glasgow	S
146. Dalli, Pietro	10.10.1893	?	?	Ayr	S
147. Danieli, Daniele	23.03.1878	Monte di Malo	(VI)	?	—
148. De Angeli, Mario	14.02.1906	Milano	(MI)	London	E
149. De Gasperis, Carlo	01.09.1906	Tivoli	ROMA	London	E
150. De Marco, Lorenzo	05.02.1885	Picinisco	(FR)	Edinburgh	S
151. De Marco, Pasquale	10.04.1898	Caserta	(CE)	Glasgow	S
152. De Rosa, Carlo	11.02.1882	Napoli	(NA)	London	E
153. Del Grosso, Giuseppe	20.04.1889	Borgotaro	(PR)	Hamilton	S
154. Delicato, Carmine	17.02.1900	Atina	(FR)	Edinburgh	S
155. Delzi, Carlo	02.10.1913	Livorno	(LI)	London	E
156. Di Ciacca, Aristide	06.10.1920	Picinisco	(FR)	Glasgow	S
157. Di Ciacca, Cesidio	20.10.1891	Picinisco	(FR)	Cockenzie	S
158. Di Cocco, Domenico	04.06.1876	Velliterro	?	Manchester	E
159. Di Luca, Pietro	29.09.1873	Rochetta Al Volturno	(IS)	Glasgow	S

273

Surname and Christian Name	Date of birth	Place of Birth		Last place of residence	
160. Di Marco, Mariano	24.11.1897	Cassino	(FR)	Hamilton	S
161. Di Marco, Michele	08.05.1890	Picinisco	(FR)	Swansea	W
162. Di Vito, Giuseppe	25.11.1874	Casalattico	(FR)	Crossgates	S
163. Dottori, Argilio	20.01.1882	Roma	ROMA	Southampton	E
164. Ermini, Armando	28.08.1890	Chitta	?	London	E
165. Falco, Celestino	01.08.1891	Cuneo	(CN)	London	E
166. Fantini, Guglielmo	03.08.1889	Napoli	(NA)	Southampton	E
167. Farnocchi, Francesco	09.06.1906	Stazzema	(LU)	Glasgow	S
168. Fellini, Ettore	25.09.1888	Savignoia	?	London	E
169. Felloni, Giulio	25.03.1905	Parma	(PR)	Aberdeen	S
170. Feraboli, Ettore Innocente	25.02.1885	Pessina	(CR)	London	E
171. Ferdenzi, Carlo	12.06.1897	Vernasca	(PC)	London	E
172. Ferdenzi, Giacomo	16.03.1898	New York	—	London	E
173. Ferdenzi, Giovanni	15.06.1879	Vernasca	(PC)	London	E
174. Ferdenzi, Giovanni	20.05.1884	Vernasca	(PC)	London	E
175. Ferrari, Francesco	19.08.1899	Zignago	?	Port Glasgow	S
176. Ferrari, Guido	01.09.1893	Valdena	(PR)	Kirkcaldy	S
177. Ferrari, Luigi	19.10.1907	Bettola	(PC)	Aberdare	W
178. Ferrero, Bernardo	14.09.1890	Montechiaro D'Asti	(AT)	London	E
179. Ferri, Fiorentino	22.01.1886	Filignano	(IS)	Bellshill	S
180. Ferri, Giovanni	12.07.1884	Vernasca	(PC)	Hull	E
181. Filippi, Mario	15.03.1910	Castelnuovo G.	(LU)	Ayr	S
182. Filippi, Simone	26.10.1878	Pieve	(LU)	Ayr	S
183. Finazzi, Anniballe	19.01.1903	Trescore	(GR)	London	E
184. Fiorini, Clement	20.01.1888	Sora	(FR)	Manchester	E
185. Fisanotti, Oreste	09.08.1897	Mathi	—	London	E
186. Foglia, Claudio Silvo	02.01.1891	Amatrice	(RI)	London	E
187. Fontana, Giovanni	18.07.1892	Frassinoro	(MO)	Carlisle	E
188. Forte, Giuseppe	03.01.1893	London	—	Belfast	NI
189. Forte, Onorio	02.05.1880	Arce	(FR)	Chorlton Medlock	E
190. Fossaluzza, Matteo	25.11.1897	Cavasso	(CR)	London	E
191. Fracassi, Gaetano	18.04.1876	Pescarolo	(CR)	Manchester	E
192. Franchi, Giacomo	06.08.1896	Bardi	(PR)	New Tredegar	W
193. Franciscono, Nicola	03.12.1884	Alice Castello	(VC)	London	E
194. Fratteroli, Giancinto	06.09.1900	Picinisco	(FR)	Ayr	S
195. Friggi, Egidio	29.11.1886	Motta Visconti	(MI)	Southampton	E
196. Frizzi, Carlo	13.12.1873	Caserta	(CE)	Manchester	E
197. Fulgoni, Giacomo	10.07.1894	Grezzo Di Bardi	(PR)	Hirwaun	W
198. Fulgoni, Giovanni	04.07.1900	Grezzo Di Bardi	(PR)	Ponty Gwarth	W
199. Fusco, Antonio	26.08.1909	Casalattico	(FR)	Belfast	NI
200. Fusco, Giovanni Antonio	03.09.1877	Cassino	(FR)	Dundee	S
201. Gabbini, Alfeo	11.10.1897	Cannero	(NO)	London	E
202. Gadeselli, Vincenzo	15.09.1885	Bardi	(PR)	London	E
203. Gagliardi, Battista	28.02.1890	Milano	(MI)	London	E
204. Gallo, Emilio	20.11.1896	Belmonte	(FR)	Edinburgh	S
205. Gargaro, Francesco	25.05.1898	Picinisco	(FR)	Ayr	S
206. Gazzi, Andrea	02.08.1900	Bardi	(PR)	Gorsewinon	W
207. Gazzi, Francesco	12.01.1922	Bardi	(PR)	Pont Newydd	W
208. Gazzi, Lino	03.06.1881	Bardi	(PR)	Ferndale	W
209. Gentile, Candido	17.08.1894	Ventimiglia	(IM)	London	E
210. Gerla, Giuseppe	10.04.1893	Abbairati	?	London	E
211. Ghiloni, Nello	25.12.1909	Barga	(LU)	Glasgow	S
212. Giannandrea, Vincenzo	16.12.1910	Belmonte Castello	(FR)	Elgin	S
213. Giannotti, Alfredo	23.10.1885	Camporgiano	(LU)	London	E
214. Giannotti, Ettore	20.05.1910	Brescia	(BS)	London	E
215. Giovanelli Luigi	24.04.1890	Bardi	(PR)	London	E
216. Giraschi, Enrico	22.02.1896	Pellegrino	(PR)	London	E
217. Gonella, Francesco	01.01.1885	Pontstaira	?	London	E

274

Surname and Christian Name	Date of birth	Place of Birth		Last place of residence	
218. Gonzaga, Luigi	11.02.1924	Bedonia	(PR)	London	E
219. Gorgone, Alfeo	02.09.1909	Venezia	(VE)	London	E
220. Gras, Davide	03.02.1882	Bobbio Pelice	(TO)	London	E
221. Greco, Domenico	13.04.1885	Santo Padre	(FR)	Middlesbrough	E
222. Greco, Tullio	26.10.1897	Arpino	(FR)	Middlesbrough	E
223. Grego, Anthony	00.00.1891	Sora	(FR)	Greet	E
224. Guarnori, Antonio	17.02.1884	Novara	(NO)	London	E
225. Guerri, Lino	11.11.1914	Via Risasoli?	?	London	E
226. Gussoni, Ercole	12.02.1902	Roma	ROMA	London	E
227. Gutkind, Curt Sigmar	29.09.1896	Manheim	—	London	E
228. Iannetta, Ferdinando	25.10.1889	Viticuso	(FR)	Edinburgh	S
229. Iannetta, Orazio	23.08.1901	Belmonte Castello	(FR)	Methil	S
230. Iannetta, Vincenzo	25.10.1902	Belmonte Castello	(FR)	Methil	S
231. Iardella, Pietro	05.07.1885	Pontremoli	(MS)	London	E
232. Incerti, Rinaldo	17.04.1884	Villa?	?	London	E
233. Jordaney, Giuseppe	06.05.1888	Courmayeur	(AO)	London	E
234. Landucci, Ernani	29.09.1894	Firenze	(FI)	Chorlton Medlock	E
235. Lanzi, Ugo	01.04.1905	Milano	(MI)	London	E
236. Lepora, Reino	29.07.1897	Alice Castello	(VC)	London	E
237. Longinotti, Giovanni	17.05.1892	S.Maria Del Taro	(PR)	Heywood	E
238. Lucantoni, Amedeo	16.02.1897	Roma	ROMA	Middlesbrough	E
239. Lucchesi, Pietro	26.01.1894	Castiglioni	(LU)	Prestwick	S
240. Luise, Raffaele	15.09.1905	Torre Del Greco	(NA)	London	E
241. Lusardi, Tomasso Angelo	29.05.1909	Blaengaru	(PN)	London	E
242. Lusardi, Vittorio	23.07.1892	Bedonia	(PR)	Llanharan	W
243. Maccariello, Elpidio	16.05.1890	Casapulla	(CE)	London	E
244. Maddalena, Marco Carlo	16.12.1909	Fanna	(PN)	London	E
245. Maggi, Cesare	22.02.1887	Torino	(TO)	London	E
246. Maiuri, Guido	30.04.1877	Napoli	(NA)	London	E
247. Mancini, Antonio	03.08.1885	Atina	(FR)	Ayr	S
248. Mancini, Domenico	22.04.1881	Sessa	(CE)	Chorlton Medlock	E
249. Mancini, Umberto	02.07.1891	Picinisco	(FR)	London	E
250. Mancini, Vittorio	19.04.1899	Picinisco	(FR)	London	E
251. Manini, Cesare	25.11.1903	Palazzolo	(FI)	London	E
252. Marchesi, Charles Domenico	17.07.1872	Codogno	(MI)	London	E
253. Marchetto, Ugo	18.04.1897	Venezia	(VE)	London	E
254. Marello, Eugenio	30.03.1893	Alfieri	?	London	E
255. Marenghi, Giovanni	23.04.1897	Bardi	(PR)	Pontypridd	W
256. Marenghi, Luigi	21.07.1893	Piacenza	(PC)	London	E
257. Mariani, Amleto	24.05.1887	Torino	(TO)	London	E
258. Mariani, Pietro	03.10.1921	Bardi	(PR)	London	E
259. Marini, Luigi	06.01.1912	Cuccaro	(AL)	London	E
260. Mariotti, Fulgenzio	23.09.1885	Costacciaro	(PG)	London	E
261. Marre, Carlo	03.08.1880	Borzonasca	(GE)	Manchester	E
262. Marsella, Antonio	15.10.1899	Casalattico	(FR)	Bonnybridge	S
263. Marsella, Filippo	07.04.1897	Casalattico	(FR)	Wishaw	S
264. Marsella, Orlando	22.08.1914	Glasgow	—	Glasgow	S
265. Martis, Orazio	18.07.1883	Sassari	(SS)	New Malden	E
266. Marzella, Antonio	06.04.1899	Filignano	(IS)	Glasgow	S
267. Massari, A	Unconfirmed				
268. Mattei, Francesco	13.10.1885	Sesso	(RE)	London	E
269. Matteoda, Leopoldo	30.07.1881	Saluzzo	(CN)	London	E
270. Melaragni, Michelangelo	18.03.1890	Cassino	(FR)	Manchester	E
271. Menozzi, Gioacchino	24.08.1894	Bardi	(PR)	London	E
272. Meriggi, Mario	17.08.1892	Portalbert	—	London	E
273. Merlo, Giuseppe	29.03.1914	San Gallo	(BG)	Trealaw	W
274. Meschi, Oscar	16.07.1920	Fornoli	(LU)	Glasgow	S
275. Meta, Pasqualino	05.02.1899	Cassino	(FR)	Paisley	S

275

	Surname and Christian Name	Date of birth	Place of Birth		Last place of residence	
276.	Miele, Natalino	25.12.1898	Cassino	(FR)	Edinburgh	S
277.	Miglio, Filippo Luigi	19.05.1883	Trinito Cuneo	(CN)	London	E
278.	Milani, Luigi	04.05.1890	Oggiono	(CO)	London	E
279.	Minetti, Giacomo	11.07.1905	Bardi	(PR)	Neath	W
280.	Mittero, Antonio	15.07.1908	Chieri	(TO)	Stalybridge	E
281.	Montagna, Giulio	31.10.1888	Napoli	(NA)	London	E
282.	Monti, Giuseppe	23.01.1889	Lacco Ameno	(NA)	Manchester	E
283.	Morelli, Luigi	01.09.1892	Borgotaro	(PR)	London	E
284.	Moretti, Giovanni	01.03.1900	Pardivarma	(SP)	Greenock	S
285.	Moruzzi, Ernesto	12.08.1879	Bardi	(PR)	Neath	W
286.	Moruzzi, Peter	31.05.1887	Bardi	(PR)	Neath	W
287.	Moruzzi, Pietro	24.11.1917	Bardi	(PR)	London	E
288.	Moscardini, Santino	02.01.1879	Barga	(LU)	Motherwell	S
289.	Musetti, Lorenzo	25.02.1897	Buenos Aires	—	London	E
290.	Musetti, Pietro	31.01.1890	Pontremoli	(MS)	London	E
291.	Muzio, Enrico	12.12.1892	Napoli	(NA)	London	E
292.	Nannini, Oreste	28.05.1891	Pievepelago	(MO)	Edinburgh	S
293.	Nardone, Antonio	20.10.1882	Cassino	(FR)	Middlesbrough	E
294.	Nichini, Giulio	04.05.1896	Orta Novarese	(NO)	London	E
295.	Notafalchi, Lorenzo	08.08.1885	Piacenza	(PC)	London	E
296.	Novelli, Vincenzo	08.07.1893	Fubine	(AL)	London	E
297.	Olivelli, A	Unconfirmed				
298.	Operti, Egidio Ferrucio	26.08.1890	Torino	(TO)	Southampton	E
299.	Orsi, Giuseppe	22.06.1890	Albareto	(PR)	London	E
300.	Orsi, Pietro	01.05.1888	Pontremoli	(MS)	London	E
301.	Ottolini, Giovanni	21.07.1876	Lucca	(LU)	Birmingham	E
302.	Pacitti, Alfonso	03.08.1887	Cerasuolo	(IS)	Glasgow	S
303.	Pacitti, Carmine	03.06.1876	Filignano	(IS)	Carfin	S
304.	Pacitti, Gaetano	10.12.1890	Villa Latina	(FR)	Edinburgh	S
305.	Pacitto, Gaetano Antonio	19.10.1875	England	—	Hull	E
306.	Palleschi, Nicola	16.12.1884	Sesto Campano	(IS)	Glasgow	S
307.	Palumbo, Gioacchino	21.03.1897	Minori	(SA)	London	E
308.	Paolozzi, Alfonso Rodolfo	29.03.1901	Viticuso	(FR)	Edinburgh	S
309.	Papa, Pietro	02.10.1909	S.Biagio	(FR)	Glasgow	S
310.	Pardini, Agostino	09.09.1901	Capezzano	(LU)	Greenock	S
311.	Parmigiani, Giuseppe	17.11.1889	Tourolo	?	London	E
312.	Pastecchi, Enrico	06.03.1896	Roma	ROMA	London	E
313.	Paulone, Amadeo	24.03.1885	Scanno Aquila	(AQ)	Southampton	E
314.	Pellegrini, Domenico	22.10.1894	Varsi	(PR)	London	E
315.	Pelosi, Paul	23.03.1882	Picinisco	(FR)	Edinburgh	S
316.	Pelucco, Francesco	12.04.1882	Quariento	?	London	E
317.	Perella, Luigi	03.12.1893	Picinisco	(FR)	Edinburgh	S
318.	Peretti, Luigi	01.10.1880	Agrano	(NO)	London	E
319.	Pettiglio, Carlo	05.05.1878	Cassino	(FR)	Edinburgh	S
320.	Piancastelli, Annino	26.07.1894	Busighella	?	London	E
321.	Picozzi, Carlo	04.10.1889	Milano	(MI)	London	E
322.	Pieri, Alfredo	08.11.1898	Lucca	(LU)	Carlisle	E
323.	Pieroni, Giuseppe	31.01.1889	Pieve	(MS)	Ayr	S
324.	Piloni, Battista	24.05.1897	Crema	(CR)	London	E
325.	Pinchera, Angelo Antonio	31.08.1898	Cassino	(FR)	Glasgow	S
326.	Pinchiaroli, Luigi	01.12.1894	Albareto	(PR)	Pontypridd	W
327.	Pino, Antonio Cesare	18.10.1889	Lonigi	(ME)	London	E
328.	Piovano, Giacomo	25.02.1892	Castelnuovo G.	(LU)	London	E
329.	Piscina, Giovanni	16.05.1884	Parma	(PR)	London	E
330.	Plescia, Andrea	16.01.1905	Palermo	(PA)	London	E
331.	Plescia, Baldassare	01.01.1915	Palermo	(PA)	London	E
332.	Poli, Amedeo	10.03.1896	Barga	(LU)	Glasgow	S
333.	Poli, Egisto	17.11.1882	Colognora	(LU)	Glasgow	S

276

Surname and Christian Name	Date of birth	Place of Birth		Last place of residence	
334. Pollini, Manlio	20.03.1883	Milano	(MI)	Southampton	E
335. Pololi, Francesco	06.03.1881	Toliggio	?	London	E
336. Pompa, Ferdinando	16.09.1876	Picinisco	(FR)	Swansea	W
337. Pontone, Domenico	13.08.1885	Cassino	(FR)	Hartlepool	E
338. Pozzo, Giacinto	20.04.1906	Viverone	(VC)	Whitton, Middx	E
339. Prati, Carlo	04.11.1877	Lugagnano	(PC)	Hull	E
340. Previdi, Lodovico	12.06.1895	Gropparello	(PC)	London	E
341. Prister, Camillo Flavio	28.06.1890	Gradisca	(UD)	Ilminster	E
342. Puchoz, Marcello	26.08.1896	Courmayeur	(AO)	London	E
343. Pusinelli, Pietro	03.04.1897	Naso	(ME)	London	E
344. Quagliozzi, Angelo	30.08.1881	Cassino	(FR)	Sheffield	E
345. Quaranta, Domenico	30.01.1883	Carbonara Napoli	(NA)	London	E
346. Rabaiotti, Antonio	20.10.1885	Bardi	(PR)	Newport	W
347. Rabaiotti, Bartolomeo	23.03.1881	Bardi	(PR)	Pontypridd	W
348. Rabaiotti, Domenico	12.02.1912	Bardi	(PR)	Ogmore Vale	W
349. Rabaiotti, Francesco	06.03.1894	Bardi	(PR)	Swansea	W
350. Rabaiotti, Luigi	11.12.1910	Bardi	(PR)	Swansea	W
351. Raffetti, Carlo	22.09.1901	Genova	(GE)	London	E
352. Raggi, Luigi	15.08.1880	Bardi	(PR)	London	E
353. Ranaldi, Antonio	16.01.1884	Arpino	(FR)	Middlesbrough	E
354. Ravetto, Carlo	09.01.1897	Alice Castello	(VC)	London	E
355. Ravina, Cristoforo	06.01.1882	Fulbrino	?	London	E
356. Ravina, Giuseppe	26.03.1884	Fubine	(AL)	London	E
357. Razzuoli, Enrico	15.12.1909	Stazzema	(LU)	Darvel	S
358. Rea, Camillo	06.10.1878	Arpino	(FR)	Middlesbrough	E
359. Rea, Domenico	07.01.1900	Arpino	(FR)	Middlesbrough	E
360. Ricaldone, Alessandro Angelo	03.12.1892	Fubine	(AL)	London	E
361. Ricci, Lazzaro	24.03.1891	Bardi	(PR)	Treharris	W
362. Rinaldi, Giovanni	31.03.1883	Artenes	—	Leith	S
363. Rivaldi, Patrocco	18.01.1879	Cremona	(CR)	London	E
364. Roccantonio, Francesco	23.10.1875	Rocca D'Arce	(FR)	Peebles	S
365. Rocchiccioli, Caesar	06.12.1909	Barga	(LU)	Troon	S
366. Roffo, Ernesto	14.01.1896	Picinisco	(FR)	London	E
367. Rosi, Guglielmo	25.12.1893	Pontremoli	(MS)	London	E
368. Rosi, Luigi	16.12.1886	Grondola	(MS)	London	E
369. Rossetto, Ferdinando	19.06.1888	Bollengo	(TO)	London	E
370. Rossi, Emilio	08.09.1888	Viticuso	(FR)	Edinburgh	S
371. Rossi, Eugenio	17.10.1893	Paris	—	Mountain Ash	W
372. Rossi, Flavio	15.06.1902	Bardi	(PR)	Port Glasgow	S
373. Rossi, Giovanni	11.09.1923	Bardi	(PR)	Cardiff	W
374. Rossi, Luigi	14.08.1908	Bardi	(PR)	Swansea	W
375. Rossi, Mario	03.04.1889	Pisa	(PI)	London	E
376. Rossi, Pietro	23.12.1875	Viticuso	(FR)	Edinburgh	S
377. Rossi, Vitale	05.05.1898	Cavaglia	(VC)	London	E
378. Rossotti, Carlo	09.03.1899	Chieri Torino	(TO)	London	E
379. Rota, Carlo	20.03.1898	Giarole	(AL)	London	E
380. Ruffoni, Giovanni Battista	05.05.1885	Chignolo Verbano	?	London	E
381. Ruocchio, Michele Andrew	06.07.1908	?	?	Larkhall	S
382. Russo, Carmine	24.07.1886	Cassino	(FR)	London	E
383. Rustioni, Oreste	09.07.1913	Milano	(MI)	London	E
384. Sagramati, Vilfrido	19.10.1910	Roma	ROMA	London	E
385. Sala, Emilio	21.10.1912	Monza	(MI)	Luton	E
386. Salsano, Luigi	14.06.1921	Tramonti	?	London	E
387. Sangalli, Gianetto	12.07.1882	Milano	(MI)	London	E
388. Santarello, Ferruccio	17.12.1892	Venezia	(VE)	London	E
389. Santi, S	Unconfirmed				
390. Santini, Quinto	29.07.1880	Pistoia	(PT)	Paisley	S
391. Santuz, Antonio	27.01.1884	Fanna	(PN)	Birmingham	E

Surname and Christian Name	Date of birth	Place of Birth		Last place of residence	
392. Sartori, Luigi	14.04.1885	Morfasso	(PC)	London	E
393. Scarabelli, Angelo Mario	19.04.1892	S.Maria Della Verra	(PV)	London	E
394. Sidoli, Giovanni	17.08.1894	Bardi	(PR)	Glyncorrwg	W
395. Sidoli, Luigi	29.12.1882	Bardi	(PR)	London	E
396. Siliprandi, Olimpio	10.01.1883	Mantova	(MN)	Pettswood	E
397. Silva, Luigi Antonio Mario	11.11.1893	Via Anano?	?	London	E
398. Silverstrini, Giovanni	24.04.1894	Verona	(VR)	London	E
399. Simeone, Francesco	27.01.1891	S.Vittorio Lazio	(FR)	London	E
400. Sola, Carlo Frederico	28.06.1882	Torino	(TO)	London	E
401. Solari, Federico	05.09.1914	Vernasca	(PC)	London	E
402. Solari, Luigi	24.04.1888	Bardi	(PR)	Neath	W
403. Sottocornola, Edmondo	02.04.1897	Gargallo	(NO)	London	E
404. Sovrani, Giovanni Jean	13.07.1882	Saludecio	(FO)	London	E
405. Spacagna, Giuseppe	09.03.1881	Cervaro	(FR)	Eastleigh	E
406. Spagna, Antonio	10.10.1894	Bardi	(PR)	Maesteg	W
407. Spelta, Giuseppe	07.03.1897	Milano	(MI)	Scarborough	E
408. Speroni, Ermete	27.11.1898	Milano	(MI)	Beckenham	E
409. Stellon, Giovanni Maria	14.09.1891	Fanna	(PN)	Newport	W
410. Sterlini, Giuseppe	31.05.1900	Bardi	(PR)	Wellington	E
411. Sterlini, Marco	17.10.1891	Bardi	(PR)	Tenby	W
412. Storto, Giuseppe	18.11.1900	Monferrato	?	London	E
413. Stratta, Giacomo	07.03.1894	Bollengo	(TO)	Croydon	E
414. Strinati, Giovanni	26.03.1880	Bardi	(PR)	Cwmaman	W
415. Taffurelli, Giuseppe	29.03.1892	Bettola	(PC)	Dowlais	W
416. Taglione, Benedetto	14.11.1883	Arpino	(FR)	London	E
417. Tambini, Giovanni	13.03.1899	Bardi	(PR)	Newport	W
418. Tapparo, Luigi	22.10.1898	Bollengo	(TO)	Edinburgh	S
419. Tedesco, Raffaele	03.09.1889	Mocera	?	Edinburgh	S
420. Tempia, Guiseppe	04.07.1896	Bollengo	(TO)	London	E
421. Todisco, Antonio	14.04.1893	Vallerotonda	(FR)	Redcar	E
422. Togneri, Giuseppe	19.03.1889	Barga	(LU)	Dunbar	S
423. Tortolano, Giuseppe	12.08.1880	Cassino	(FR)	Middlesbrough	E
424. Tramontin, Riccardo	24.11.1890	Cavasso Nuovo	(PN)	London	E
425. Traversa, Italo Vittorio	06.06.1918	Carisio	(VC)	London	E
426. Trematore, Severino	24.05.1895	Torre Maggiore	(FO)	London	E
427. Trombetta, Pietro	01.08.1892	Minori	(SA)	Chertsey	E
428. Tuzi, Pasquale	01.04.1898	Picinisco	(FR)	Edinburgh	S
429. Vairo, Cesare	26.07.1891	Milano	(MI)	London	E
430. Valente, Adolf	15.06.1900	Cervaro	(FR)	Edinburgh	S
431. Valli, Giovanni	20.09.1901	Novarro	?	London	E
432. Valmaggia, Elio	12.11.1896	Gemonio	(VA)	London	E
433. Valvona, Enrico	05.09.1885	Villa Latina	(FR)	London	E
434. Vercelli, Emilio Giacomo	01.08.1894	Mombercelli	(AT)	London	E
435. Viccari, Antonio	28.02.1890	Pontremoli	(MS)	London	E
436. Viccari, Giulio	31.05.1901	Pontremoli	(MS)	London	E
437. Viccari, Pietro	27.09.1889	SS.Cosmo e Damiano	(FR)	London	E
438. Virno, Giovanni Battista	07.10.1888	Cava Dei Tirreni	(SA)	London	E
439. Zambellini, Luigi	04.12.1887	Como	(CO)	London	E
440. Zanelli, Ettore	03.11.1893	?	?	Tonypandy	W
441. Zanetti, Antonio	09.07.1898	Varsi	(PR)	Swansea	W
442. Zangiacomi, Italo	16.04.1879	Verona	(VR)	London	E
443. Zani, Guido	30.11.1900	Pontremoli	(MS)	London	E
444. Zanolli, Silvio	09.04.1880	Monteforte	?	London	E
445. Zavattoni, Ettore	19.08.1882	Villate	(TO)	London	E
446. Zazzi, Luigi	03.01.1895	Borgotaro	(PR)	London	E

Total Men Lost = 446   From England   296   From Scotland   94   From Wales 50
From Northern Ireland   2   From Unknown Locations   4

Bibliography

Alberoni, F. 1970. Aspects of Internal Migration Related to Other Types of Italian Migration. In: Jansen, C. J. (ed.). *Readings in the Sociology of Migration*. Pergamon, Oxford, 285–316.

Ambrose, M. 1989. An Italian Exile in Edinburgh, 1840–1848. In: Millar, E. A. (ed.). *Renaissance and Other Studies*. Department of Italian, University of Glasgow.

Armfelt, E. 1902. Italy in London. In: Sims, G. R. (ed.). *Living in London*. Cassel & Company Limited, London.

ATI 1979. Association of Teachers of Italian. Special Edition on Italian Immigration to Britain, **29**.

Barone, A. 1989. *Italians First: From A to Z*. Paul Norbury Publications, Kent.

Barr, J. 1964. Napoli, Bedfordshire. *New Society*, 2 April 1964, 7–10.

Boissevain, J. 1970. The Italians of Montreal. Social Adjustment in a Plural Society. *Studies of the Royal Commission on Bilingualism and Biculturalism,* **7**.

Bottignolo, B. 1985. *Without a Bell Tower*. A Study of the Italian Immigrants in South-west England. Centro Studi Emigrazione, Roma.

Brown, J. 1970. *The Unmelting Pot*. Macmillan, London.

Cavallaro, R. 1981. *Storie senza Storia*. Indagine sull'Emigrazione Calabrese in Gran Bretagna. Centro Studi Emigrazione, Roma.

Cavalli, C. 1973. Ricordi di un Emigrato. Edizioni, *La Voce Degli Italiani in Gran Bretagna*, London.

Chadwick-Jones, J. K. 1964. The Acceptance and Socialization of Immigrant Workers in the Steel Industry. *Sociological Review,* NS **12**, 169–83.

Chadwick-Jones, J. K. 1965. Italian Workers in a British Factory: A Study of Informal Selection and Training. *Race,* **6**, (3), 191–8.

Chappel, C. 1984. *Island of Barbed Wire*. Hale, London.

Child, J. 1943. *Italian or American?* The Second Generation Conflict, Yale University Press, New Haven.

Chistolini, S. 1986. *Donne Italo-Scozzesi: Tradizione e Cambiamento*. Centro Studi Emigrazione, Roma.

Clarke, T. N., Morrison-Low, A. D. and Simpson, A. D. C. 1989. *Brass and Glass*. National Museums of Scotland, Edinburgh.

Cocozza, E. 1987. *Assunta. The Story of Mrs Joe*. Vantage Press, New York.

Colpi, T. 1979. The Italian Community in Glasgow with Special Reference to Spatial Development. *Association of Teachers of Italian*, **29**, 62–75.

Colpi, T. 1986. The Italian Migration to Scotland: Fact, Fiction and the Future. In: Dutto, M. (ed.). *The Italians in Scotland: Their Language and Culture*. Consolato Italiano Generale Edimburgo. Edinburgh University Press.

Colpi, T. 1987. The Social Structure of the Italian Community in Bedford, with Particular Reference to its Places of Origin and Migration. Unpub. D. Phil. thesis, University of Oxford.

Colpi, T. 1991. *Italians Forward*. A visual History of the Italian Community in Great Britain. Mainstream, Edinburgh.

Colpi, T. 1991. Origins and Campanilismo in the Bedford Italian Community. In: Sponza, L. and Tosi, A. (eds). *A Century of Italian Immigration to Britain: Five Essays*. The Italianist. Reading University Press.

Dickens, C. 1838. *The Adventures of Oliver Twist*.

Di Giovanni, C. 1989. *Eravamo Terroristi. Lettere dal Carcere*. Edizioni Paoline, Milano.

Di Mambro, A. M. 1989. Tally's Blood. Play for stage commissioned by the Traverse Theatre, Edinburgh.

Dutto, M. (ed.). 1986. *The Italians in Scotland: Their Language and Culture*. Consolato Italiano Generale Edimburgo. Edinburgh University Press.

Farrell, J. 1983. Italian. In: McClure, J. (ed.). *Minority Languages in Central Scotland*. Association for Scottish Literary Studies, Occasional Paper Number 5.

Foerster, R. 1919. *The Italian Migration of Our Times*. Harvard University Press.

Forte, C. 1986. *Forte*. An Autobiography of Charles Forte. Sidgwick and Jackson, London.

Gans, H. 1965. *The Urban Villagers*. Macmillan, New York.

Gough, V. 1990. Interned Italians and the Sinking of the *Arandora Star*. Unpub. M. A. Dissertation. Polytechnic of Central London.

Garigue, P. and Firth, R. 1956. *Two Studies of Kinship in London*. Athlone Press, London.

Gillman, P. and Gillman, L. 1980. *Collar the Lot*. How Britain Interned its Wartime Refugees. Quartet Books, London.

Guida Generale. 1939. Guida Generale degli Italiani in Gran Bretagna. Terza Edizione. E. Ercoli & Sons, Londra.

Hall, R. 1926. *Adam's Breed*. Cassell & Co., London.

Hickey, D. and Smith, G. 1989. *Star of Shame*. The Secret Voyage of the *Arandora Star*. Madison, Dublin.

Hughes, A. C. 1988. The Italian Community in South Wales 1870–1945. Unpub. M. A. Dissertation. Cardiff University.

Hughes, A. C. 1991. *Lime, Lemon and Sarsaparilla*. Seren Books, Bridgend.

Il Giornale di Barga. Voce Independente. 1949–1991. Barga.

King, R. and King, P. D. 1977. The Spatial Evolution of the Italian Community in Bedford. *East Midland Geographer,* **6,** (7), 337–45.

King, R. 1978. Work and Residence Patterns of Italian Immigrants in Great Britain. *International Migration,* **16** (2), 74–82.

King, R. 1979. Italians in Britain. An Idiosyncratic Immigration. *Association of Teachers of Italian,* **29,** 6–16.

King, R. and Zolli, L. 1981. Italians in Leicester. *Association of Teachers of Italian,* **53,** 3–14.

Kochan, M. 1983. *Britain's Internees in the Second World War*. Macmillan, London.

Lafitte, F. 1988. *The Internment of Aliens*. Libris, London. (First published Penguin Books 1940.)

La Voce degli Italiani. Quindicinale degli Italiani in Gran Bretagna. 1948–1991. London.

La Voce degli Italiani. Direttorio. Guida Pratica Degli Italiani in Gran Bretagna. 1991. London.

Lawrence, D. H. 1920. *The Lost Girl*. William Heinemann Ltd, London.

Leoni, P. 1966. *I Shall Die on the Carpet*. Leslie Frewin, London.

Levi, C. 1948. *Christ Stopped at Eboli*. Cassell and Company Ltd, London.

Levi, C. 1959. *Words are Stones. Impressions of Sicily*. Victor Gollancz, London.

Londra Sera. Giornale d'Informazione. 1976–1991. London.

Lopreato, J. 1970. *Italian Americans*. Random House, New York.

Lotti, S. 1988. Internati e PoW Italiani in Gran Bretagna. *Rivista di Storia Contemporanea,* **17** (1), 110–17.

Macdonald, J. S. and Macdonald, L. D. 1964. Chain Migration, Ethnic Neighbourhood Formation and Social Networks. *Milbank Memorial Fund Quarterly,* **42** (1), 86–97.

Macdonald, J. S. and Macdonald, L. D. 1972. *The Invisible Immigrants*. Runnymede Industrial Unit, Special Publication, London.

Mack Smith, D. 1981. *Mussolini*. Weidenfeld and Nicolson, London.

Maclean, A. 1985. *The Lonely Sea*. Fontana Collins, London.

Marin, U. 1975. *Italiani in Gran Bretagna*. Centro Studi Emigrazione, Roma.

Mark, R. 1978. *In the Office of Constable*. Collins, London.

Mayhew, H. 1851. *London Labour and The London Poor*. 4 Vols.

Millar, E. A. 1988. La Scozia, 1908. In: Millar, E. A. (ed.). *Renaissance and Other Studies*. Department of Italian, University of Glasgow.

Nelli, H. 1964. The Italian Padrone System in the United States. *Labour History*, **5**, 153–67.

Open University. 1982. *Bedford: A Portrait of a Multi-Ethnic Town*. Educational Studies: A Third Level Course. Ethnic Minorities and Community Relations. Open University Press.

Palmer, R. 1978. The Italians: Patterns of Migration to London. In: Watson, J. (ed.). *Between Two Cultures*. Migrants and Minorities in Britain. Blackwell, Oxford, 242–68.

Rea, A. 1989. *Manchester's Little Italy*. Memories of the Italian Colony of Ancoats. Neil Richardson, Manchester.

Ria, A. 1990. *Italians in Manchester*. History, Traditions, Work. Musumeci Editore, Aosta.

Rodgers, M. 1982. Italiani in Sco[z]zia. The Story of the Scots Italians. In: Kay, B. (ed.). *Odyssey: Voices from Scotland's Recent Past*. The Second Collection. Polygon, Edinburgh.

Rogerson, R. W. K. 1986. *Jack Coia. His Life and his Work*. Lindsay & Co., Edinburgh.

Rossi, G. 1990. Ricordano il 1940. *La Voce Degle Italiani in Gran Bretagna,* February 1990.

Russo, J. 1970. Three Generations of Italians in New York City: Their Religious Acculturation. In: Tomasi, S. and Engelm, M. (eds). *The Italian Experience in the United States*. Centre for Migration Studies, New York, 195–213.

Salvoni, E. with Fawkes, S. 1990. *Elena. A Life in Soho*. Quartet, London.

Sereni, B. 1974. *They Took the Low Road*. A Brief History of the Emigration of the Barghigiani to Scotland. *Il Giornale di Barga,* Barga.

Sereni, B. 1979. *La Storia dei Barghigiani fra Ottocento e Novecento. Il Giornale di Barga,* Barga.

Sibley, D. 1962. The Italian and Indian Populations of Bedford. A Contrast in Assimilation. *Northern Universities Geography Journal*, **3**, 48–52.

Sponza, L. (ed.) 1979. Italian Immigration to Great Britain. *Association of Teachers of Italian*, **29**.

Sponza, L. 1988. *Italian Immigrants in Nineteenth Century Britain: Realities and Images*. Leicester University Press.

Stent, R. 1980. *A Bespattered Page?* Internment of His Majesty's most Loyal Enemy Aliens. Andre Deutsch, London.

Suttles, G. D. 1968. *The Social Order of the Slum: Ethnicity and Territory in the Inner City*. University of Chicago Press, Chicago and London.

Tagliasacchi, P. 1990. *Coreglia Antelminelli*. Patria del Figurinaio. Nuova Grafica, Lucca.

Tedeschi, V. 1987. *Un Bacio a Silvia e Altri Racconti*. BMG, Matera.

Tolaini, V. 1982. *Voyage of an Alien*. Published privately, London.

Tosi, A. 1979. I Matune di Bedforde o Le Fondamenta di una Comunità di Italiani in Gran Bretagna. *Association of Teachers of Italian*, **29**, 76–84.

Tosi, A. 1984. *Immigration and Bilingual Education*. A Case Study of Movement and Population, Change and Education within the EEC. Pergamon Press, Oxford.

Tosi, A. 1991. *Italians Overseas*. The Language of the Italian Communities of the English Speaking World. Giunti, Firenze.

Valgimigli, A. 1932. *La Colonia Italiana di Manchester 1794–1932*. Enrico Ariani, Firenze.

Wetton, J. 1991. Scientific Instrument Makers in Manchester c.1790–1870. Forthcoming. Manchester Literary and Philosophical Society, *Memoires and Proceedings*.

Wilkin, A. 1979. Origins of the Early Italo-Scots. *Association of Teachers of Italian*, **29**, 52–61.

Wilkin, A. 1989. Further Definitions of the Origins of the Earliest Italo-Scots. In: Millar, E. A. (ed.). *Renaissance and Other Studies*. Department of Italian, University of Glasgow.

Zorza, P. 1985. *Arandora Star*. Supplemento a *Italiani in Scozia*. Glasgow.

Index